SOCIAL CHANGE AND ECONOMIC LIFE INITIATIVE

Series Editor: Duncan Gallie

THE SOCIAL AND POLITICAL ECONOMY
OF THE HOUSEHOLD

THE SOCIAL CHANGE AND ECONOMIC LIFE INITIATIVE

This volume is part of a series arising from the Social Change and Economic Life Initiative—a major interdisciplinary programme of research funded by the Economic and Social Research Council. The programme focused on the impact of the dramatic economic restructuring of the 1980s on employers' labour force strategies, workers' experiences of employment and unemployment, and the changing dynamics of household relations.

ALSO PUBLISHED IN THIS SERIES

THE SOCIAL
AND POLITICAL ECONOMY
OF THE HOUSEHOLD

Edited by

MICHAEL ANDERSON, FRANK BECHHOFER,

and

JONATHAN GERSHUNY

OXFORD UNIVERSITY PRESS
1994

Oxford University Press, Walton Street, Oxford OX2 6DP

Oxford New York
Athens Auckland Bangkok Bombay
Calcutta Cape Town Dar es Salaam Delhi
Florence Hong Kong Istanbul Karachi
Kuala Lumpur Madras Madrid Melbourne
Mexico City Nairobi Paris Singapore
Taipei Tokyo Toronto
and associated companies in
Berlin Ibadan

Oxford is a trade mark of Oxford University Press

Published in the United States
by Oxford University Press Inc., New York

© the several contributors 1994

All rights reserved. No part of this publication may be reproduced,
stored in a retrieval system, or transmitted, in any form or by any means,
without the prior permission in writing of Oxford University Press.
Within the UK, exceptions are allowed in respect of any fair dealing for the
purpose of research or private study, or criticism or review, as permitted
under the Copyright, Designs and Patents Act, 1988, or in the case of
reprographic reproduction in accordance with the terms of the licences
issued by the Copyright Licensing Agency. Enquiries concerning
reproduction outside these terms and in other countries should be
sent to the Rights Department, Oxford University Press,
at the address above

This book is sold subject to the condition that it shall not, by way
of trade or otherwise, be lent, re-sold, hired out or otherwise circulated
without the publisher's prior consent in any form of binding or cover
other than that in which it is published and without a similar condition
including this condition being imposed on the subsequent purchaser

British Library Cataloguing in Publication Data
Data available

Library of Congress Cataloging in Publication Data
The Social and political economy of the household / edited by Michael
Anderson, Frank Bechhofer, and Jonathan Gershuny.
(The Social change and economic life initiative)
Includes bibliographical references and index.
1. Households—Economic aspects—Great Britain. 2. Family—
Economic aspects—Great Britain. 3. Sexual division of labour—
Great Britain. 4. Sex role—Great Britain. I. Anderson, Michael,
1942- . II. Bechhofer, Frank. III. Gershuny, Jonathan.
IV. Series.
HB820.S6 1994   339.292—dc20   94–18361
ISBN 0–19–827938–8
ISBN 0–19–827935–3 (pbk.)

1 3 5 7 9 10 8 6 4 2

Set by Hope Services (Abingdon) Ltd.
Printed in Great Britain
on acid-free paper by
Bookcraft (Bath) Ltd.
Midsomer Norton, Avon

FOREWORD

This volume is part of a series of publications arising from the Social Change and Economic Life Initiative—a programme of research funded by the Economic and Social Research Council. The major objectives of the programme were to study the nature and determinants of employer labour force policies, worker experiences of employment and the labour market, the changing dynamics of household relations, and the impact of changes in the employment structure on social integration and social stratification in the community.

The research programme focused on six local labour markets: Aberdeen, Coventry, Kirkcaldy, Northampton, Rochdale, and Swindon. These were selected to provide contrasting patterns of recent and past economic change. Three of the localities—Coventry, Kirkcaldy, and Rochdale—had relatively high levels of unemployment in the early and mid-1980s, whereas the other three experienced relatively low levels of unemployment.

The data collected by the Initiative give an exceptionally rich picture of the lives of people and of the operation of the labour market in the different localities. Three representative surveys were carried out between 1986 and 1987, providing fully comparable data across the localities. The first—the Work Attitudes/Histories Survey—was a random survey of the non-institutional population aged between 20 and 60, involving interviews with about 1,000 people in each locality. It provides information on work histories, current experiences of employment or unemployment, and attitudes to work. This was taken as the point of departure for the other two surveys, focusing respectively on the household circumstances of respondents and on the policies of their employers. In the Household and Community Survey approximately a third of the original respondents were reinterviewed to develop a picture of their household strategies, their organization of domestic work, their leisure activities, their friendship networks, and their attitudes towards welfare provision. Where people had partners, interviews were carried out both with the original respondents and with their partners. The Employers' Survey was based on telephone interviews with senior management in the establishments for which respondents in the original Work Attitudes/Histories Survey worked. A further non-random follow-up survey was carried out involving 180 of the establishments that had taken part in the initial survey. The details of the research design and sampling for the different phases of the programme are provided in an Appendix at the end of this volume.

In addition, related studies were carried out in individual localities, focusing in greater depth on issues that had been covered in the common surveys. These included studies of the historical context of employment practices, current processes of technical change, managerial/employee relations policies, industrial relations, gender segregation, the relationship between employer and employee perceptions of employment conditions, and household strategies with respect to labour market decisions and the organization of work within the household.

The team that implemented the programme consisted of thirty-five researchers drawn from fourteen different institutions. It brought together sociologists, economists, geographers, social historians, and social psychologists. The major common research instruments were collectively constructed through a series of working groups responsible for particular aspects of the study. The programme involved, then, a co-operative interdisciplinary, research effort for which there are few precedents in British social science.

DUNCAN GALLIE
National Co-ordinator and Series Editor

CONTENTS

viii   *Contents*

LIST OF FIGURES

LIST OF TABLES

NOTES ON CONTRIBUTORS

MICHAEL ANDERSON is Professor of Economic History, University of Edinburgh.

FRANK BECHHOFER is Professor of Social Research, and Director, Research Centre for Social Sciences, University of Edinburgh.

BRENDAN BURCHELL is Lecturer in Social Psychology, Faculty of Social and Political Sciences, University of Cambridge.

DUNCAN GALLIE is Foundation Fellow in Sociology, Nuffield College, Oxford.

JONATHAN GERSHUNY is Professor of Sociology and Director of the ESRC Research Centre on Micro-social Change, University of Essex.

MICHAEL GODWIN is a part-time Lecturer in Economics and Statistics, School of Social Sciences, University of Bath.

SARA HORRELL is Assistant Lecturer, Faculty of Economics and Politics, University of Cambridge.

SALLY JONES is Research Officer, School of Social Sciences, University of Bath.

STEPHEN KENDRICK is Senior Health Information Scientist in the Information Statistics Division, National Health Service, Scotland.

DAVID MCCRONE is Reader in Sociology in the University of Edinburgh.

BRIAN MAIN is Professor of Economics in the University of Edinburgh.

JILL RUBERY is Senior Lecturer, Manchester School of Management, University of Manchester Institute of Science and Technology.

CAROLYN VOGLER is Lecturer in Sociology at the City University, London.

Introduction

MICHAEL ANDERSON, FRANK BECHHOFER, AND
JONATHAN GERSHUNY

The chapters in this book all use information and ideas generated as part of the Social Change and Economic Life (SCEL) Initiative. This multi-institution, interdisciplinary research programme was funded by the Economic and Social Research Council between 1985 and 1990. Teams from eleven universities co-ordinated three major surveys, conducted in six British travel-to-work areas: Aberdeen, Coventry, Kirkcaldy, Northampton, Rochdale and Swindon. In each area, about 1,000 randomly selected adults aged 20–60 were interviewed for on average about ninety minutes; most of the initial interview was concerned with work-related themes. About 300 of the 1,000 respondents in each area were then reinterviewed about aspects of their households' economic and social relations, and in these second interviews the partners of those who were married or co-habiting were also asked a range of questions; both partners were also asked to complete a diary covering in some detail their activities over the course of the following week. Thirdly, telephone interviews were held with a sample of employers in each locality, and some of these were followed up in more extended face-to-face interviews. In most of the original six localities, and also in several others, some supplementary studies were conducted, often involving further and more qualitative interviews with a subset of the household samples. Fuller details of the studies and of the resulting data sets may be found in the appendix to this volume.

The work of the Social Change and Economic Life Initiative has been published in a number of volumes, each concerned with a particular area of the research. All the contributions collected here are in one way or another concerned with aspects of what we have called 'the social and political economy of the household'. By this we mean that they address some of the ways in which households organize their economic activities (defining these in a broad sense—as will be clear below) and the ways in which they are thus able to sustain themselves over time, by gathering in and maintaining the resources (material and human) that they use and by deploying these resources in pursuit of individual and collective ends.

It is sometimes claimed that to treat households as collectivities in this way raises a number of analytical problems. First, there is a potential issue of reification, of treating households as if they had character or collective attributes in ways which disregard the fact that they are made up of individuals who may be expected to act according to their own individual values and aspirations. We return to this question below, where we argue that households do indeed have some characteristics which only make sense at the level of the collectivity, and that it is necessary to understand these 'emergent properties' if we are to be able adequately to interpret behaviour. Secondly, there is a danger that discussions which treat the household as a unit give too little attention to power relationships. In particular, there is a risk that if all individuals are, so to speak, given equal weight, central issues of the unequal access of different household members to resources and to the processes by which decisions are made may be ignored. We accept that this is of great importance, but not that it is fundamentally damaging to our approach. Rather, the power differentials within the household are an appropriate and central topic for study. We believe our authors have been well aware of this in their contributions to this book.

Thirdly, accepting the validity of the enterprise, there is the question of whether it is possible to obtain data which will allow us to comprehend the 'household-elements' of household behaviour. It is indeed the case that most of the data utilized in this book come from interviews with individuals, and there is a particular problem because the constraints of the collective large-scale interview process made it impossible for us to include, within our main programme of work, interviews with children and with members of households not related to the prime respondents. What we were able to do, however, was interview the partners of a substantial proportion of our respondents and we are thus often able to cross-check their responses and our interpretations. We can sometimes also explore the interestingly different reasons for discrepancies in their views, as Carolyn Vogler does in her discussion of control over decisions within households, or as Anderson, Bechhofer and Kendrick do in their analysis of partners' different accounts of the factors influencing the timing of important demographic events in their lives.

It is also very apparent from the data that almost all our interviewees were well aware that the kinds of actions about which we were asking questions took place within the context of the household, and that this affected the making of the decisions. On some specific occasions, the views or anticipated reactions of other household members had not (or so we are told) in fact influenced a particular decision, but the legitimacy of such views potentially to influence that decision was nevertheless recognized. Also, of course, the anticipated reactions of other members of the household, including decisions that *they* may take in their turn, impact on the decision maker, and this process of interaction is fundamental to the idea of households as collectivities, as we have already suggested above.

It is, moreover, not surprising that this should be so. At any point in time it is only in a tiny minority of households that the members are seeking to behave as atomistic individuals taking no account of each other—and such situations are inherently fragile. Most households, most of the time, develop highly complex sets of rules governing what is or is not acceptable behaviour by members. For example, they reach understandings about membership and rights of membership (who is entitled to invite who to sleep in the house and share in access to communal facilities and food, for example). They develop working practices about the allocation of tasks such as cleaning or paying bills, or bringing in resources by work or other means, which are necessary to maintain the household's environment and provide it with resources. They evolve mechanisms to order the time-sequencing of behaviour (who, and on what terms, can use which facilities when). And they develop often very precise shared expectations over members' access to property and other 'rights' within the household (food, consumer durables, space, etc.). Put a different way, households in general have to co-ordinate and accommodate the attitudes, beliefs, and behaviours of their members. The sets of rules by which this accommodation and co-ordination take place emerge through social interaction and have the characteristics of an 'emergent property' which does not belong to any one member of the household.

We have already suggested above that some individuals influence the outcomes of these rule-making processes more than do others, and this is a crucial aspect of the social and political economy of the household—as Carolyn Vogler in particular shows in her discussion of budgetary outcomes. Just as in any other social organization, household relationships involve power which arguably, as in other areas, derives from market and work situations inside and outside the household, from status considerations and from the formation of alliances between members. These power-related processes, which especially affect the allocation of resources, are one of the key themes of work within the social and political economy of almost any social organization. Where households are especially interesting, however, is that both their membership and the power relationships between their members change over the life-cycle, as partnerships are formed and end (through death or dissolution), and as new members are added and depart for other reasons. We see as particularly important the process whereby children gradually gain independence, and in most cases eventually leave the household (although, for reasons already outlined, many of the questions which arise will have to be left to future researchers). A further set of interesting questions arises from the impact of life-course-related changes in patterns of employment, and these are discussed in several of the chapters in this volume, although there remains much to be learned about the interaction between these employment changes and the economy of the household.

THE SOCIAL AND POLITICAL ECONOMY OF THE HOUSEHOLD: AN AGENDA

Central to our concerns in this volume are issues of the *organization* of household economic behaviour, how this varies between sections of the population, and how it changes over the household's life course and over historical time. We have chosen to describe our concerns as 'the social and political economy of the household' in order to stress our view that a sociologically informed understanding of household behaviour needs to address a range of issues rather wider than those conventionally considered by most modern economists, and needs to view them from a range of analytical perspectives which is broader than theirs. In particular, there are many activities which take place in households (and which are vital for their continuance over time) that are ignored in, for example, the national accounts of the 'formal economy' because they involve no direct cash transactions of any kind. For example, in addition to operating directly in labour and product markets, households deploy their labour on a whole range of activities required to sustain their members. These include:

1. The direct production within the household of commodities and services by 'self-provisioning' (e.g. by preparing food, gardening, or knitting) and 'self-servicing' (e.g. in childcare, washing clothes, or shopping).
2. Exchange or other means of acquiring resources or services by non-market relationships with other households.
3. Non-market direct acquisition of commodities from external sources, by means ranging from foraging through to theft. One primary set of concerns of the social and political economy of the household must therefore be the factors which influence the (widely different) allocation of household labour between these tasks (and therefore, incidentally, between the market and non-market elements of the economy), as well as the total amount of labour allocated to each of them.

Secondly, when resources enter the household, or when goods and services are produced by whatever means, a whole series of allocative processes come into operation. It is the outcome of these processes which result both in the total amount of particular kinds of goods and services that are available for consumption (as opposed to saving or investment) and, especially important, in some household members getting more access and some less access to them. Some of these consumption-related allocative processes themselves, over time, impact on and are affected by changes in the ways in which households allocate their labour, and by developments within the wider economy. Thus, for example, there are complex interrelationships between the development of mass-production techniques, the domestic supply of devices that are labour-saving in areas which have primarily been women's work, and women's involvement in the extra-household labour market. Or, as another example, consider how changes in consumption patterns of food (what is eaten in households, when it is eaten and in whose company) need to take account of innovations in agricultural and food products and food manufacturing practices, changes in the patterns of food retailing, changes in food preferences and beliefs about nutritional standards, changing levels of household income and decisions about its allocation to food rather than other purposes, and trends in the division and organization of domestic labour and in the involvement of different household members in extra-household activity in the labour market, the education system, voluntary associations, and leisure activities.

In considering these issues, it immediately becomes clear that all these activities involve to a greater or lesser extent allocative processes within households, and thus, like all allocative processes, imply that *choices* have to be made. This is not to imply that *on each and every occasion* when a household member performs an 'economic activity' a conscious choice is made. Indeed this is very far from the truth because, as we observe later, for much of the time for most people many activities involve simply the continuation of habitual practices, and this is what makes everyday life possible. Nevertheless over time it is clear that all households have an element of choice in their resource allocation and consumption decisions, and that this applies both in the aggregate (how much time and effort the members of the household should put into which kinds of 'work', for example) and, in households with more than one member, at the level of each individual (who does or gets what). Less obviously, perhaps, there are also elements of choice in the membership of the household itself. Addition or subtraction of members of the household (whether by having additional children, taking in relatives or lodgers, or sending children away from home) alters both the 'resource consumption' and the 'resource generation' sides of the household economy. Though we do not develop it fully in this volume, there are thus some key aspects of household demography which a full-scale analysis of the social and political economy of the household would need to take into account. Finally, households, with a greater or lesser degree of ease, also have elements of choice in how they interact in broad economic terms with external agents, be these kin, neighbours, employers, customers, or the State (in this context primarily as a welfare body though it also influences household behaviour profoundly through taxation and the regulation of household behaviour by, for example, child-employment legislation). While some data on such relationships were collected in the Social Change and Economic Life Initiative, they have not proved easy to analyse as yet within the kinds of frameworks that we are adopting here.

ISSUES IN THE ANALYSIS OF CHOICE

As its title suggests, this book tackles issues of interest to both economists and sociologists. In discussing the relationship between economics and sociology, James Duesenberry once wrote that 'economics is all about how people make choices; sociology is about how they don't have any choices to make'. The chapters in this book illustrate well the general position taken by Granovetter (1985) who quotes Duesenberry's quip in a seminal article. His approach to economic sociology is set firmly in the European tradition best exemplified by Max Weber in his insistence that economic action is a central but special case of social action. It may be a fair reflection of much economics to say that it is all about how people make choices but it is also a common criticism levelled at many economists that they operate with an atomized, undersocialized conception of social action. The authors of the chapters in this book cannot be accused of taking such a stance.

Duesenberry's position, however, is not only overgenerous to many economists; it is a caricature of good sociological practice. Over the years, sociologists have raised a whole series of different questions about choice: whether and when and why members of particular societies are provided with the opportunity to make choices; what are the circumstances in which they do indeed make choices (rather than maintaining 'habitual' practices); how the various modes of decision making are distributed among those members of societies that do indeed 'make choices'.

As Granovetter points out, the suggestion that sociology is about how people do not have any choices to make reflects an 'oversocialised conception of man' which was admirably disposed of thirty years ago by Wrong (1961). Much of the argument turns on the notion of a 'norm'. 'Norms' are a particular set of beliefs and may be defined as 'people's perceptions of understandings of what behaviour is normal for, or expected by, members of their group, and hence collectively sanctioned'. Crucially, norms are perceptions or beliefs about what behaviour is or should be normal, and, from them, people infer rules guiding everyday conduct. There are thus two quite distinct elements: the belief about normalcy, and the inference to propriety.

There are, of course, some normative means of controlling behaviour which are clearly codified, and in the extreme case of 'laws' these both define what is deviant and prescribe sanctions on the deviant. However, the main means by which social behaviour is controlled is through norms 'internalized' by an individual and reinforced through ongoing processes of interaction and interpersonal indication of support or of negative sanctions (threatened or actual). It is easy to see how some commentators can portray this process as one which indeed leads to a view of human behaviour as norm-driven, one in which, once a norm has been internalized by an individual, in Wrong's words 'he both affirms it and conforms to it in his conduct'. If norms really did constrain behaviour in this comprehensive way, then Duesenberry's comment about sociology would be no joke: there would be no economic *action* to explain, there would merely be habitual economic behaviour—and there would be thus no choices to be made in any meaningful sense. In an extreme case, there would also be no variability in behaviour across a society, as everyone conformed to exactly the same set of prescriptions for action.

In practice, it is self-evident that norms do not work like this. Normative action is underpinned by a desire to avoid sanctions, to win the approval of significant others, and to maintain a favourable self-image. This is not, however, as Wrong points out in his classic paper, the one fundamental motive in human conduct. To take such a position is, paradoxically, to fall into exactly the same trap as the adherents of the undersocialized model who see individual, atomized, self-interest pursued through rational action as the sole fundamental motive in human behaviour. Also, as Granovetter (1985: 485) again points out, in the oversocialized model there is an implication that once behavioural patterns are established and internalized, 'ongoing social relationships . . . have only peripheral effects on behaviour', leaving us with a conception of the actor as atomized as that in the undersocialized model.

Economic (and probably all) decision making must be seen as a rational activity conducted within a framework of normative behaviour but modified by the network of social relations within which the individual is embedded; the household, as we have already pointed out, is a (possibly the) crucial part of this network. Only with such a view of making choices can we get a grasp both on the way that norms change and the ways in which economic choices are made.

Most people most of the time act in conformity with their own conception of what behaviour is normal for, and expected by, members of their group, and hence collectively sanctioned. However, any one of these elements may be subject to pressure for change over time, and each may be a source of variability at a point in time. Consider, for instance, the case of a non-employed married woman with a small child in the mid-1960s, asked whether a married woman with a small child should take a job. In most parts of British society she would probably have answered in the negative, perhaps adding that there are some circumstances in which it would be acceptable to go against the norm (for example, if the husband was chronically sick or unemployed, or if a female relative lived in the house and could do the household chores and help with childcare). Suppose this mother was offered a job which in the abstract would be attractive to her. In the mid-1960s she would probably have refused, perhaps pointing out that she did not belong to one of the categories who 'needed to work'. In a sizeable sample of women in similar situations asked the same questions, a small proportion of those who say that a woman with a small child should not take a job will nevertheless agree to do so. Some will justify their breach of a norm, which they acknowledge, referring to the 'exceptional' circumstances which apply in their case. Note here that there will always be an element of judgement involved, and that women interpreting their situation as one which 'justifies' taking the job will be affected by the network of ongoing social relations around them. Some of the women who agree to take the job will not attempt to justify their action by appealing to 'exceptional circumstances' but simply contravene the norm; again this may be buttressed by the network in which they find themselves. For whatever reason then, there will be a small group whose members affirm the norm but do not conform to it.

If the same question is asked every year for a long time, perhaps twenty years, a slowly rising number of women will be seen not to conform to the norm. They will continue to acknowledge the norm because nothing seriously challenges their belief that employment of married women with small children is unusual (and in some way undesirable, at least for the majority of households). They will continue to justify their behaviour by reference to their particular circumstances, especially household circumstances or by the particular trade-off which working provides in their case. In part the process is driven by changes in 'external' structural factors: for example, changes in the female labour market such as availability of part-time jobs or provision of child care, changes which are themselves in part employers' responses to the norms. There are also analytically similar changes internal to the household: for example, access to new forms of domestic technology which allow changes in the times of day at which key domestic activities can take place, or greater use of partly processed food.

As time goes on, the circumstances under which it is acceptable to deviate from the norm become wider, even if the norm is still affirmed as 'what most women do'. In subgroups of the population it becomes so common for married women with small children to work that cultural changes start to take place, reinforced by the networks of social relations, so that the norm becomes something adhered to by others but not 'people like us'. Perceptions of what is 'normal' in a statistical sense are lagging behind this process, but finally as numbers of working mothers continue to increase, at some point perceptions 'catch up', probably very rapidly, with what is going on, and many of the working mothers identify themselves as part of a group that is so large that it cannot possibly perceive itself as deviant. Indeed within their own network of social relations they may even begin to view non-working mothers as deviant. When this point is reached, a further rapid acceleration in married women's employment may be observed which in no way reflects changes in structural opportunities or constraints, but is a direct reflection of normative change. This is of course a greatly simplified model, ignoring in particular generational change, the role of the media, the impact of social movements, and so on. It nevertheless parallels at least some of the views of what has happened in the UK over the past three decades (e.g. Dex 1988).

The outcome of a shift in norms of this kind is a substantial degree of variation in behaviour within a national population and, as a result, a situation where a significant degree of 'choice' exists. This does not mean, however, that, at the level of the individual or the household, behaviour becomes random: people continue to behave according to their views as to what is normal and in line with their beliefs, reinforced through ongoing social interaction, about what is proper for people like themselves. They do nevertheless frequently recognize that they are *choosing to follow one system of beliefs rather than another*. So, while we must reject an 'oversocialized' conception of man, we must also reject an approach, which has been not uncommon in economists' analyses, that ignores belief systems altogether (or that explains them away in terms of a model of maximizing utility, without asking what the elements are that comprise utility for any particular set of respondents).

CHOICES WITHIN HOUSEHOLDS: SOME EMPIRICAL ILLUSTRATIONS

Because of the rapid changes that have been taking place in household economic behaviour over the past fifty years (changes that in great part stimulated the inception of the Social Change and Economic Life Initiative), we live in a world where there is very substantial variability in household behaviour and in belief systems associated with it. Many examples of this appear in the work contained in this book. Thus, for example, as Carolyn Vogler shows in her chapter in this volume, a wide range of different financial allocation systems is in operation within households, even controlling for class and other standard background variables. Or, as Sara Horrell and her colleagues reveal, among dual-worker couples with children under the age of five, while substantial numbers solve their child-care needs by alternating their work periods through some kind of 'shift' system, many others appear to synchronize closely their working (and therefore also their non-work) hours, thus using third parties for child-minding during working hours in order to maximize the 'free' time that they can spend together. Or, as Brian Main shows, faced with hard times, different households exploit different kinds of options in order to make ends meet (and are more likely to change their expenditure patterns than their labour market activity).

Charting this variability is an essential starting point for any understanding of the social and political economy of the household in Britain today. But, beyond that, we need also to understand as much as we can of the factors and processes which produce this kind of variation. This inevitably means that we have to confront issues about choice: indeed, much of this book is about the circumstances under which people make choices and how, in these various circumstances, the choices are made.

There are two particular aspects which we pursue here. The first is the study of structural factors external to the household or arising from its own composition and membership, which open up or constrain options. The nature of the local labour market and of individuals' involvement in it, the availability of assistance from relatives, the presence or absence of dependent children, the skills and earning potential of the various household members now and into the future, and the security of their employment are just a few of the factors which influence the outcomes which we observe. Examples of the operation of factors of this kind abound in the chapters of this book: for example, the limited options that most local labour markets offer for rapid recovery from unemployment (see chapter by Brian Main); or that children's ages impact not merely on the frequency of their mothers' employment, but also on the kinds of work which they are willing to take (see chapter by Sara Horrell *et al.*).

These structural factors constrain or facilitate some forms of behaviour rather than others and therefore influence outcomes in ways that help to explain the diversity of behaviour which we observe. They do not, however, provide an adequate sociological account of our observations. For, as we noted above, while it is not *determined* by belief systems, behaviour is profoundly *influenced* by them. Indeed, at any point in time, as in any other social organization, household behaviour is severely 'rule-governed'. But, crucially, as a result of some of the processes which we have discussed above, what is treated as a 'rule' in one household may be treated as highly 'deviant' in another. Households each have their own 'subcultures' and these significantly affect the ways in which they will operate in terms of task allocation, how they will internally allocate resources, and how they will react to opportunities which may arise in the outside world.

Thus, for example, while, as we indicated above, viewed statistically there is a wide diversity of reactions by a non-employed married woman with children to an offer of employment, from the perspective of the individual household at any particular point in time there will normally be a clear set of expectations as to what would and what would not be acceptable behaviour. The same would apply to any other area of household activity: for example, the main outlines of the domestic division of labour, the circumstances under which additional members might be added to the household, the budgeting system to be employed, or who has access to which parts of domestic space or to priority over access to which aspects of household consumption.

Empirically, it is clear that some of the variation in belief systems must be influenced by the kinds of structural options and constraints outlined above. However, it is also clear that this kind of explanation by itself is insufficient. Variations in belief systems are themselves a crucial influence, varying outcomes even between households which appear to be in very similar structural sets of circumstances. Moreover how people interpret the guidance of their belief systems under particular circumstances (and thus how they react to new possibilities) is also a function of a wider set of principles through which they orient their behaviour in the world.

We noted above some of the ways in which people develop and modify their beliefs about what is normative behaviour (both in the sense that it is acceptable and also normal for their reference groups within the population). Some of the beliefs that people hold about appropriate household behaviour are probably acquired through early socialization and certainly it is clear from work done within the SCEL Initiative that parental role models do play a significant part in influencing at least initial practices in such areas as budgeting (though for some kinds of households more than others, as Carolyn Vogler shows) and the household division of labour (see the discussion in Jonathan Gershuny's chapter). It is also obviously the case that couples actively create shared belief systems through ongoing interaction and that these modify and constrain the options that are available to each other and to individual family members (see the discussion of the impact of partners' views on respondents' labour market plans in the chapter by Anderson, Bechhofer and Kendrick, or Gershuny's demonstration of the extent to which partners can be shown to tend to equalize their total working hours once a wide definition of 'work' is adopted). It is also clear that many aspects of household behaviour are subject to frequent discussion with peers, notably among women with close female relatives and often also with friends and workmates. In some cases, relatives, notably mothers, play an important role. To a significant extent, it appears from our data that household belief systems about appropriate behaviour are sometimes also modified in the light of past experiences (of the impact of unemployment, of mishaps which occurred when particular lines of action were followed, for example, over the use of baby-sitters, or of particular forms of credit). One example of this, discussed by Gershuny below, is the way in which the allocation of domestic work in households is affected not only by current employment patterns but also by the female partner's work history.

This is one aspect of a broader set of considerations: that behaviour is oriented not simply to the present but also to the past and to the future. As we have just suggested, past experiences influence views on what is appropriate in the present, and, as is explored further in David McCrone's chapter, together with the other kinds of normative pressures outlined above, these experiences provide a repertoire of devices around and through which households organize their daily lives. For most members of most households, however, aspirations and plans for the future also serve to structure at least some parts of present activity, by opening or closing particular options as acceptable lines of action. As Main shows, for example, most women are able to articulate preferences about the timing of their re-entry into employment—even if many fail to achieve them.

The evidence cited in the chapter by Anderson, Bechhofer and Kendrick confirms what earlier research has suggested, that there is substantial and structured variation within the population in the extent to which households 'plan' their activities in other than a short-term, day-to-day way, and in the degree to which individual actions are set within longer-term 'strategic' frameworks. Yet, we would argue, it is impossible fully to understand how and why household members react as they do to new situations, unless one knows something about the household's own cultural framework within which such decisions are made. In particular, it is clear that many households operate with what Anderson and his colleagues call 'strategies', more or less integrated sets of general prescriptions for action, oriented towards desired medium- or long-term goals, which they use to guide choices in the context of particular situations that they face, whether these relate to opportunities for a change in employment, the possibility of having a third child, or whether to spend money on home improvements rather than on some good or service with a more immediate but shorter-term utility. Put differently, most of our respondents, to a greater or lesser extent, do perceive themselves as actively and with foresight seeking to organize and influence the paths taken by their lives. These perceptions are the factors which they take account of in their actions (even though, as is also clear from the work which follows, they do not wholly determine them).

CONCLUSIONS

In sum, household economic behaviour, especially when this is defined within the wider perspective employed here, is influenced by a range of factors wider than those which even economists like Gary Becker have normally taken into account. Household behaviour within modern societies is highly diverse, and this diversity arises from diversity in beliefs and expectations as well as from the widely varying structural constraints and opportunities offered by the capacities of the household members and the environments within which they interact. The chapters in this volume show the extent to which insights into these diverse factors can be obtained from large-scale modern survey data; they also show how important are survey data in charting the patterns of the diversity. However, the work discussed here also shows the importance of integrating large-scale questionnaire work with data gathered by other research methods. It shows the value of assembling information on the life history of individual families by the collection of detailed accounts of the timing of events in people's past lives. The collection of detailed diaries provides insights into processes with many analogies to actual observation, but without at least some of the distorting effects of the presence of a direct observer. Finally, as the work reported by McCrone shows, much of our understanding of the processes of household organization and choice can only come from much more qualitative intensive interviewing. It is from the simultaneous employment of this diversity of methods that much of the new insight into the social and political economy of the household reported here has come.

PART I
Choice and Constraint in Household Strategies

1

Individual and Household Strategies*

MICHAEL ANDERSON, FRANK BECHHOFER,
AND STEPHEN KENDRICK

INTRODUCTION

In the last twenty years, sociologists, social anthropologists, economists, demographers, and social historians have all (and increasingly) attempted to understand certain aspects of behaviour through the use of the concept of 'strategies' (see for example Bourdieu 1976; Levine 1977; Tilly 1979; Anderson 1980; Oppenheimer 1981; Pahl 1984). Underlying this usage is a wish to escape from the strait-jacket of rigorous structuralism without recourse to extreme voluntarism; the fundamental problem is thus the age-old dualism of structure and action. More recently, a sociologist, Crowe (1989) has provided a valuable theoretical examination of the concept, published together with an insightful comment by Morgan (1989). Crowe points out the varied ways in which the concept has been employed ranging 'from sophisticated investigations of some of the tenets of game theory to *ad hoc* usages of the term "strategy" in which little or no attention is paid to its theoretical grounding'. While accepting that there is nothing intrinsically wrong with this, he suggests that there is merit in taking the term to 'imply the presence of conscious and rational decisions involving a long-term perspective' (1989: 19). Morgan ties the concept back to the Weberian categories of action in a discussion of what might constitute non-strategic behaviour, and usefully reminds us that strategies are inextricably bound up with decisions about the use and distribution of resources.

* We are very grateful for the support of the other members of the Edinburgh team throughout the Social Change and Economic Life Initiative, and especially for their help in constructing those parts of the Household and Community questionnaire asked only in the Kirkcaldy area.

These contributions started, perhaps inevitably, a debate. Shaw (1990) argues that the origins of the term 'strategy' lie in its military usage and suggests that as a method, strategic analysis is flawed. Sociology should therefore be about 'the limitations' of strategy. Knights and Morgan (1990) also warn that the concept is not unproblematic and that in the military and corporate context, 'strategy reveals its intimate relation with power and domination'. They agree with Shaw that strategy should be a topic for analysis rather than an analytic tool.

We agree that in using the concept of 'strategy' one should be aware of the issues raised by these critics. Nevertheless, in our judgement, 'strategy' is a useful shorthand for the overall way in which individuals, and possibly collectivities, consciously seek to structure, in a coherent way, actions within a relatively long-term perspective. Strategies, then, are higher order constructs which form general prescriptions for action. It is important to note, however, that empirically these may manifest themselves in conscious decisions not to act. For instance, someone may review their position in the labour market, and decide that over the next period of time they will remain in their present job. This may be because that is the most appropriate thing to do in order to achieve the longer-term pursuit of a better job, or because their position in the labour market is somewhat precarious and their strategy is one of preserving what they have got.

Our usage of the term must be distinguished from two influential bodies of work. Particularly in the work of some economists and historical demographers, strategies are simply logical deductions derived by the analyst and used to provide coherent and rational interpretations of patterns of behaviour observed in the course of econometric analyses of cross-sectional data. No attempt is made to investigate whether respondents actually base their behaviour on the rational calculations posited by the model. In consequence, while heuristically useful, the interpretations are not empirically grounded in social research and offer little help in understanding how people respond to new sets of circumstances. Pahl's use of the phrase 'household work strategies', in contrast, is thoroughly grounded but, in his description of the way in which households organize their domestic division of tasks, the concept becomes effectively a convenient summary term for more or less interlinked sets of practices. This is a long way from most of the more sociological interpretations of the idea, which all seem to imply that strategies are not behaviours or practices but systems of rationally grounded decisions leading towards desired medium- to long-term goals.

We follow Crowe in requiring strategies to be at least to some degree 'conscious'. As noted above, by no means all scholars have seen it as necessary that actors should have actively created for themselves and be aware of any 'strategies' that may underlie their behaviour. Bourdieu, for example, has suggested that, in many traditional societies in particular, people may operate 'either by consciously reinventing or by subconsciously imitating already proven strategies as the accepted, most respectable, or even the simplest course to follow. Those strategies that have always governed such practices finally come to be seen as inherent in the nature of things' (Bourdieu 1976: 118). To the extent that this is the case, methods much more subtle than the large-scale survey are required to elucidate the principles underlying behaviour.

We, however, are concerned to gain an understanding of the ways in which people plan and attempt to structure their lives in a changing world. In this context, one is concerned with the extent to which they, rightly or wrongly, perceive themselves as actively and with foresight seeking to organize, plan, control, or influence the paths taken by their present and especially their future lives. We seek to establish whether, in various different areas of life, they have plans to achieve particular goals and whether they have given thought to various alternative futures. *Strategies* we take to be more generalized than plans, general prescriptions which actors take into account when making plans within structural constraints. Actors may not themselves refer specifically to strategies; we infer their existence from the accounts they give of their plans.

Plans and strategies are, however, not static. When faced with actual choices in their lives, people may be unable to respond in ways which are consistent with their strategies. This is of course especially likely to occur when there are rapid and far-reaching changes in their social circumstances whether these be macro-structural such as changes in the labour market, or at the individual level such as illness or marital breakdown.

Our thrust in this chapter, however, is not a theoretical one and we do not wish our argument to become lost by entanglement in these theoretical thickets. To us it seems that central to any research concerned with social change and economic life must be an attempt to explore those situations in which people have at least a shadowy awareness of the possibility of organizing their futures in a rationally grounded, goal-directed manner.

Our reading of the work of the diverse group of scholars described at the outset suggests three important issues which demand further work. This chapter explores these issues in a general way; some of their detailed investigation will require further analyses of our data and more research.

First, it is striking that empirical investigation of strategies in the general area of family and the household is comparatively sparse. Yet evidence is what we need if we are to gain any real insight into the significance, if any, of strategies as bases for social action. Secondly, hardly any of the work has been conducted through large-scale survey research; as a result, almost nothing is known about the extent and forms of variability of the strategies of individuals in the population. Thirdly, while a number of authors have deployed the concept of 'household strategies', this idea is both conceptually and empirically problematic, though something of this kind arguably must exist for families and households to be able to operate over the longer term as effective social entities.

We here explore two related questions. Can large-scale survey evidence relating to individuals' operation of their household economies throw light on the empirical existence and distribution of something to which we feel we can legitimately apply the label 'strategy'? And what are some of the main conclusions which we can draw about the nature and distribution across the population of such strategies as they existed in the six areas studied in this research in the late 1980s?

We employ data collected in both of the main Social Change and Economic Life Initiative surveys. After appropriate weighting to allow for the oversampling of the unemployed and for variations in household size, and for most purposes pooling the results for all six survey areas, there is the equivalent of 6,112 respondents from the first survey and 1,816 for the second. Certain of the questions that we analyse here were only asked in Kirkcaldy, and for these there are 1,011 respondents to the first survey and 309 to the second. As the chapter proceeds, we try to throw light on some of the conceptual issues which are raised by the concept of 'household strategies' and here we are able to call upon data on the partners of all married or cohabiting respondents to the second survey. For this purpose, we have 1,330 couples for the six areas and 226 for Kirkcaldy alone. A number of the questions which we use in the analysis were included in a 'self-completion' section of the survey, where male and female partners filled in responses independently on separate schedules which each had in front of them. Finally, for Kirkcaldy, we have information from a series of intensive interviews conducted among a subset of couples; these enable us to elucidate further the meaning of some of the responses given and also throw some light on some of the more taken-for-granted elements in our respondents' 'strategic thinking'. These interviews are discussed further in the chapter by our colleague David McCrone.

ELICITING RESPONDENTS' PLANS FOR THE FUTURE

In this section we show that our survey questions do appear to elicit respondents' thoughts about how they will organize their lives in the future. However, as one might expect, this is an area where question wording may be critical. It is always difficult (arguably it is impossible) to prove in a survey that anyone holds any particular set of perceptions of the world and of their position in it. Among many other relevant factors, respondents may wish to please the interviewer by making a positive response or they may wish to conceal something of which they think the interviewer will disapprove. In addition, the questions asked may not in practice stimulate the expected response, or despite careful piloting may tap something different from what was anticipated at the time of their design. Given the very limited amount of empirical survey research that has been conducted into strategies, there were few well-validated questions that could be included within our surveys and although most of the questions were thoroughly piloted, subsequent analysis has produced some puzzles, not all of which we can reconcile, even with the aid of our intensive interview material.

Accepting all this, however, perhaps the most striking conclusion of our analysis is that responses to a number of our questions suggest not only that a high proportion of respondents do think ahead and do plan in significant areas of their lives but also that they are aware that they do and are able to reconstruct these thoughts for the interviewer. Illustrative examples are that 68% of males aged 30–39 respond 'yes' to the question 'Have you thought about what sort of job you want to be doing in five years time?', and that in the group aged 50–60, around two-thirds (68%) respond that 'I tend to plan out my finances carefully', rather than that 'I just take things as they come'. Three-quarters (76%) of males aged 20–29 and living as part of a couple reply positively to the question 'Do you have any plans for yourself and your household at the present time' and then go on to give the interviewer an account of these plans. Finally, some preliminary idea of the extent to which respondents seek actively to control their own lives can be derived from a rather different question. Around three-quarters of the men (76%) and of the women (73%) replied that 'What happens to me is my own doing', compared with the remainder who felt 'that I have little influence over the things that happen to me'. Taking these four questions together, almost 96% of all respondents responded in a positive manner to at least one of them.

We see each of these questions as tapping some component of a 'strategic' orientation to life, and are encouraged in our view by the way the responses are structured in our sample. As we shall see, in our data, as in much earlier work on this topic, compared with the sample as a whole, the unemployed, unskilled manual workers, and older respondents of both sexes are especially likely to have few 'plans' of any kind, even in areas where the vast majority of the population give positive responses to our inquiries. The elucidation of these differences and the reasons for them is a complex issue, to which we return towards the end of the chapter.

However, there is a strong case to be made for the view that life is only manageable if large areas are part of the taken-for-granted world and there are aspects of our respondents' lives where the responses suggest a much lower level of active planning and organization. There is one especially clear example of this, though it relates to the organization of a present activity and may thus be related only tangentially to strategies in the longer-term sense. We asked how people arrived at their present arrangements for dividing up or sharing the work around the house. The responses suggest a high degree of 'traditional' behaviour. Among both male and female respondents only 30% said other than that they just 'did what seemed natural' when they first set up home together. At the other extreme just 23% of male respondents and 25% of female respondents admit to discussing their current arrangements and changing as a result of what had been decided.

Another area where people less often tell us that they 'plan' their behaviour is in their marital and child-bearing lives. The life-history demographic information available to us, however, suggests that some planning does indeed occur but respondents appear to play it down in the interview. In part this may be a result of the questions asked, but even our intensive interviews found that few respondents admitted to a high level of actively planned behaviour in their family-building history. We explore this issue further below.

We are, then, reasonably confident that our survey questions are tapping components of strategies. However, the precise wording of a question may be crucial in determining the nature of the response. For example, in the first survey, respondents in Kirkcaldy were asked: 'Thinking about your working life over the next five years or so, would you say you know definitely what you want to do / you have a rough idea of how you want things to go / you're not very sure what you want to do in relation to work in the next five years?'. In the second survey, respondents were asked the superficially rather similar question: 'Have you thought about the kind of job that you want to be doing in five years time?'. Responses to these two questions, broken down by age group and sex, are shown in Table 1.1. In both cases, the data are limited to Kirkcaldy respondents who were interviewed at the first and the second surveys and, in order to compare the same respondents, the age variable refers to age at the first survey.

With the sole exception of women in the 20–29 age group, more respondents in each comparable category said that they knew or had a rough idea about what they wanted to do in their working lives than responded that they had thoughts about the sort of job they wanted in five years' time. Given, as we shall argue further below, the possibly greater generality of the first question, these results seem reasonable. With the same exception,

TABLE 1.1 *Thoughts about future working life (%)*[a]

	Age group				
	20–9	30–9	40–9	50–60	All
Thoughts about working life over the next five years (K52)					
Know definitely what want to do					
Male	22	42	40	44	37
Female	18	16	31	24	21
Rough idea of how want things to go					
Male	48	32	39	21	35
Female	27	43	8	0	23
Not very sure what want to do					
Male	30	26	19	14	22
Female	45	42	50	.19	42
Don't intend to work					
Male	0	0	2	22	6
Female	10	0	10	57	14
Know definitely + rough idea					
Male	70	74	79	65	72
Female	45	58	39	24	44
Thought 'yes' about what sort of job wanted in five years' time (R40)					
Male	50	59	38	41	47
Female	58	42	21	21	40
Number:[b]					
male	(39)	(36)	(37)	(42)	(154)
female	(53)	(43)	(35)	(22)	(153)

Note: The age variable refers to age of respondent at the time of the first survey in order to ensure that exactly the same two groups of respondents are being compared across the two questions. The results for the second question (R40) would be very slightly different if it was cross-tabulated against the respondents' age at the time of the second survey.

[a] Kirkcaldy respondents only.
[b] Number of cases on which percentages are based in each cell of the table.

women were less likely to respond positively than men, again a not surprising finding.

However, when the responses to the two questions are cross-tabulated with each other, the association is very weak for females and there is absolutely no relationship at all for males.

Indeed, at first glance, the only encouraging finding is that all ten males who indicated in the first survey that they did not intend to work had, a year later, no thoughts about a job in five years' time (as did nineteen of the twenty-one women).

It might be tempting to conclude that responses to questions about plans and thoughts of this kind are entirely random or alternatively represent views which are highly transient and of no social significance whatsoever. For some of the population, this may, indeed, be partly true. However, the fact that, as we have already mentioned, such responses are significantly related to respondents' past experience and locations in the social structure suggests a need to look further for an explanation. There are two possible answers to the superficially puzzling discrepancy. The question in the first survey was asked in the context of questions about the labour market in general and was phrased in a way which encouraged respondents to think about the future course of their working life *in general*. The question in the second survey followed a series of questions which were much more focused on *specific* jobs. Respondents who were contemplating retirement, or a significant change in direction, for instance, might well reply that they knew or had a rough idea about their future working life, while not having thought specifically about the sort of job that they wanted to be doing in five years' time. This explanation points to the importance of question wording and context. An alternative interpretation points to a more general and extremely important issue in the understanding of strategies.

The two surveys were conducted more than a year apart and people's perceptions of their employment futures can easily change, especially in an insecure employment market like Kirkcaldy where in many cases the job that one hopes to have in five years' time can vanish entirely from the local labour market with much less than a year's warning. While most of our respondents did indeed have quite clear and detailed plans or aspirations for many areas of their lives, events were continually forcing a reconsideration or even the abandonment of these ideas so that, in the area of employment in particular, detailed plans seldom turned out in practice as intended. However, at any particular moment in time the majority, albeit clearly a changing majority, of our respondents continued to see an orderliness in both their past and their future work lives.

To summarize this section, there is evidence that in some areas of their lives the bulk of our respondents give answers to the survey questions which suggest the existence of some kind of strategic thinking and that these responses are socially structured. The absence of strategies in some areas is itself a matter to be explained but caution is necessary as the data are sensitive to question wording and question context. Finally, it is central to our argument that, although they concern the long term, strategies are nevertheless not fixed and unchanging but subject to constant re-examination and revision.

PATTERNS AND TIME SPANS OF STRATEGIC THINKING

In this section of the chapter we shall review some of the major dimensions along which our respondents appear to develop plans for their lives and the way they are structured, focusing of course on medium- and long-term plans.

In her still important book, *Fertility and Deprivation: A Study of Differential Fertility amongst Working-Class Families in Aberdeen*, Janet Askham (1975) examines two different approaches to family planning and suggests that they are part of more general orientations to life rather than, as had previously been suggested, cultural differences in values and norms. In particular it is, as she calls them, characteristic beliefs which mark out her group of respondents with well above average family sizes. The relationship to our discussion of strategies is clear. These respondents have, she writes, 'a present rather than a future time-orientation because for them the future is more uncertain and insecure than it is for other social groups'; this in turn encourages them to 'take things as they come', and to have no clear sense of control over their destiny. Thus they believe 'one should leave decisions to those with the know-how', have low self-esteem and lay great emphasis on 'luck' as the main factor influencing the path of their lives. Finally, Askham (1975: 96–8) notes that this group of respondents has a general unwillingness to make plans, with few thoughts about the future for their children or of their own jobs.

A parallel contrast between households which 'take life as it comes', and households which do not, has been explored by

Wallman (1984, 1986). She describes two households, both headed by young English working-class couples, in one of which the female partner is ' "quite happy as I am" ' while the other is ' "quite happy about how things are going" '. The former couple 'deliberately live in the present' and 'feel that they have control of their lives one day at a time'. The latter 'can't just live from day to day', 'talk in terms of problems and problem solving', and express 'great faith in planning'. As Wallman sums up, these households 'can be said to have the same economic options. But because one is resolutely present-oriented and the other just as consistently looks towards the future, they organize those options in quite different ways' (Wallman 1986: 62–3).

It might be argued that 'taking things as they come', while clearly present-oriented, could be seen as a kind of short-run defensive strategy. However, we think it more useful to restrict the term 'strategy' to forward-looking approaches to the organization of life. This is not to say that the short-term adaptations implied by 'taking things as they come' are unimportant. Indeed, the data from our intensive interviews show that they occur in the lives of *everyone* interviewed, both planners and non-planners. We prefer to talk of them as *coping devices*, mechanisms for handling the day-to-day problems of life. The crucial point is that for the non-planners they are the main way of organizing life and they see themselves as generally 'taking things as they come'. We are certainly not implying, however, that one form of organization is superior to the other. This distinction between coping devices which enable people to 'get by' on a day-to-day basis and strategies which are part of the process of 'making out', of attempting to achieve long-term goals, is developed and illustrated at length in the following chapter.

Next in this chapter we look in more detail at work-related strategies, then turn to family-building strategies and finish up with more general orientations and those more focused on home and the household. But first we highlight some important points.

As we shall show below, strategic thinking is linked to age, to gender and, to some extent, to marital status. Variation arises from changes over the life cycle of the household, from differences in expectations and domestic task allocation by gender, and from the different pressures and opportunities affecting the lives of single men compared with single (and also widowed and divorced) women and, more sharply, male and female partners in couples. Our semi-structured interviews in Kirkcaldy show clearly that while early in their partnerships men and women have many plans and aspirations, as time goes by (often by their mid-thirties) most seem to have achieved more of an equilibrium. They may continue to have particular aspirations (not always shared by both partners), but their efforts seem directed more to staying roughly as they are rather than seeking to change their futures in any radical way. However, just as downward mobility should not be overlooked in favour of upward mobility, we should not underestimate how important it may be to people to remain roughly as they are and how difficult this can be. In particular, as couples become older, where they have strategies these seem often to be defensive or aimed at maximizing the opportunities offered by their present position rather than being highly proactive.

Strategic thinking is also related to the possession of resources, and deprivation and insecurity are serious deterrents to planning. One would expect both current patterns of perceived deprivation (notably unemployment) and past experience to be relevant. Although our attempts to separate past experience of deprivation from current deprivation have been markedly inhibited by, for example, the small proportion of currently employed respondents with a history of unemployment, our strong impression is that current employment status is significantly more important than past history.

Work-related Strategies

We have already reviewed a considerable amount of data relating in various ways to our respondents' medium-term plans or thoughts about their work lives. For example, among those who were currently in employment (the question was not asked of the unemployed or the non-employed), 61% of men and 40% of women think of themselves as having a career, potentially a very long-term plan. Alongside this, 62% of men in employment have thought about the kind of job that they want to be doing in five years time; so have 54% of women. When this latter group is combined with those who believe they have a career, four-fifths of the men (81%) and two-thirds of the women (68%) have given at least some thought to the long-term trajectory of their working experiences.

There are groups—for example, those approaching retirement, and women in the early stages of child-rearing—in which one would expect a smaller proportion to concern themselves with such thoughts because, for very different reasons, they think it unlikely that they will be working within that time span. In other groups—for example men in established professional occupations as opposed to those in more insecure labour markets—we would expect a higher proportion of respondents to have such longer-term perspectives. Another example here is young men once established into an occupational group as opposed to young, and especially young married, women. In general these predictions are borne out by the data.

Thus, for example, men at all ages are more likely to be thinking about jobs in five years' time and/or that they have a career than are women, and the young are more likely to do this than the old. Of those in employment at the time of both surveys, more than four-fifths (86%) of men in their twenties and three-quarters (77%) of women respond positively to at least one of these two questions. There is only a small change among those in their thirties (84% and 72% respectively), then a significant fall, especially for women, among those in their forties (76% and 59%). Notably, however, there is no real difference between those in their forties and those aged between 50 and 60 (76% and 61% respectively).

A main finding of this chapter is that the late thirties or early forties seem to form some kind of watershed. By the time they reach this stage, a significant proportion of our respondents appear to have begun to view life in a less proactive and more defensive kind of way, something which comes out even more clearly in our intensive interviews.

Turning to socio-economic matters, Table 1.2 shows the strong relationships between these data and respondents' occupation, classified according to the Registrar General's Social Class categories. (Similar results are obtained using the conceptually preferable Hope–Goldthorpe categories but some cell sizes are rather low.) Given the more career-structured nature of many middle-class jobs, this is not entirely surprising but much the same effect is apparent if we confine ourselves just to those with thoughts

TABLE 1.2 *Thoughts about employment*

	Most recent job[a]					
	1	2	3N	3M	4	5
Have thoughts about job in five years or believe have career (%)[b]						
Males	92	95	91	74	61	50
Females	....	90	62	66	60	33
Number:[c]						
males	(50)	(228)	(60)	(228)	(104)	(27)
females	(6)	(150)	(190)	(30)	(94)	(41)
Have thoughts about job in five years (%)[d]						
Males	79	73	65	58	45	44
Females	....	68	50	52	51	28
Number:[c]						
males	(52)	(233)	(62)	(235)	(112)	(32)
females	(6)	(157)	(205)	(37)	(114)	(45)
Believe they have a career (%)[d]						
Males	86	80	73	53	35	21
Females	78	72	36	34	18	8
Number:[c]						
males	(178)	(547)	(231)	(810)	(285)	(80)
females	(38)	(511)	(716)	(160)	(405)	(144)

[a] By the Registrar General's Social Class categories.
[b] The two questions were asked at different times. The data presented are for respondents who were in employment (self-employed or employed) on both occasions. The class data are those recorded at the second survey and the figures would be slightly different but the overall pattern the same if class data at the first survey were used.
[c] The total number of respondents by sex for each column.
[d] The data are for respondents in employment at the time the question was asked and the class variable is as recorded at that time.

about their jobs in five years' time. The fact that the marked disjunction for women falls between the service class (Classes 1 and 2) and the rest should be noted.

While, a priori, one might expect structuring by family status, this is not the case. Indeed, although some of the variables are significantly intercorrelated, no clear differences by family status have been located in these data so far. Admittedly, women who were not members of couples were rather more likely than women who had partners to see themselves as having a career (55% compared with 37%) but almost exactly the same proportion of the former group as the latter had thoughts about a job in five years' time (56% and 53% respectively). To give comparability, these latter data are for women in employment but the same finding holds for all female respondents (the figures are 49% and 46%). Furthermore there is no clear correlation with family size for any group.

We have discussed earlier the question which asked people to think about their working life over the next five years and tell us whether they knew what they wanted to do. We also know something about how confident or fatalistic respondents were about these goals, which may, of course, have involved an element of fantasy. Respondents who said they knew definitely what they wanted to do were asked whether they expected to be able to do it, while those who had a rough idea were asked whether they expected that things would turn out that way. In what follows we have excluded those who said they did not intend to work. Further, the figures differ slightly from those in Table 1.2 as we are able here to utilize the entire Kirkcaldy sample obtained in the first survey. Overall, 73% of our male respondents and 58% of the females had at least a rough idea of how they wanted their working lives to go and a substantial majority of these expected to achieve their aspirations. At the extreme, around a third (30%) of the male respondents and a fifth (22%) of the females had, and expected to be able to achieve, definite plans. On the other hand, those who were not very sure what they wanted to do and felt they would just have to take whatever came up, made up over a fifth of all male respondents (22%) and over a third of the females (36%). Interestingly these gender differences reflect women's greater uncertainty about the direction of their future working lives rather than the proportions expecting to achieve particular outcomes. Indeed, while only 26% of women as opposed to 38% of men knew definitely what they wanted to do over the next five years, 86% of them expected to realize their ambitions as opposed to 78% of men.

In general, and taking into account small cell sizes in some cases, the proportions expecting to achieve definite plans vary very little by age, by employment status, or by occupational class. The two notable exceptions are the unemployed, both male and female, and men over 50 where only around two-thirds expected to achieve their goal. Similarly, among those who were not very sure what they wanted to do, the proportion who thought they would have to take whatever came up varies little by these variables. Just as with the gender differences, it is the extent to which respondents know what they want to do that is structured. Thus while over half of the self-employed of both sexes knew definitely what they wanted to do in their work lives over the next five years (as did 39% of the employed men and 32% of the employed women), this figure falls to 26% of the unemployed men, 18% of the unemployed women and 12% of the non-employed women. Only 24% of young men aged 20–29 knew definitely what they wanted to do as opposed to 43–45% of men in the three older age groups. For women the pattern is somewhat different, certainty growing after the age of 40. Around one-fifth of women in the two younger age groups (21% and 19%) are in the category knowing definitely what they want to do, one-third (31%) of the 40–49 year-old group and only with the oldest group, 50–59, does the proportion reach the male fig-ure with 47%. The pattern by occupational class is somewhat obscured by small cell sizes but in general those in non-manual occupations are more likely to know definitely what they want to do than those in manual occupations.

So far we have considered only current and prospective ques-tions, but some of our respondents claim to have looked a long way ahead in their lives. We have two questions that cover very long periods of time, albeit retrospectively. First, over a third of men and women (37% of men and 38% of women) replied 'yes' to the question: 'When you were in your last year at school did you have any clear idea about the type of job you'd like to have later on in life—say by the age of 40?'. Significant possible prob-lems of recall and retrospective rationalization arise here, but our confidence in the validity of these data is somewhat increased when we note that while, for men, there is no marked age effect, only 31% of women in their fifties and 37% in their forties (com-pared with 41% of women aged 20–29 or 30–39) had such a view, findings which intuitively fit changing employment patterns over time. Furthermore, as one would expect, answering 'yes' to this question is clearly related to father's occupation. Twice as many respondents with fathers in higher non-manual occupations answered in this way than did those with fathers in unskilled manual occupations (52% and 26% of the men; 60% and 30% of the women).

A somewhat similar question, asked only in Kirkcaldy, appears in the first survey with similar results. Around one in six of the men and women alike (18%) responded that when they first started work they had a definite plan of what they wanted to do with their working life, and 36% of men and 27% of women had 'a rough idea'. However, 46% of men and 56% of women replied that they had 'no real idea'. Thus slightly over half of the men and slightly under half of the women had at least a rough idea of what they wanted to do with their working life.

We also asked about the outcomes. Among those who had at least a rough idea when they started work, around half of the men (48%) and of the women (53%) said that their work life had turned out as expected. Among those who had no real idea about their working life when they started work, a similar proportion (56% of the men and 54% of the women) had generally been able to get the jobs they wanted. Clearly we are not dealing with exactly analogous situations here as the latter group probably had lower expectations and certainly less fixed ideas about what they were aiming at, making it easier to feel they had got the jobs they wanted. Nevertheless, in terms of their perceptions, it is clear that for around half of our respondents either they had failed to achieve the specifically desired outcomes or generally to get the jobs they wanted. It is important to repeat that strategies, in our view, should not be seen as immutable blueprints for action over a lifetime. Rather they are guiding principles which are constantly being revised in the light of events and structural changes, for instance in the labour market.

We have a question about medium-distance plans which also throws light on outcomes and yields not dissimilar results. In the second survey we asked about the background to respondents' last job change. Because of the complexities of asking such a question in a comprehensive way given the limited space of our survey, the question was limited to starting or voluntarily stopping work or changing from full- to part-time or the reverse. Among those to whom the question applied, the opportunity had 'just come up' for 34% of males and 40% of females, whereas

47% of men and 43% of women said that they had 'been thinking about changing [their] situation in this way for some time'. In keeping with the life-cycle effects noted above, this last response was particularly given by women in the 40–49 age group, 51% of whom replied that the opportunity 'had just come up'. By no means all those who responded that the opportunity had just come up were 'non-planners'. Many almost certainly did have ideas about what they wanted to do, but something else had come up and they had taken it. It is amply clear that plans and outcomes are not the same thing and that, for many men and women, strategies are only poorly related to the actual behavioural outcomes. As David McCrone shows in the next chapter, our intensive interviews in Kirkcaldy support this interpretation of the survey findings.

We can now pull these various findings together. It is undoubtedly the case that the picture which emerges from the above data is one which suggests that most individuals do have consciously articulated work-related plans which they describe to us. So how do we understand the situation where a considerable proportion of those whom we interview tell us that in practice 'opportunities just come up'? The latter statement is, of course, compatible with most sociological interpretations of the work lives of the mass of the population which assert that people, even middle-class people, do not have much control over their lives in the world of work. Ray and Jan Pahl in their study of managers (Pahl and Pahl 1971: 103), stress the role of luck and the limited extent to which even this group can in fact plan and affect their own life chances in the world of work. In their work among manual workers, Blackburn and Mann (1979) again and again stress the lack of orderliness of labour markets and the very limited extent of real choice available in practice to most of the men that they studied.

This raises in turn the question of why a substantial majority of these same groups of the population are still able to respond that, for example, they see themselves as having careers or that they have thoughts about the kind of job that they will be doing in five years' time.

We see two reasons for this. The first is that most people may well believe that, even if unable to plan their precise position in a job market, they will be able to find employment within broad sets of jobs which might indeed legitimately be viewed by respondents, when replying to our questions, as 'kinds of jobs'. Similarly, the steps from job to job may be seen by many respondents, in retrospect, as having sufficiently logical a structure to be classifiable as involving the following of a 'career', especially as we allowed respondents to use their own definition of career.

Our second interpretation reflects more fundamental orientations to life. While, in practice most people may be unable to plot in advance their employment trajectories with any great accuracy, yet there are very strong pressures on them to act as if they are doing so. In modern Western societies, there is a strong expectation that economic rationality will hold sway in the world of work. People are, we would argue, expected to at least try to control this area of their lives. They thus want to control the world of work and there is a substantial literature on alienation which suggests that they do not like being unable to control it. An essential prerequisite to any attempt to control and to exercise choice is the possession of forward-looking sets of plans, expectations, or hopes. Thus only those who have 'legitimate reasons', such as retirement or child-rearing, or those whose labour market position is so weak that they are manifestly unable to control their future existence, can readily admit, probably even to themselves, that they do not have ideas about their future employment.

'Demographic' Decisions

In contrast to the world of work, the world of marriage and children has strong private, romantic cultural overtones. Under these circumstances, we suspect that many people find it unacceptable to appear too rational about these areas of one's life, and overtly articulated strategies and plans and forward thinking are thus likely to be much less prevalent. Nevertheless sociological and economic analysis conventionally sees this as an area where actual behaviour is in fact highly structured by economic and other rational factors.

In the self-completion element of the second survey we offered respondents and their partners a list of twelve possible reasons which might be important in influencing the point in their lives when they first set up home together. We asked them to tick those which applied to them. How did they react to this question which, like all the self-completion questions, they answered separately without consultation? Wherever possible throughout this chapter we present the data manipulated so as to combine all males and all females together, be they respondents or partners.

By far the most cited response to this question was 'We fell in love and couldn't live without each other', mentioned by roughly three-quarters of the men (71%) and of the women (77%); no other single response is mentioned by more than one in three people. Thus only a quarter of men and women alike (24%) cited 'We'd got enough money together to get a house', while 25% of men and 12% of women opted for 'I was at a suitable point in my working life', and 11% of men and 14% of women 'My partner was at a suitable point in his/her working life'. Only 40% of the men and 35% of the women, a group we may for present purposes perhaps think of as 'strong planners', offered one or more of these three responses. Around one in seven people (14% of men, 16% of women) said that rented accommodation became available, which probably implied a degree of planning but could just be happenstance. We might also wish to include as planning indicators, 'The time had come when I wanted to live with a regular sexual partner' (cited by 29% of men and 20% of women), and 'I wanted the security' (22% of the men and 25% of the women), both rather ambiguous in these terms. If we include these, to obtain a group of 'weak planners', the proportions citing one or more of the six 'planful' responses rise to a more substantial 64% of men and 62% of women.

It is important to be clear about what is being claimed here. It is not that those people who gave us the romantic, if conventional response were very much less likely to be planners in some sense than those who did not, although there is such a relationship. Thus among the 'romantics', 38% of the men are 'strong' and 61% 'strong or weak' planners compared with 47% and 76% among the rest. The corresponding figures for the women are 35% and 60%, 37% and 71%. The point is rather the high proportion who give an emotional 'non-rational' response (two-thirds or more even among 'strong planners'), and that even among those who did not give this response, less than half of the men and just over a third of the women are 'strong planners'.

Moreover examination of the patterns of variation by occupational class, employment status, and age fails to identify any major subgroup within the population who confess to a strong rational economic basis in their marriage decisions. All social groups give 'fell in love' as by far the most frequent response.

There is some patterning by age, of a kind which intuitively at least increases our confidence in the data. Older men are slightly more inclined to say that they 'fell in love' (66% in the youngest and 76% in the oldest group) although this does not hold for women; the youngest group of men and women are roughly twice as likely as the oldest to cite having enough money for a house or feeling that the time had come to live with a regular sexual partner; and roughly one and a half times as likely to say they wanted the security, (the latter two responses of course among our 'weak' measures of planning). There are also differences in the percentages admitting that their partner's pregnancy was the reason ranging among men from 10% of the youngest group to 6% of the oldest, and among women from 13% to 8%.

We also, in a similar kind of question in the self-completion element of the second survey, asked respondents to tell us the things that were important in influencing the point in their lives when they had their first child together. Of the eleven alternatives offered, only five attracted more than 15% of respondents. Four could be said to suggest some degree of premeditation and each was cited by a substantial minority of those interviewed. A response which claims fairly precise, long-term planning, 'I'd always planned to start a family at that time', was cited by around a third (33% of males and 31% of females); 'I felt the time had come when we could manage on only one income for a while' was said to have influenced over a fifth (21% of males and 23% of females); the rather more general 'I wanted to start a family before we were too old' was given as a reason by 45% of men and 39% of women; and 'We thought we were then in a position to give a child the time and attention he/she deserved' was cited by 42% of males and 45% of females. However, a substantial number did not plan: 30% of males and the 34% of females reported that the female partner became pregnant unexpectedly. (Of course, this is not an entirely satisfactory measure as it must be admitted that in some cases the pregnancy will have been the result of contraceptive failure rather than lack of planning.)

Although there are some discernible differences by age, employment status, and most recent occupational class, it is perhaps the relative absence of such structural patterning which is more striking. Admittedly, it seems the currently unemployed are particularly likely to claim that their partner became pregnant unexpectedly. Two in five currently unemployed men (41%) compared with under a third currently employed men (30%) cited this response, indicating either a lack of planning or contraceptive failure even though the event in many cases happened many years ago. The proportion of unemployed men giving this response is also a rather higher figure than the 33% of men in Goldthorpe-class categories 5, 6, and 7 who do so and may in turn be compared with the 25% in classes 1 and 2. By contrast, while 34% of employed men claimed that their timing was what had always been planned, only 25% of the currently unemployed did so. It may then be that within the populations we have studied there is a subgroup who are and have for many years been likely to lead unpredictable lives in a number of different ways, a point perhaps meriting further investigation. Nevertheless the differences in general are not large and for females no clear patterns at all emerge.

Thus, as one might expect, the data on the timing of their first child suggest rather more planning than was evident for the timing of marriage but around a third of couples experienced an unexpected pregnancy, and the planning exercised by the remainder, at least as reported to us, was frequently only in general terms.

Finally, the same lack of emphasis on planning one's family life is very clear when we look at answers to a question which we asked of all respondents and partners in Kirkcaldy: 'When you first set up home together how much idea did you have of how you were going to fit together your working lives and your family life in terms of having children?' Only a small minority of either sex (around one in six men and one in ten women) responded by choosing the option offered that they had a 'definite plan' of when they were going to have children and how they would fit working around it. A further one in twenty men and women planned 'not to have children because of commitments to working', giving, overall, 24% of men and 15% of women with a clear plan. This contrasts with those who reported only a rough idea

(39% of men and 36% of women) and a rather surprising 37% of men and 50% of women with 'no real plans about fitting together work and having children' at the time of first setting up home together. There is a very marked age effect here with, as one would expect, the percentage with no real plans at the time they set up home together being significantly higher in the older age groups (seven in ten women aged 50 to 60 reported that they had no real plans at that time compared with three in ten women aged 20 to 29; the corresponding proportions for men are just under half and just over a quarter). Interestingly (and perhaps partly because any variation is masked by the age effect), at least in terms of current class categories, there are no marked class effects here, nor do such effects become apparent even when we look at the extent to which those who then had some plans or rough idea had actually succeeded in carrying them out. Few couples, then, seem to have given serious attention at the outset to fitting together work and children and it seems likely that the process is one of continuous adaptation to changing circumstances.

In the intensive interviews, in which Dr Straw and Mrs Sinfield clearly obtained excellent rapport with their respondents, very little reporting of clearly developed demographic life plans occurs, although the survey evidence shows that the majority of the couples interviewed did seem to have tried to plan the intervals between and the number of births of their children. There is also, however, a strong sense in those interviews that the birth of the first child is seen in many cases as a 'taken for granted' aspect of and reason for marriage and something which is expected to follow relatively soon after marriage. To that extent some of the reasons given may be retrospective rationalizations.

If, then, we draw together the threads of this section, it seems we should distinguish the broadest and long-term sense of 'family planning' from the specific sense of the timing of one's first child, and presumably subsequent children. Demographic behaviour in the broad sense still seems to a great extent to be responsive to opportunity and those interviewed volunteered little information about planning in this area of life. When it comes to the specific and generally controllable issue of the timing of their first child, the sample splits into those where the woman became unexpectedly pregnant and the roughly two-thirds whose responses suggested a degree of rational planning.

This area of life is in many ways the obverse of the world of work discussed in the previous section. Ideologically, romance and spontaneity are expected to dominate at least most people's thoughts about these key aspects of their lives, and indeed chance, at most structurally constrained, is probably still an important determinant of actual outcomes. Unlike the world of work, however, where people seem to wish to be in control but chance plays a greater part than people think it should, in the world of children and the family it is likely that rational decision making and a degree of planning do exist but are played down.

Organization of Domestic Life

In this section, we are particularly interested in areas which involved property and where therefore we might expect many respondents to exercise 'rational forethought'. However, for the more affluent, we hypothesized that there would be a tension between their greater ability to organize their lives in a planful way, and their capacity to operate in an *ad hoc* manner with less risk of disaster.

We look first at a question asking respondents 'Which of these statements best fits the way you organize your financial affairs?' The alternatives offered were 'I just take things as they come' and 'I tend to plan out my finances carefully'. While it is possible that some of those giving the second response had short-term planning in mind, the structuring of the responses and some evidence from the intensive interviews suggest that this response involves longer-term planning. Overall, 55% of males and 62% of females replied that 'they plan their finances carefully'. As might be expected from the greater flexibility open to them, men and women in the 20–29 age group plan rather less, the tendency being particularly marked for young men rather than young women, while men and women in the 50–60 age group plan rather more. The effect on planning of living in a couple is very different for males and females. Male respondents in couples tend to plan more than those not in couples (57% compared with 46%). Women not in couples, on the other hand, plan slightly more than those in couples (67% compared with 61%). We suspect that the men in couples feel a greater responsibility for others than those not in couples, and the women not in couples a greater responsibility for their own actions, but we do not have data with which to pursue this further. We have already seen that, whereas two-thirds of single women plan, this is the case for less than half of single men. For both sexes the divorced and (at least for women) the widowed are also above-average planners. Household standard income, a measure which standardizes for household composition, is on average higher among the planners, after controlling for sex and membership of a couple, or after controlling for sex and current marital status broken down into single, married, separated, divorced, or widowed.

Table 1.3 shows a clear association between the perceptions of those interviewed of the ease or difficulty with which they can make ends meet and their reporting that they plan their finances carefully. Those who see themselves as coping least well are also least likely to plan. Taking all these findings together, it is clear that the tendency for greater resources to make planning easier is stronger than the ability which greater resources bring to run more risks by taking things as they come.

TABLE 1.3 *Respondents and partners in couples who plan their finances carefully (%)[a]*

| | Ease or difficulty of making ends meet | | | | |
	Very easy	Quite easy	Neither difficult nor easy	Quite difficult	Very difficult
Males	66	64	56	50	39
Females	62	63	64	52	50
Number:[b]					
males	(86)	(336)	(582)	(256)	(60)
females	(80)	(310)	(606)	(263)	(60)

[a] Categorized by ease or difficulty in making ends meet, and by sex.
[b] The total number of respondents by sex for each column.

We also asked those who had bought their own home why they had done so. Half of the men and the women alike (49% and 51%) gave 'It was a good investment' as the most important reason and another quarter (26% of men and 29% of women) mentioned this factor as their second choice. Around half of the men and of the women (51% and 54%) gave the rather ambiguous 'I liked the idea of owning my own property' as a first or second reason; 'You are freer to do what you want with it' was the third most popular first or second choice (mentioned by 20% of men and 21% of women). This response was especially selected by women currently not members of a couple (31%). Analysis by employment status shows little variation for women but among men the good investment aspect was most stressed by the self-employed followed by the employed and was less stressed by the non-employed, who instead were more likely than the self-employed and the employed to mention freedom and the fact that it was cheaper than rent. For neither men nor women was there any substantial variation by Goldthorpe category. Clearly on this basis the long-term consequences of house purchase are high in the minds of those who purchase across most of the social spectrum and at all ages.

However, Pahl's work on housing careers would go further and suggest that for many people housing does not just involve a once-for-all long-term decision but in addition can frequently be seen as part of a progressive strategy involving conscious planning over significant parts of their lives. Unfortunately, lack of time led to severe cuts in the housing section of the questionnaire and the only information we have on housing careers relates to the reasons our respondents gave for their last move.

Around a third of men and of women (30% and 36%) said that they had moved because they had wanted a different size of home, and a fifth (21% of males and 22% of females) said they had wanted a different type of home. Wanting to buy a house or flat resulted in a move for 18% of the men and 16% of the women, while 20% of males and 14% of females said it made financial sense to buy a better home, and 18% of males and 21% of females said they had wanted to move to a better area. Interestingly, there were no large variations by age group here, suggesting considerable consistency of pattern over time.

Can we draw any conclusions from these data about our respondents' housing strategies? Would we expect these more planning-oriented options to receive more responses in a situation where respondents could mention as many options as they liked (and where in reply to some other questions they clearly did go for significant multiple response)? If we take 'I wanted to move to a better area' or 'It made financial sense to buy a better house' as indicating the existence of a housing career, a quarter of the sample (26%) gave one or both of these responses. We can take this as the first level of a rather crude indicator. If we create a second level by adding 'I wanted to buy a house/flat', which may be simply a one-off decision, 36% of our respondents give one or more of these three replies. Including the rather more ambiguous replies indicating wanting a different type or size of property to create a third level, raises the figure to 62%. These figures are virtually identical for men and women but they are structured in other ways. At the first level we find around a fifth of the unemployed and the non-employed (19% and 21%), just over a quarter of the employed (28%) and a third of the self-employed (34%). At the second level the corresponding figures are 28%, 26%, 39%, and 47%. At the third level, the differences are considerably reduced, the figures being 52%, 68%, 66%, and 60%. By age, 10 percentage points more of those aged 30–39 and 40–49 give these responses at the first and second levels than those aged 20–29 or 50–60. Apart from the self-employed, there are no systematic differences by Goldthorpe categories.

We might thus tentatively conclude that between a quarter and a third of our respondents may have (or have had) a clear long-term planned housing career. That this estimate may be too high is, however, suggested when we note that fewer than one in six of our respondents mentioned house moves in response to the general question 'Do you have any plans for yourselves and your household at the present time?' Even more significantly, most of these were young people; only 9% of men and women in their forties and living in couples made any mention of moving in response to this question. And, as we shall see later, most of those who mention moving wish to do so because they are very dissatisfied with the area in which they live or with their current house.

Control and its Effects on Planning

There is many a slip between plan and achievement. It is quite clear in Askham's work, for example, and also in much of the literature on the 'culture of poverty', that one reason why many people do not make detailed plans is that they perceive that they have very little chance of carrying them out. Do our data suggest that our respondents feel able to control their lives and how does this affect their willingness to make plans for the future? There are two possible approaches to this question.

The first is to ask people how realistic they think their thoughts and aspirations are or have been in practice.

We have already noted the two sets of questions, asked of people in Kirkcaldy only, about how they thought their working plans had and would work out in practice. Looking ahead, of those who had at least a rough idea of what they thought they would achieve in their working lives over the next five years, three-quarters of the men and of the women expected to realize their aspirations, while among those who were not very sure what they wanted to do, 35% of the men and 65% of the women thought that they would have to take whatever came up. We have already discussed (see p. 35) the rather similar question about the plans people had when they first started work and whether these ambitions had been achieved. Of those who had at least a rough idea, half said their working life had turned out as expected, and of those with no real idea around half had been obliged to take whatever jobs had turned up. Making the necessary caveats for comparability, the contrast between these answers suggests that people's labour market plans are often unrealistic. This may be especially true, as we hinted above, in an economy such as that of Kirkcaldy where frequent shocks occur.

As for long-term family plans, while fewer people claimed to have had them, the outcomes in as far as we can measure them do today seem to have been rather more achievable. For example, fifty-two men reported that when they first set up home with their present partner they had clear plans of relating children to work life and forty-five of these reckoned that things had worked out as they had planned. The corresponding figures for women are twenty-seven out of thirty-three. Ten of the women and fourteen of the men said that these plans had involved not having children, and in the case of four women and one man this had not worked out as planned.

A second way of exploring this issue of control and its effects is to ask directly how much people think that they are in control of their lives. Within the self-completion section of the second survey respondents and their partners were asked: 'Which of these statements best describes the way you feel: "What happens to me is my own doing" or "I feel that I have little influence over the things that happen to me"?' 'What happens to me is my own doing' was the response of three-quarters of the men and the women (75%, 74%).

These feelings of control are certainly associated with other life experiences in ways one would expect, though not always strongly. Thus, if we contrast the group who believe what happens to them is their own doing with those who feel they have little influence over what happens to them, two-thirds of the men in the first group compared with half of the second believe they have a career (the corresponding figures for women are 50% and 29%); 62% compared with 52% have thought about the job they want to be doing in five years' time (51% and 35% in the case of the women). If we examine the data relating to the last job change, of those men who believe what happens to them is their own doing, 61% had been 'thinking about the change for some time', whereas the 'opportunity just came up' for exactly the same percentage of those who believe they have little influence over the things that happen to them. For women this relationship does not hold, possibly reflecting the more happenstance way in which many return to the labour market or move from full- to part-time work or vice-versa.

Further analysis of this question reveals an important dimension to feelings of control: they are to a considerable extent structured by age, marital status, and occupational class. With the material available we cannot unravel the complex processes involved, but we may hypothesize that the older, the separated, widowed, and divorced, the unemployed and non-employed, and the working class are less likely to possess the resources (using the term in the widest sense) needed to organize their lives; they are also more likely to feel by virtue of adverse experience that they do not control their lives. The data support this general interpretation. Thus, for example, men and women in their fifties are less likely to feel that what happens to them is their own doing (67% of men and 62% of women aged 50–60 compared with 77% of men and 76% of women aged 20–49). Separated, widowed, and divorced women and widowed and divorced men are less likely to feel in control than do the single and the currently married. For both sexes, the self-employed clearly feel much more in control, the unemployed and non-employed markedly less so. Four in five men (83%) with occupation in Goldthorpe categories 1 and 2 feel that what happens to them is their own doing compared with two-thirds (69%) of men in categories 5, 6 and 7. For women the parallel figures are 88% and 68%. And the mean household standard income, perhaps our most direct measure of resources, is higher among those who felt in control: 24% higher in the case of men and 16% in the case of women.

HOUSEHOLD STRATEGIES

We turn now to a rather different dimension of the problem of elucidating strategies from empirical research. Much of the literature refers to 'household' strategies ('household work strategies', 'household resource generation strategies', and so on). Conceptually there are some difficulties in this idea, as one of us demonstrated more than ten years ago (Anderson 1980) and has been elaborated in the more recent critiques discussed earlier. Nevertheless strategies, at least as we use the term, clearly have strong cultural aspects and thus must have an element of sharedness in their existence: the question then becomes with whom are the beliefs shared? Since households by definition share living space and in most conceptualizations also jointly engage in consumption at least of food, there must also be mechanisms to govern these aspects of behaviour. The fact that the State, financial institutions, and indeed marriage and child legislation lay certain expectations on at least some members of households as a group is also clearly relevant. Thus households, like all enduring groups, must have emergent properties which we can treat as existing above the individual level. It therefore makes perfectly good sense to assume that households can indeed have (or at least be treated as having) strategies which are more than the sum of the individual aspirations of their members, in the same way as we may assume that the members of any other group or organization share belief systems which, once shared, are experienced by members as external constraints. None of this denies that some members at some points in time may be more committed to the shared belief systems than are others, nor that beliefs may be more shared in some areas of activity than others, nor that sometimes this sharing may be the consequence of patriarchal hegemony or even a desperate lack of alternatives. These raise questions for empirical investigation but nothing is gained in our view by pretending that 'household' strategies cannot usefully be conceptualized at least in principle, since if this view is taken, a number of questions of significance both to the sociology and the economics of the household cannot be addressed.

However, while we believe that the study of household strategies is both relevant and significant, this is by no means a straightforward task. We began our work in the hope that we would be able to explore certain aspects of the organization of the household economy from the point of view of all its members. In practice, designing a questionnaire which would satisfy the needs of many investigators made it impossible to include any more than fairly marginal information on the involvement and beliefs of anyone other than the respondent and partner. This is regrettable since it means that we cannot directly explore the changes imposed on the culture of the household by, for example, children moving into work nor the extent to which children share the aspirations and career plans which their parents have for them. Nor in our intensive interviews did we have the time to explore this aspect of the problem in depth, though we have gathered some clues about factors which may operate in this area. There is, however, a number of ways in which we can get a little insight into the kinds of beliefs that couples share and do not share, into how people perceive their lives are constrained by these beliefs and, if only through our intensive interview data, how if at all they seek to react to them and even to limit their constraining effects.

Plans for Self and Household

Right at the end of the interview in the second survey, respondents were asked: 'Do you have any plans for yourselves and your household at the present time?' If they said 'yes' they were asked: 'Could you tell me about them'. In all, 54% of both male and female respondents replied 'yes' to this question. There are two justifications for seeing this question, asked of individuals, as nevertheless containing strong 'household components'. The first is that members of couples were more likely to respond positively to this question (for males: 59% for members of couples, 38% for the rest; for females: 58% and 44%) and were more likely to name more than one plan. This effect (see Table 1.4) is especially marked among young males in couples who, as we might expect in the light of earlier discussion, are particularly likely to be thinking proactively at this time in their lives.

TABLE 1.4 *Respondents replying 'yes' to the question: 'Do you have any plans for yourself and your household at the present time?' (%)[a]*

	Age				
	20–29	30–39	40–49	50–60	All
Couples					
Males	76	62	58	46	59
Females	62	64	56	45	58
Number:[b]					
males	(98)	(211)	(195)	(134)	(638)
females	(166)	(216)	(167)	(130)	(679)
Others					
Males	40	44	15	36	38
Females	54	52	23	24	44
Number:[b]					
males	(145)	(50)	(17)	(30)	(242)
females	(110)	(55)	(28)	(48)	(241)

[a] Categorized by age, sex, and whether in couple.
[b] Numbers of cases on which percentages are based in each cell of the table.

Secondly, when respondents were asked, with both partners present, to elaborate their plans, a large proportion of the responses seem best interpreted as referring to the household and they are structured in a way which supports this inference. The responses given by men are very similar to those given by women.

The responses were classified in great detail and most respondents mentioned more than one item. The coding was done in such a way that the plans can be combined in a meaningful way to give the eight categories shown in Table 1.5. Home improvement and decoration, nearly always of a do-it-yourself kind, forms the bulk of the first category; purchases or change of con-

TABLE 1.5 *Respondents having a particular type of plan for themselves and their household*

Type of plan	%
Home improvement	24
Holidays and leisure	18
Housing-related	16
Work-related	10
Own family	6
Children	3
Education	2
Money and status	2

Notes: These are percentages of the entire sample (N = 1,792). Thus 24% of all respondents mentioned one or more items classified as 'home improvement' among the plans they had for themselves and their household. If we confine ourselves to respondents who claimed to have such plans, this category is mentioned by just under half of them.

A description of the content of the categories is to be found in the text.

sumer goods are also included here but only make up around 5% of these responses. The second main category is holidays, travel and other leisure interests although the first two make up around 85% of this category. Housing plans refer to moving house or area, buying or selling a house and so on. The last large category is work-related plans. Plans for one's family in general make up a smaller but significant category and three small groups are plans specifically for one's children, for education and for money or status. In the analysis, respondents are classified as having, say, work-related plans if they mentioned one or more things in that category.

As Tables 1.4 and 1.6 show, couples give rather different responses to those not living in couples. For couples by far the commonest plans (especially among young couples) were for home improvements. Thereafter, holiday or leisure plans are the next most frequently mentioned (and were particularly important for older age groups) and then plans to move house or area which, as we have seen earlier, were predominantly focused among the younger respondents. Indeed, we can see a clear pattern where younger men and women focus their hopes and expectations on acquiring and improving their accommodation and to

TABLE 1.6 *Respondents with specified plans for themselves and their household (%)[a]*

	Age				
	20–29	30–39	40–49	50–60	All
Home improvement					
Couples					
Males	42	36	25	16	29
Females	38	35	26	24	32
Others					
Males	4	13	1	18	8
Females	4	21	10	2	8
Housing-related					
Couples					
Males	24	22	10	11	16
Females	22	19	10	9	16
Others					
Males	15	3	0	18	12
Females	24	16	7	12	18
Holidays and leisure					
Couples					
Males	15	20	24	22	21
Females	18	20	20	21	20
Others					
Males	9	14	11	14	11
Females	12	17	5	11	12
Work-related					
Couples					
Males	14	12	10	4	10
Females	10	12	5	3	8
Others					
Males	18	20	3	17	17
Females	17	7	1	4	10
Own family-related					
Couples					
Males	13	7	3	4	6
Females	14	3	4	2	6

	Age				
	20–29	30–39	40–49	50–60	All
Others					
Males	7	3	0	0	5
Females	18	10	2	3	11
Number[b]					
Couples					
Males	(98)	(210)	(195)	(134)	(637)
Females	(166)	(216)	(163)	(129)	(674)
Others					
Males	(145)	(50)	(17)	(30)	(242)
Females	(109)	(55)	(28)	(48)	(240)

[a] Categorized by age, sex, and whether in couple.
[b] Number of cases on which percentages are based in each cell of table.

a more limited extent on family, work, and leisure. Then, as they enter middle age they become much more restricted in their proactive planning and focus it largely on continued home improvement and plans for holidays and travel, probably because they have either achieved their housing, work, and family ambitions or have come to believe that this is no longer possible. As we have no data enabling us to compare respondents with their partners we cannot be certain that these really represent 'household' plans, but the great similarity of responses for men and women is at least compatible with this reasonable hypothesis. The presence of both partners at the interview increases our confidence in this interpretation.

Our focus here is, of course, mainly on couples, as those not living in couples are presumably dealing mainly with individual plans. However, a brief look at the latter group is relevant as we find a quite different pattern, rather less clearly age-related, but slightly different for men and women. Given the sample size, one must be careful not to overinterpret small differences. For men not living in couples, work-related plans are consistently highly salient, although the meaning of these plans doubtless changes as, for instance, they approach retirement. For women, between the ages of 30 and 49, home improvement is of importance, while for the youngest women housing-related plans seem crucial along with family-related plans, generally concerned with marriage. The finding that the pattern is different for single men compared with single women and for both from that for couples increases our confidence that much of the data earlier reported do reflect 'household' plans of some kind.

It appears then that many couples do have plans for themselves and their households that may be said to form part of their strategies, are clearly related to the life cycle, and are different from those held by persons not living in couples. We earlier came to the tentative conclusion that although it may be tempting to imagine that those with the fewest resources are forced by harsh necessity to plan their lives, this is not so. Our findings here are equally in line with the previous literature suggesting that resources are necessary if one is to plan.

As the two types of plan most commonly mentioned by couples are self-evidently resource-dependent—this applying even to do-it-yourself home improvement—it is not surprising to find this finding replicated again (see Table 1.7). The higher-income groups have more plans giving on average more than twice as many responses to the general question than the low-income groups. Those with more resources are more likely to report having home improvement or holiday and leisure plans, be these resources higher household standard income, being employed or self-employed, or being of higher social class. These variables are of course interrelated, but employment status or occupational class involve more than income alone.

Compared with these clearly consumption-oriented plans for home improvement, holidays, and so on, the existence of housing-related plans is less resource- or class-dependent. We believe this is not hard to explain. While the level of resources available is likely to determine the action which couples hope to take with respect to their housing, there is a wide range of possibilities for action with very different resource implications. Thus, for instance, council tenants face a different situation from owner-occupiers and the resources that the former need to improve at least a little on a desperately bad housing situation may be far less than those already in expensive properties require to move up-market.

It is dissatisfaction with one's house or flat or with the area in which one lives which is a crucial determinant of housing-related plans. Nearly two-fifths (38%) of those under 40, who place

TABLE 1.7 *Respondents with home improvement or leisure plans (%)*[a]

	Household standard income (£)						
	<3 000	3 000–4 999	5 000–6 999	7 000–8 999	9 000–10 999	11 000–12 999	≥13 000
Home improvement plans							
Age <40	24	19	37	42	48	51	46
Age ≥40	5	7	23	23	30	28	44
Holiday and leisure plans							
Age <40	8	6	15	22	16	37	25
Age ≥40	10	8	20	28	32	29	30
Number:[b]							
age <40	(32)	(67)	(134)	(142)	(70)	(49)	(56)
age ≥40	(31)	(50)	(90)	(90)	(69)	(35)	(57)

	Most recent Registrar General's social class					
	1	2	3N	3M	4	5
Home improvement plans						
Age <40	54	40	42	33	29	25
Age ≥40	6	35	28	16	18	14
Holiday and leisure plans						
Age <40	29	25	17	13	15	11
Age ≥40	43	32	24	15	16	11
Number:[b]						
age <40	(32)	(205)	(173)	(114)	(125)	(31)
age ≥40	(15)	(160)	(129)	(135)	(130)	(47)

	Employment status			
	Self-employed	Employed	Non-employed	Un-employed
Home improvement plans				
Age <40	33	43	19	29
Age ≥40	16	27	17	10
Holiday and leisure plans				
Age <40	18	21	14	9
Age ≥40	27	25	16	2
Number:[b]				
age <40	(45)	(462)	(118)	(65)
age ≥40	(35)	(424)	(121)	(41)

[a] Categorized by various variables by age.
[b] Number of cases on which percentages are based in each cell of the table.

themselves on one of the five points towards the dissatisfied end of an eleven-point scale of satisfaction with their present house or flat, indicate plans to do something about their housing, compared with less than one in six (15%) of those towards the more satisfied end of the scale. The differences are even greater among those of 40 and over (34% compared with 7%). Very similar results are found if we compared those relatively satisfied with their town or area as a place to live with those relatively dissatisfied.

The existence of plans for home improvement involves spending time and money on do-it-yourself activities and other ways of improving one's home, and is markedly more common among those satisfied with their present house or flat, or area in which they live compared with those relatively dissatisfied. This suggests that those dissatisfied are more likely to react to their situation by moving than by improving their house or flat, and are thus more likely to report housing plans. This is exactly what we find. Thus, among those dissatisfied with their present flat or house, twice as many have housing plans and no home improvement plans than the reverse situation of home improvement plans but no housing plans. Among those satisfied with their house or flat the relationship is reversed and the proportion rises to three and a half to one.

Work plans are the last of the frequently mentioned groups. The question asked about 'plans for yourself and your household', so we would expect those mentioning work plans to be the groups in which such plans are most likely to impinge strongly on their families. The data support this interpretation. For instance, twice as many of the unemployed and the self-employed compared with the employed and non-employed mention work plans. In the case of the unemployed group one would anticipate that getting employment would have a great impact on the lives of their families, and in the case of the self-employed their families are frequently heavily involved in the running of their businesses. Given that many of the questions about work strategies discussed earlier will be perceived as personal and individualistic we would not expect by any means all those having such strategies to mention work plans but would expect some positive relationship between the responses. This is indeed the case. Only a minority of those with thoughts about their job in five years' time refer to work plans in answer to the question under discussion. However, if we focus on those mentioning work plans, the ratio of those with thoughts about their job in five years' time to those without is nearly four to one in the 20–39 age group, and nearly five to one in the 40 and over age group.

Discussion between Partners

A prerequisite for the existence of a 'household' strategy (in our sense) should be some degree of prior discussion between household members. They may or may not agree, but for there to be a household strategy members must be at least dimly aware of what strategy the others wish to follow. The survey asked only two questions which throw light on this issue and, for reasons we have already explained above, these were limited to partners living in couples. Both were originally included for quite other reasons so that the wording is not exactly what we should have desired for the present purpose, but the data nevertheless support our claim that we are tapping 'household' strategies a good deal of the time.

First, as a follow-up to the question (asked to both respondents and their partners) asking people their thoughts about what sort of job they wanted to be doing in five years' time, each person claiming to have given the matter some thought was asked whether they had discussed it with their partner. We have once again reorganized the data by sex regardless of whether the data come from respondent or partner. Men in couples are more likely than women to have thought about their job in five years' time, but 72% of males and of females alike who had given the matter thought had discussed them with their partner. There were no exceptional variations by age here. Among men, Goldthorpe's service-class employees (77%) and the self-employed (75%) were slightly more likely than the working class (66%) to have discussed this issue, possibly as a result of differences in communication between spouses or from a greater perceived potential impact of job changes on wives in the higher social groups. The patterns for women show no systematic variability, with high figures for all groups; it seems that most women still continue to feel that they must or would wish to take their husbands' views about possible areas of employment into account.

A similar follow-up was asked to the questions about last job change and once again we have pooled the responses from respondents and their partners. This showed that 73% of males and 82% of females said that their last job change was discussed with their partner. As noted earlier, this variable is really only meaningful for women and, as with current thoughts about future jobs, no outstanding differences are apparent by socio-economic group. Indeed, women of almost all social categories show a very high propensity to discuss their changes with their partners.

Sharing of 'Strategies' by Partners

We would expect the accounts given by partners of their strategies to agree to a greater extent where these strategies are shared between partners and form part of a 'household strategy'. A final way then in which we can explore strategies at a level higher than the individual is by comparing the relationship between the declared plans and aspirations of respondents and their partners. At a number of points in the second survey, questions were asked of both respondents and their partners, and, as we mentioned earlier, self-completion schedules were frequently used. These were filled in by the couple without reference to each other, and in the presence of the interviewer, thus minimizing the danger of contamination between the two sets of responses.

Even on the demographic variables the consistency of responses between partners is not always very high. The data can be viewed in two ways. We can ask what proportion of the wives gave a particular response also given by their husbands or vice versa. These data relating to the question asking why the couple had their first child when they did are presented in Table 1.8 for the five most popular responses.

Interpretation is again not straightforward for a number of reasons. We have no baseline telling us what level of agreement one might expect, respondents were allowed to tick as many items as they wished and partners may have varied in the importance they gave to a particular response, and finally one would expect a degree of evasiveness. It is easy to suspect that one can see these issues reflected in the data: for instance, in the larger proportion of wives who admitted to pregnancy in the cases where their husbands mentioned this than the reverse. But the

TABLE 1.8 *Husbands or wives giving a particular response where the item was mentioned by their partner*

Response	Husbands		Wives	
	(%)	Number[a]	(%)	Number[a]
I/my partner became pregnant unexpectedly	71	(348)	81	(304)
I'd always planned to start a family at that time	55	(317)	52	(338)
I wanted to start a family before we were too old	61	(399)	53	(457)
I felt the time had come when we could manage on only one income for a while	44	(229)	47	(213)
We thought we were then in a position to give a child the time and attention he/she deserved	58	(459)	62	(429)

[a] Number of cases on which percentages are based.

lack of agreement that the couple had 'always planned to start a family at that time' is striking. The most likely explanation is that one partner did indeed have a strategy and prevailed, by whatever means, on the other partner to go along with them. The other partner may have been relatively indifferent or power may have been exercised in some way but it is tempting to conclude that only around half of our sample had a shared strategy in this central area of life.

Nevertheless there is some contrary evidence. It comes from a rather more straightforward question which asked partners to classify themselves as having children and wanting or not wanting more, or not having children and wanting or not wanting to have any. Here the level of agreement is far better although not perfect. We restrict the analysis to couples where the woman is aged less than 40. Thus, for those who have children, 93% agree on whether they hope to have more or not. For those without children, exactly the same percentage agree on whether they hope or do not hope to have any. If we take these data at face value it looks as if couples may indeed have a joint strategy on whether or not to have children but may disagree on the timing or on the explanations they offer for the timing.

The ways in which couples organize their finances is, as Carolyn Vogler shows later in this volume, both complex and highly structured, but we have already discussed a question which taps their broad perceptions. Thus we know the extent to which couples agree or disagree over the way in which they organize their finances. Of all couples, there is agreement in 39% of partnerships that they plan their finances, while 21% of partners both agree that they take things as they come. This, however, leaves four in ten where there is disagreement.

We also know what proportion agree over their views as to whether what happens to them is their own doing: in 59% of couples both agree that what happens to them is their own doing while in 10% both agree that they have little influence. While it is entirely possible that couples will differ in their perception of the amount of control they have over their lives, it is unlikely that there can be much by way of a joint long-term strategy where one partner believes herself or himself to be in control and the other takes the opposite view of their situation. Once again, then, for around six couples in ten there may be a joint strategy.

One would, of course, expect that some couples in the population will develop and sustain joint strategies underpinning their behavioural patterns and others will not. The crucial question is the proportions falling into each group. It would be unwise to make too much of the data here, and the proportions will differ in various areas of life, but a working hypothesis for future research and analysis is that the population may be roughly equally divided in this regard.

PLANNERS AND NON-PLANNERS

We return now, in the last main section of this chapter, to the level of the individual and the question whether low or high levels of planning are highly structured in the population.

We noted early in this chapter that influential work such as that of Askham identified certain selected groups of the population as 'chronic non-planners'. However, even when Askham was writing about it, their demographic behaviour was already very much that of a minority and we might infer that, in more general terms, such groups were a small subgroup of the population. We might then guess that, in the intervening years, their numbers have further declined. The increase in marital dissolution may have especially affected the lower working-class groups which Askham described, resulting in fewer non-planning couples. As we have already hinted, our data are consistent with this line of argument.

Our first approach is to see whether there are groups of the population which have well below or well above average tendency to 'plan'. We have taken four questions relating to very different areas of life which we have already discussed in detail above, and counted the number of questions to which each respondent replied in a 'planful' manner. The four positive indicators were: answering 'yes' to the questions 'Have you thought about what sort of job you want to be doing in five years' time?' and 'Do you have any plans for yourself and your household at the present time?'; and responding 'I tend to plan out my finances carefully', and 'What happens to me is my own doing' to the questions on financial planning and control over one's life. Table 1.9 shows the results of this investigation, in each case giving the percentage of all respondents in any category who replied positively to none, one, two, three, or all four of these questions; it also gives the mean household standard income for each level of the index.

If we take a somewhat extreme position and a score of zero as indicating the chronic non-planners, then the data support the argument we have just advanced that they are relatively uncommon, amounting to around 4% of our sample. Nor is it easy to point to a particular group as falling into this category despite a hint that they are slightly more common in the working class and among unemployed and non-employed women. The similarities are more striking than the differences, and the lack of clear structural differentiation suggests that chronic non-planners, while not entirely a thing of the past, no longer fit the neat patterns once attributed to them. We must, however, urge some caution as our measurement is somewhat crude, and such structural variation as exists is in line with the older research.

On the other hand, a score of zero or one, corresponding to around one in five of our sample, certainly indicates a low level

TABLE 1.9 *Respondents giving 'planful' responses on one or more of four questions (%)*

	Number of questions on which respondents gave a 'planful' response					
	0	1	2	3	4	Total number[a]
Males	4	17	31	31	18	(858)
Females	4	19	30	30	17	(891)
Males 20–29	4	18	36	24	18	(240)
Males 30–39	1	11	32	35	21	(255)
Males 40–49	6	14	28	31	21	(266)
Males 50–60	3	25	24	33	14	(157)
Females 20–29	3	18	28	34	17	(275)
Females 30–39	3	16	27	32	22	(259)
Females 40–49	5	16	37	26	15	(188)
Females 50–60	6	28	32	24	10	(169)
Males in couples	3	14	29	32	21	(621)
Males not in couples	4	23	34	27	12	(237)
Single men	4	23	31	28	14	(207)
Females in couples	4	18	31	31	16	(657)
Females not in couples	4	23	27	27	18	(234)
Single women	3	17	23	32	25	(148)
Self-employed men	4	7	29	36	23	(82)
Employed men	3	15	31	31	20	(631)
Unemployed men	4	26	32	27	10	(98)
Non-employed men	4	38	24	21	12	(47)
Self-employed women	0	20	23	23	34	(17)
Employed women	3	12	31	34	20	(531)
Unemployed women	5	32	25	25	13	(82)
Non-employed women	6	30	30	25	9	(261)
Males						
Service class (1, 2)	2	7	27	36	28	(295)
Intermediate (3)	0	17	34	24	26	(53)
Working class (5, 6, 7)	6	23	33	27	12	(434)
Females						
Service class (1, 2)	1	10	19	40	30	(178)
Intermediate (3)	4	16	32	31	18	(356)
Working class (5, 6, 7)	7	26	34	26	8	(320)

	Mean household standard income (£s) for each level of the index of planning and control (to nearest £100)					
	0	1	2	3	4	Total number[a]
Males	6 400	6 400	8 300	9 200	9 800	858
Females	6 000	6 500	7 500	8 600	9 000	891
Number[b]	(67)	(311)	(532)	(531)	(308)	(1 749)

[a] Number of cases on which percentages are based.
[b] Number of cases in each level of planning and control.

of planning. The data are now far more clearly structured and the trends reinforce some of the points which have emerged in earlier analysis. Older men and, especially, women, the unemployed and non-employed of both sexes, and working-class people generally are all over-represented in this group. Once again it seems to be resources of all kinds that are necessary for planning and this is especially clear in financial terms, with the mean household standard income of those scoring one or two on the index well below that for those scoring higher.

This same trend is apparent among those who score highly on the planning and control dimension. Around one in six of the sample reach the maximum score, and just under half score 3 or 4. It is the self-employed, both men and women, and the service class who are overrepresented here and, of course, the mean household standard income for those scoring 3 or 4 is high. The proportion with high scores is higher in the 30–39 age group than the 20–29 age group, especially for men, and then declines steadily. This makes intuitive sense in terms of the need to plan. There is, of course, considerable intercorrelation between these independent variables, and further analysis is needed to unravel the trends completely. Indicative of this is the finding that well over half of single women (57%) fall into this group, whereas single men tend to be underrepresented (42%).

However, another way of looking at these data is to note that even among working-class women, to take an example, although a third score in the bottom two categories, there are still a third in the top two. In all social groups examined there is a wide spread of scores and it is clear that the correlations between the four variables making up the index cannot be very high. In other words, while it seems reasonable to argue that someone scoring three on the index is more inclined to plan than someone scoring zero or one, it is not the case that planning in one particular area of life strongly implies planning in another.

We have taken the four variables used in the index and cross-tabulated them for all possible pairs for men and women separately. For four of the tables, chi-square is not significant despite the relatively large sample sizes of around 850–900. If we calculate a correlation coefficient for all twelve tables, we obtain gammas of more than 0.3 in only three cases with three more around 0.2. Only the association between having thoughts about one's job in five years' time and having plans for oneself and one's household is sizeable (gammas of 0.38 and 0.46).

It is, of course, possible that a single underlying dimension of 'planning/strategies' does exist and these weak relationships arise because our questions are tapping it imperfectly. However, the evidence from our semi-structured interviews and the general line of argument we have been developing, together with preliminary results from some more detailed modelling we have carried out of the social determinants of different strategies, lead us to prefer the interpretation that for most couples there is not a single dimension of planning/not planning.

FINAL REMARKS

In this chapter we have presented the broad sweep of results from what is probably the first attempt to use large-scale survey methods in the systematic investigation of plans and strategies at the individual level and, to some extent, at the household level. The research was fortunately timed to do this as it was able to build on some outstanding pioneering work. We make no claim to have solved the many problems which arise in this area but only to have taken a number of steps firmly in the right direction.

We have deliberately painted with a broad brush in order to provide an adequate description as well as some interpretation of the extensive material collected in this study. Accordingly, in these final remarks we shall not attempt to summarize what has gone before but rather address once again the debate on 'strategies' in order to make our position on some important issues as clear as possible.

We started this chapter by defining strategies as more or less rational principles which actors can articulate and describe: higher order constructs which form general prescriptions for actions leading towards desired medium- or long-term goals. We believe the data fully support our argument that the concept of strategy is helpful in understanding the actions of individuals and their households. It is, however, all too easy to slip into implying that there is one, single strategy which is an unchanging blueprint and is the sole determinant of action across all areas of life. Everything in that statement is incorrect.

First of all, it is clear that at the very least there are different sets of strategies which apply to the world of work and the world of the family and household. This rather conventional dichotomy, closely related to the public and the private, and well established in sociology, was built into our research methodology and thus not surprisingly shows up clearly in the data. Future research should, however, bear in mind that these two worlds are themselves in all probability subdivided in ways which we have not been able to address.

Secondly, it is important not to reify strategies. In the last analysis they are constructs with which people make sense of their world. Conceptually, they do indeed help social scientists to bridge the dichotomy between structure and action for they are to a considerable extent structured and they do guide action. Human beings, however, unless they happen to be social scientists, do not fret too much about bridging this gap. The evidence suggests that many people do attempt to define goals, that they do have some more or less rational plans to achieve these goals, and that these plans cohere loosely at a higher level and help these people to cope with their everyday lives. But we should beware of the tendency to become prescriptive, to imply, as some of the earlier literature perhaps does, that those people without a strategy are necessarily somehow incompetent.

Thirdly, strategies are always being reviewed and amended in the light of events. It is quite clear that plans held one moment in time are frequently not achieved. It is important to note that this does not seem to lead to the abandonment of plans and strategies in principle, so to speak, but to their revision. People who told us that they had failed to achieve plans held earlier in their lives still told us about their plans for the future. Human beings appear only to have difficulty in coming to terms with the changes and inconsistencies in their apparently firm and rational plans when they happen to be looking at them as social scientists.

Finally, and here we are on more controversial ground, we should remember that strategies are not the only stimuli to action. This is not the place to enter into the debate on rationality but to restrict all human action to a means–end dichotomy is in the end to make human beings less human. People cope with the exigencies of day-to-day existence in many ways, and in 'getting by', more is involved than purely rational action.

Some of these ideas are developed further in the complementary chapter by David McCrone. It is worth commenting that just as we had completed the present chapter yet another paper about strategies appeared in *Sociology* (Edwards and Ribbens 1991). Writing from a feminist perspective and focusing their discussion on 'strategic discourse in the lives of women', much of their argument relates to some of the last few paragraphs. Their major aim is to encourage 'sociological analysis which, when it looks at women's lives particularly, works outwards from the domestic instead of from the public inwards'. Despite this gendered focus, they do not deny that an overrational view of men, generally though not always by male social scientists, may similarly have distorted analysis. Some of their critique may apply to what we have written in this chapter and it is striking that we felt impelled to draft these cautionary final remarks before their paper appeared.

In only one crucial regard do we differ completely from Edwards and Ribbens. They have chosen to stop using the term 'strategy' and this will doubtless be applauded by some of the authors whose writing we discussed in the first few pages of this chapter. We can appreciate the reasons for their decision. Yet they admit to having found it exceedingly difficult to find a suitable substitute word or phrase. We prefer to continue using the word while making every effort to bear in mind the caveats we have just outlined and our view that the term is best confined to longer-term prescriptions for action. While it is true that the context in which words have developed is important and Shaw may be right to see the spread of the term as a form of military imperialism, the debate on strategies reveals that the word has already been used in many ways. For the time being we retain it in the hope that it will continue to acquire the kind of resonance which we believe is useful and shed its more undesirable overlays. Nevertheless it should be borne in mind that the sociological core of what we have written here is dependent not on the word strategy but on the underlying processes to which we have tried to draw attention. The question of how human beings make sense of and structure their lives is too important to become entangled in the thickets of semanticism.

2

Getting By and Making Out in Kirkcaldy*

DAVID McCRONE

That individuals and households make plans and devise strategies
has long been a central concern of sociologists. More specifically,
as Straw and Kendrick (1988: 44) have pointed out, 'contrasting
the cultural traits of middle-class forward-planning with working-
class short-term hedonism is a sociological commonplace.' This
chapter argues that while 'strategies' exist in many households
and provide broad prescriptions for action, they can best be
understood not as neat blueprints but as ways of seeking to control and make sense of life's exigencies. It is a key part of the
argument that strategies are frequently partial and changing, and
need not connect together all aspects of people's lives in an articulated and explicit way. To grasp in a fairly preliminary way
clear examples of the distinction between less strategic and more
strategic perspectives, consider these two contrasting observations:

I'm no' really a planner. Just whatever comes, comes. I think that things
change that much nowadays [that] ye canna plan too much ahead. Some
o' them do; an awful lot o' people do, but I don't think I'm that type.
(Male: self-employed joiner)

I think most people in life have a set plan, and ye try to achieve yer
aims. But again, there's lots o' things that actually happen, like o' the
[miners'] strike, for instance. We were goin' along quite well, an' things
could've moved faster certainly, but again, as I say, the financial side is
so uncertain. Best thing is to have a long-term outlook, and short-term
planning towards it. (Male: mining engineer, currently unemployed)

While both respondents experience life as rapidly changing and
hence difficult to control, they undoubtedly differ with regard to

---

* The intensive interviews on which this chapter is based were carried out by
Pat Straw and Dorothy Sinfield. I am indebted to Michael Anderson and Frank
Bechhofer for their helpful comments in writing this chapter.

their perspectives on it. While the second respondent tries to behave strategically (expressed as having a 'set plan', a 'long-term outlook'), the first, while recognizing that 'planners' exist, does not include himself among them.

These examples highlight nicely the presence and absence of strategic thinking, but, as we shall see, things are rarely as clear-cut and carefully articulated as in these comments. Nevertheless the argument will be that strategies undoubtedly exist, and are used by some individuals and households to make sense of and impose structure onto their lives, to give some forward projection. A central part of the argument, however, is that whereas virtually all households are involved in 'getting by', often in quite complex and ingenious ways, only some exhibit a sense of strategy, and attempt to 'make out'. The key point here is that getting by is about coping in the short term, say, on a day-to-day or week-to-week basis. Coping with everyday living, solving the problems which households and individuals encounter on a day-to-day basis confronts 'planners' and 'non-planners' alike. Everyone has to use 'coping devices' some of the time, and some households rely on these all of the time, making little or no attempt to 'plan'. However, the more one plans successfully, the easier it is to get by; the less one plans successfully, the more one relies on coping devices.

Making out, on the other hand, involves taking a longer-term perspective, taking decisions in the short term which have deliberately long-term implications, marking off, as it were, milestones of progress along the way, indulging in strategic thinking and behaviour. Clearly people can be more or less strategic, and where the former is the case and where they have achieved their aims, we can say that they have 'made out'. In practice, however, most people behaving strategically will still have their goals to achieve, which is why the idea of a process, of 'making out', is preferred. The focus here, then, is on the plans and strategies people use rather than what they actually achieve.

This chapter will argue that while virtually all those interviewed do manage to 'get by', only some are 'making out', that is, operating within broader, even implicit, sets of goals and aspirations they set for themselves. It is important to recognize that getting by and making out are not permanent states in people's lives. Some people trying to make out, for example, will be unsuccessful in their strategy, which will then require them either to persevere with it, or to change their strategy, or give up the attempt in favour of simply 'getting by'. Neither do strategies necessarily emerge at the outset fully formed. Rather, opportunities to make out may occur by happenstance during the life course, and if the circumstances and resources of the household allow, plans can be made and longer-term strategies begin to form.

There is also the logical possibility that those trying to get by fail to do so, and become effectively unable to cope with the situation in which they find themselves. In practice, however, no one in our sample fell unequivocally into this category, although a couple of respondents came close to doing so.

This chapter will have two main tasks: first, to show just how people do get by, the mechanisms and coping devices they employ in handling day-to-day and week-to-week living. The main aim of this part of our argument will be to show that 'getting by' involves some intricate and highly competent routines. The notion that those who do not indulge in 'strategies' are somehow socially and economically incompetent, that they indulge in short-term hedonism, is no part of our argument. The second part of the chapter focuses on those spheres of social life—working, having and raising children, organizing domestic affairs, making ends meet, and housing arrangements—through which we can show the existence and operation of 'strategies' in some households and not in others.

THE DATA

The analysis is based on intensive interviews with thirty-four households in Kirkcaldy which had already been interviewed twice, firstly in the Work History/Work Attitudes survey in 1986/7, and then for the Household survey about one year later. The semi-structured 'intensive' interviews were carried out about one year after the Household survey, thus providing a check on the more structured data provided by the two earlier surveys, an update on what had happened to and in the household, and, above all, an opportunity to tap the social meaning of earlier responses with particular emphasis on the integration of the life and work histories which had been a central part of these surveys.

We were especially interested in how male and female partners saw their individual and collective life courses, their plans, strategies and aspirations. We paid close attention to work histories, particularly how partners integrated these, and fitted them around household demands, especially the planning and raising of children. In this context, women's experience of working, part-time as well as full-time, was crucial, related as it was to broader household strategies and plans. The day-to-day organization of the household, especially how it managed its financial budgeting and provisioning, and how household labour was divided, shed light on how power was distributed between household members. These interviews provided the main information on how housing histories and plans connected with work and life histories, as information on housing in the two formal surveys was slight. We hypothesized that housing provided households with the opportunity to develop alternative, even compensatory, strategies to those of the labour market, and that housing 'projects' would figure prominently in household plans (Saunders 1990). These 'projects' could refer to housing as a productive resource, as a means of capital accumulation traded in the marketplace, as well as housing as a consumption good, a means of improving the quality of life of the household.

Manifestly, work, life, and housing histories were bound to vary according to the life experience of household members, and hence we wanted to exclude certain life-cycle effects and highlight others. Consequently, the couples who were selected for intensive interview were aged between 25 and 45 and had at least one dependent child. The modal household, then, consisted of a couple in their late thirties with one or more early-teenage children, although the sample ranged from those in their mid- to late twenties with young children to those in their mid-forties, some of whose children had already left home.

From the 300 sample for the Kirkcaldy Household survey, seventy-two households were selected which fitted these criteria. The intensive interviews involved talking to the male and the female partners separately, and these interviews lasted on average two hours each. There was some resistance on the part of household members to this process, coming as it did on top of two previous, lengthy interviews, and it was not always possible to carry out intensive interviews with both partners. Consequently, the analysis here is confined to those cases where both partners were interviewed and in which the female partner was in full-time employment (N = 14), in part-time employment (N = 15) and five households in which the female partner was not in employment at all. In general, then, we had information on these households gathered over four interviews, lasting on average six or seven hours in total, a particularly rich and informative data set, consisting as it does of material from structured as well as semi-structured interviewing.

As Anderson, Bechhofer and Kendrick have made plain in the previous chapter, the structured interviews contained a number of useful indicators of 'planning' behaviour and attitudes, and in particular, responses to the following questions: whether they had thought of the sort of job they wanted to do over the next five years; whether they had any plans for themselves and their household at the present time; whether they tended to plan out their finances carefully rather than 'take things as they come'; and whether respondents felt that 'what happens to me is my own doing' rather than that 'I have little influence over the things that happen to me'. If we apply their measure of at least one positive response to these questions, we obtain, as we would expect, comparable results. Anderson, Bechhofer, and Kendrick found that 96% of all respondents responded positively to at least one of these four questions; 32 out of our 34 respondents (94%) did likewise. Again, most people opt for an intermediate position, with 25 out of 34 (74%) giving two or three positive answers out of the four. The starting point of the analysis of the thirty-four households, then, is that very few households fall into the categories of 'ultra-planners' or complete non-planners.

If we distinguish between those who score highly on the survey indicators (the 'planners') and those with low scores (the 'non-planners'), we find a rough correspondence between access to resources and the propensity to 'plan'. Hence, those in more secure and better-paid occupations are more likely to be found among the 'planners', as are men rather than women, and, within the latter group, women in full-time rather than part-time employment.

However, while we would be broadly correct to conclude that

there are occupational, even class, differences between the two groups—indeed, a key part of our argument will be that having resources is a vital ingredient in planning behaviour—there are, of course, exceptions to a distinction on simple class or resource lines. For example, among our respondents there is a GP's household which does not fall into the 'planning' category and there are others in which someone is self-employed. Nor, on the other hand, do all of the more financially straitened households in our sample of thirty-four fall into the 'non-planning' category.

THE NON-PLANNERS: COPING WITH LIFE

A central argument of this chapter is that virtually all households in the sample, planners and non-planners alike, adopt coping devices in order to get by. In the words of one respondent, 'We don't plan but we're careful'. In this section we focus on the 'non-planners', respondents with low 'planning' scores in the surveys. We find households who, by and large, are nevertheless highly competent. No household seemed to indulge in short-run hedonistic behaviour. In other words, even respondents who are ostensibly least planning-oriented on the evidence of the two main surveys use coping devices to get by.

One household which scored only 1 item on the 'planning' scale, and in which the female partner says 'we didnae plan no tae have a family, y'know. We just took it as it came along', nevertheless uses some complex and intricate devices for getting by. As non-locals, they do not have access to child-support networks among kin, and have evolved an elaborate routine of child care among friends and each other (complicated by the fact that the husband is a travelling sales representative). The female partner has developed intricate budgeting systems, and the family has been upwardly mobile in the housing market.

A similar pattern has been adopted by a couple in their early thirties with two young children. The female is an assembly operative in a local electronics factory, and the husband is a fireman. While they showed little sign of adopting a long-term strategic perspective, the female partner kept careful and rigorous accounts.

How I work is—I budget for my mortgage, my house insurance, my electric, my TV licence weekly, so I take that all off G's pay at the start when he gets it every week, and I put so much in one account, so much in this account, so much in that account, and I pay my TV stamps, and I've got my payment thing, y'know, for the electric.

This is a family without credit cards and without a cheque book: 'We don't want bills comin' from everywhere, y'know. We just work on what money we've got'.

Here we see an example of a household which clearly does not claim to plan but which has, to date, managed successfully to control the exigencies it encounters. What may seem to some to be 'traditional' behaviour (no credit cards, no cheque account, for example) is a rational adaptation to an insecure labour market, one in which both individuals and the community have experienced serious upheavals in recent years. The secret is to keep a tight rein on much expenditure either by using traditional methods like putting money in biscuit tins for specific expenditure, or, indeed, employing the modern equivalent, bank budgeting, which allows households to smooth out 'lumpy' expenditures throughout the year. We shall return to this theme when we focus on precisely how people in Kirkcaldy get by and make out.

Those who do not claim to 'plan' are generally well aware that it is possible, and, in many cases not planning is the result of conscious recognition that circumstances do not allow it. Take, for instance, the cases of two households who had tried to make the adjustment from life in the armed forces to life as civilians. Both recorded low planning scores in the survey. Each, however, tries to reduce the impact of the considerable contingencies confronting them.

In one case, the respondent, a female bar cook aged in her late thirties with two sons, is married to an ex-soldier invalided out of the army, who is currently employed as a security guard. The intensive interview revealed considerable economic stress. The husband's income was being used to pay off a substantial credit card debt, and this household was the nearest we had to one failing to get by. In trying to set up home and adjust to life outside the army, it is clear that this family has run up considerable debt. Ironically, the need to 'plan' for life outside has been the cause. As the male partner said, 'Once upon a time we used to plan things, but we can't plan for anything now.'

In this context, there seems little point in looking beyond the immediate. He continued with what seems in his circumstances a realistic and appropriate response: 'I don't sort of think I'll be living in some big mansion, or, y'know, something like that. I take each day, week, month, year, as it comes, really.' Nevertheless, the disappointment runs deep. When asked about his aspirations for his sons, he replied: 'I wouldn't want them to be clones of me because I'm not particularly proud of myself and what I've done. I've achieved minimum success. Nothing I can really shout about to the moon, y'know.'

Similar sentiments were expressed by the second respondent in this position, an unemployed man in his late forties with two sons who was in the RAF for over twenty years. Since leaving, he has been in a series of unskilled jobs in the electronics industry. Once more, he sought to make the adjustment by buying a house, and has invested considerable savings in home improvements, notably double glazing and cavity-wall insulation, suggesting evidence of a longer-term perspective. His wife has had a series of part-time jobs in a supermarket, and as a cloakroom attendant. His current attitude he judges to be quite rational: 'The way things are at the moment, you've got to take things more or less on a day-to-day or week-to-week sort o' thing. You can't afford to make big mistakes now.' What of the future? By and large it does not belong to him: 'It's really all in the past, innit? It's up to the children now how they do, you know. I would be delighted to see them both doing well. At the end of the day, it's their lives, and if they make a mess of it, it's up tae them. There's nothing we can do about it.'

In both of these cases, the adjustment to new ways of life and making a living have taken their toll, and long-term planning has been abandoned. Both households have sought to control as many exigencies as they could, only to discover that too much was against them in making the transition. What they cannot be accused of is careless hedonism, of wilfully failing to make plans for an uncertain future. The message is clear. Even respondents who are ostensibly the least planning-oriented on the evidence of the two formal surveys employ short-term coping devices to get by.

This section has tried to make two key points; first, that non-planning cannot be equated with a lack of due attention and care for contingencies. Careful and complex coping devices are necessary if households are to 'get by' on a day-to-day basis. Secondly, those who claim not to 'plan' are not necessarily unaware of what planning means. The two cases we have described of the ex-servicemen who made quite elaborate plans to ease the adjustment to civilian life and who, certainly in their own eyes, failed, makes the point. It is possible that their military training inculcated in them the importance of 'planning', while they appear to have underestimated the considerable transition required to adjust to civilian life. Having a strategy (what respondents articulate as 'plans' in these cases) made good sense in principle but was unattainable in practice. In other words, non-strategic thinking generally results from force of circumstances rather than inappropriate social values or a commitment to hedonism (indeed, ironically, both the ex-servicemen were staunch Conservative voters).

THE PLANNERS: MAKING OUT

In this section we turn to the 'planners', those who score highest on the survey indicators of planning, and illustrate the way in which their approach to life events differs. This is not to say that these couples do not make use of 'coping devices' on an everyday basis. This is for two reasons. First, 'planning' by its very nature is not concerned with short-term responses to day-to-day events, although it may make coping easier. Secondly, planners will have longer-term perspectives, but unforeseen and unforeseeable events force them to reassess their 'plans' and use short-term devices in the transition from one strategy to another.

The eight respondents are drawn from quite diverse households, each with particular social characteristics and life trajectories. Nevertheless, certain common themes emerge. First, a commitment to 'planning' their lives included a desire to plan for contingencies. Most obvious is the case of one male respondent in his early forties, a senior civil servant suffering from cancer. While the overarching strategy of the household has been to fit into a fairly peripatetic career which has taken them from Dumfries to Wick to Kirkcaldy, his illness has necessitated a new strategy whereby his wife developed her own career in the last few years with a view to becoming the main breadwinner.

A female social worker in her early thirties with two young sons had to take account of her husband only having a part-time job. Rather than become a house-husband, he had developed a career as a poet and writer, something 'charismatic rather than bureaucratic', as he put it. Planning, he said, was something his partner did. He commented, 'I'm really a bit sceptical of planning, apart from my writing projects.' His wife, on the other hand, had developed her own career, without too much enthusiasm, to enable her to be the main wage-earner. Having children was a way of enriching her life despite these demands. Getting pregnant, she thought, 'gave me some sort of change in my life. It was the only way I could see about changing it.'

She returned to work soon after her children were born, and she organized child care with her husband's mother. There were, however, limits to this 'planning'.

INTERVIEWER: Did you say that you planned the children?
RESPONDENT: Well, I planned to have children,

an important and subtle distinction.

Planning for contingencies is also important in the context of the history of the household. Another 'planner', a lower-grade civil servant in her early thirties, shared her house with a community worker with a varied working history. He had been divorced once, and she twice. They had lived together for two years, in what appeared to be still a fairly fragile household relationship. He commented: 'I'm not a person that plans ahead very much' (reinforced by agreeing that he did not plan financially, and that he took things as they came). On the other hand, she said: 'I like to know ahead. I like to plan ahead whereas you don't.' She considered herself a careful planner of her finances, and believed that what happened to her was her own doing. Her long-term plans involved getting promotion, buying her own house and giving financial stability to her own daughter (from a previous marriage). Her partner's plans were vague and focused on encouraging his own son (who lived with his ex-wife) into a career as a professional footballer, something he himself had pursued when younger. Here we have a case that is fairly rare in the sample of a household in which two individual plans (one very weak) are clearly identified, but no overarching 'household' plan accepted by both partners is visible. Both have independent incomes and each is responsible for specific items of expenditure, giving an example of what Pahl has called an 'independent management system' (Pahl 1984).

In each of these cases, 'planning' is undoubtedly present. Each involved the female partner taking on a vital income-earning role. More commonly, however, the 'household strategy' is geared around the male partner's work career. For example, a male school-teacher in his early thirties with two young children was married to a radiographer who worked full-time (there being no part-time posts available in her field locally). The man had taken two years after marriage to try to become a farmer like his father before him, but had given it up owing to a lack of capital, and returned to teaching. He felt 'trapped' in teaching because there were few opportunities for promotion, despite the family strategy having been built round his career.

Similarly, a full-time clerk in her early forties with two children had adapted her working life to that of her family and husband who had made a number of career changes and who had ended up as a teacher in a further education college. He had taken an Open University degree as well as developing a leisure career as a swimming coach. His wife scored highly on the 'planning' measures while commenting: 'I don't really think a lot about the future. I just take it as it comes', the implication being that others (her husband and sons) had made plans to which she had to accommodate.

Such male-centredness in household strategies, while not surprising, is quite widespread and often implicit. A man in his late twenties who currently worked as a chargehand in a ceramics factory but who had had a varied career in manual trades spoke quite unselfconsciously about his own medium-term work plans:

As I say, I wanted to be a joiner, sort o' thing, wi' somethin' behind me, and I could do things masel'. I think I'm gradually gettin' to the stage that I'm goin' t'be in a factory fur the rest o' ma life. I don't relish the prospect o' that so I don't think I'll be there very much longer.

The family was complete. Were more children planned? He replied, 'We won't have any more than that. That's been sorted out. That's been planned, yes.' His wife who worked full-time as a branch assistant in a building society office, having been a secretary, fitted into this perspective. She replied: 'I don't really plan that much ahead. I'm quite happy on a day-to-day basis as long as we're happy and things are OK with the kids and ma husband. . . . The family is important, it's number one.' We can contrast this adjustment by the female partner to her husband's and family's plans with this fairly self-centred account by her husband:

Now it's jist at the stage that I'm wantin' t'do somethin' which I would like to do probably for the rest of ma life. I'm at that stage now. I've achieved everything household-wise and everythin'. It may sound selfish but now I'm . . . thinkin' about doin' somethin' I would enjoy daein.

This brief insight into the plans and aspirations of those who score highly on the indicators of 'planning' reveals that, in general terms, household plans are frequently oriented around individual (male) work plans. There are a few cases where these work plans cannot be relied upon in the longer term, and female partners develop alternative working strategies, such as the woman whose husband had cancer. Given future uncertainties, she had taken on new responsibilities at work: 'It's more of a career. I can see if I do such and such, this'll happen, and I'm sort of hoping to plan for the future.' This move acknowledged her other responsibilities: 'It has been a career move, yes. The other ones have just sort of fitted around the family, but this time I've decided to think for myself.'

While household strategies are much more likely to be built around the work history of the male partner, this is not to say that there are no household strategies as such, merely individual, male ones. Even men convey a sense of adapting (or having once adapted) their work patterns and aspirations to the needs of the household, as we can see from the case of the factory chargehand we quoted earlier ('It may sound selfish but now I'm . . . thinkin' about doin' somethin' I would enjoy daein.')

This chapter has tried so far to show that virtually all respondents in our thirty-four households seek to impose some control on their lives. Even those who can be described as minimal strategists in the major surveys can be seen to employ quite intricate ways of getting by. Similarly, those who show long-term strategic thinking are also engaged in not dissimilar mechanisms of damage limitation and adjustment to the circumstances they

find themselves in. What is not at all in evidence is the stereotypi-
cal pattern of middle-class long-term forward planning and working-class short-termism. It we want strategies to be placed in a
more sociologically sound context, we must examine the devices
households use to get by and make out in different spheres of
their lives. This will be the theme of the following section.

HOW TO GET BY AND MAKE OUT

In using the terms 'getting by' and 'making out', in distinguishing
between coping and planning, it is important to expand a little
on what we mean. We are interested here in how households
assess their own situation in terms relative to their own pasts or
to other comparators such as relatives and friends, and crucially
within a future time span. Hence, how people compare themselves with their own families of origin will be a useful bench-
mark of social and economic advance. While 'getting by' implies
a short-term perspective, of coping on a day-to-day basis as it
were, 'making out' requires a much longer-term orientation to
the future. The distinction is, however, not between those who
simply survive and those who achieve. Neither are we referring to
some degree of absolute achievement, but to a measure of relative gratification, to adapt Runciman's (1972) useful term.

Secondly, as our interviews make plain, whether someone gets
by or makes out is in practice divided by a very fine line, for the
circumstances which allow those with strategies to make out, as
opposed to falling back, like non-strategists, on getting by, are
often difficult to distinguish clearly. Since much may hinge on
opportunities arising, or being in a position to take advantage of
them, we ought not to discount the importance of happenstance
and serendipity in making out. What seems crucial is being prepared for such events. If, for example, someone describes a
grasped opportunity as simply having 'come up', we should not
dismiss this as necessarily indicating unstrategic behaviour.
Putting oneself in a position to exploit unforeseen future opportunities may be a vital part of longer-term strategic success.
Moreover it is important to bear in mind that strategies will
adapt and change. We are not talking here simply of long-
cherished dreams, but also of new strategies which make them-

selves available if circumstances permit. For example, it became plain in our interviews that when the female partner went back to work, especially full-time, new horizons opened up for the household, and these frequently led to a reassessment of future plans, most obviously in terms of housing aspirations.

Thirdly, an important criterion in deciding whether a strategy is operating or not relates to the time-scale which is being used. Most obviously, a sense of a future is crucial, at least as it relates to a life trajectory. Hence, those who articulate a sense of strategy place their social aspirations in some kind of future-oriented time-frame. This might be expressed in terms of an individual's own work plans, a household's achievements, or aspirations for the children.

Fourthly, we ought to be sensitive to the ways in which individual plans and strategies articulate with those of the household as a collectivity. We wish to retain the notion of household strategy because it is frequently the case that the sum is greater than the parts. For example, there are very few households which operate separate 'management systems' in which neither partner has access to all the household's money. As Caroline Vogler points out later in this book, respondents in Kirkcaldy show a higher propensity than those in the other five areas studied to operate a 'pooling system' in which, at least in principle, financial responsibilities are not segregated.

There are, of course, sets of social limits which constrain the operation of strategies within households. We have already mentioned that it is exceedingly rare for the female partner to become the 'breadwinner' even though she may have a superior market position to the man.

Finally, being able to have a strategy will depend on the amount and kind of resources which households and individuals have at their disposal. Resources are generated both from within and outwith the household, including, most obviously, labour market skills and educational qualifications which, in the classical Weberian way, can be turned into marketable skills for income. The availability of these markets will depend on the local employment structure as well as access to wider labour markets.

However, resources do not only come in a monetized form. Most obviously, access to systems of social support and aid are very important. Households which do not have local access to kin networks have to find child care from their own internal resources by developing friendship patterns or purchasing help from professionals (such as nurseries) or from amateurs (school-children earning pocket money, for example). It is much more difficult to pursue a strategy if resources are inadequate or are missing altogether. Nor should we forget that households are repositories of resources themselves. Decisions will have to be made and arrangements negotiated between household members concerning how domestic labour is divided up, what is 'traded' between whom and at what 'price'. This is particularly important in the negotiation between individual and collective aspirations within the household. The availability of resources, however, whether monetary or social, is important in allowing strategies to be developed and pursued, but does not determine whether or not people have strategies.

These are treated here not as outcomes but as aspirations, however modest in relative terms.

GETTING A JOB

Over the last twenty years, the town of Kirkcaldy has seen great changes in its labour market which are reflected in the working lives of those in the surveys. Whereas it once had a sizeable tex-tile industry with associated trades, a well-known linoleum indus-try which developed out of it, and also furniture makers, virtually all these have gone, and with them the local job oppor-tunities. The closure of the last local colliery in the late 1980s removed an important source of employment in the town. At the same time, the development of the new town of Glenrothes to the north has brought new employment, particularly in the expanding microelectronics industry which provides employment mainly for younger people and female workers. These crucial changes in the economic history of the Kirkcaldy area are reflected in the lives of the people we interviewed.

Both men and women followed well-worn paths into local industries—men into the pits, engineering, and cabinet making; women into spinning and weaving, and assembling, as well as office work. It was common to have someone 'speak for' a rela-tive, and it is noticeable from the intensive interviews that many got jobs that way, such as the engineer who followed both his father and uncle into the paper-making factory, or the woman whose aunt got her a job behind the counter in a local shop. Local employment was important, particularly for women because they were not expected to work after they married. In many cases, a 'marriage bar' operated to prevent married women working, as in the case of the woman respondent who had to leave her warehouse employment in the mid-1960s 'because they didn't take married women'. The expectation was that bringing up a family was the proper full-time occupation for a woman.

Although such bars on married women working have long since disappeared, it is clear from our interviews that women's employment is largely subordinated to that of their male partners. The clear sense of strategy as it relates to the development of a man's career can be seen to advantage in the case of the maths graduate mentioned previously who, having got his degree behind him ('If you get a degree, you're going to get a better job, even though you don't know what it is at the start'), then took two years to work in farming. He returned to maths teaching on realizing that he did not have the necessary capital to buy a farm. His wife, who was a radiographer, subordinated her career to his: 'I mean, the most important thing was that he ended up doing something he was happy doing.' She added, almost unnecessarily: 'I don't really put my career first.'

Apart from the few cases where the woman has had to become the main breadwinner, in most households the woman's work patterns have to accommodate to the man's. This can take the form of uprooting the household to follow the male career, or adapting working hours and practices to fit in with male routines of work. This is particularly noticeable among women who were working part-time at the time they were interviewed. They appeared to have quite fragmented and diverse work histories, with a series of part-time jobs chosen to fit in with family obligations. Most commonly among these women, returning to work after having children is to a completely new job, as in the case of the supermarket shelf-filler who became a cloakroom attendant, or the production worker who became a home-help. In most cases, taking on full-time employment would require necessary redivision of household responsibilities. One husband spoke these warning words to the interviewer in the presence of his wife:

'There's too much for her to do. She's got a lot o'work in here too, y'know' (referring to household chores).

This pattern of returning to part-time work after childbirth seems to be a fairly common one, as confirmed by Martin and Roberts (1984) in the *Women and Employment* survey where they found that twice as many women returned to part-time as to full-time work. Having gone back to work part-time, they discovered, many women eventually made the transition to full-time working (Martin and Roberts 1984: 136). Because women commonly have to fit in employment around their household responsibilities, it is not surprising that they express less commitment to 'careers'. Our findings confirm those of Brannen and Moss that 'long-term and career-like perspectives were significantly absent from women's accounts before and after their return to work' (Brannen and Moss 1987: 86).

In contrast to those in our sample working part-time, those women who do work full-time appear to have less fragmented work histories. Similarly, there appears to be greater continuity in terms of employment before and after child-rearing, suggesting that domestic arrangements have been adapted to take account of full-time employment. The point remains, of course, that the 'career' largely belongs to the male partner, and the woman usually accommodates to the man's work demands. At its most extreme, this can involve women giving up work altogether as in the case of one respondent whose husband was made redundant after the miners' strike in the mid-1980s. She gave up her part-time job, partly because it interfered with the household social benefit arrangements, but above all because having that job increased the constraints on her husband finding a job elsewhere. In all but one of the cases in which the female partner was not currently employed, work had ceased prior to child-rearing and had not been resumed.

What varying sense of 'strategy' with regard to work, then, is conveyed through the interviews? Clearly, the notion of 'career' quite explicitly carries this sense of a trajectory through past, present, and future. There is also an implicit sense of strategy embedded in some people's accounts of their working lives. This comment from a GP reflects it: 'There never was any time that I felt I should have been doing something different'; in contrast to his wife who was, he claimed, 'happy enough that the main thing was how my job would develop rather than her own'. Perhaps an extreme case of reactive rather than planned behaviour is a miner-turned-milkman. Having been made redundant after thirty years in the mines, he had got a job as a milkman through his next-door neighbour, the first job he had been offered. 'Ye don't particularly like it', he thought, 'but ye get accustomed. It's a job and it's better than signin' on the dole.' His non-strategic perspective can also be gauged by this exchange between the same man and his wife:

M R S: I don't think we've ever really thought about the future. We just take things as they come. I never plan fur the future.

M R S S: It never works oot.

M R S: Well, the job I've got fur a start, like, there's no' ony great future in it. Ye canna build on this job. Well, things could always be better, I suppose, but they could be an awful lot worse.

M R S S: Ye jist count yer blessin's that everythin's goin' fine.

Mr and Mrs S undoubtedly are concerned with 'getting by' rather than 'making out'. On the other hand, we can find individuals who have, often initially, through serendipity, found exploitable opportunities on which they can subsequently base longer-term objectives. One woman had solved her child-minding problems by organizing a playgroup, which allowed her to become a play-leader, and then to move into community work after taking an HND course. She said, 'I think being involved in the play-group association really opened up lots o' different areas that I never knew were there.' To achieve this she had been obliged to reorganize her household routines to the extent of working out a household rota for family chores, and teaching her husband to cook. She was about to embark on another social work qualification at the time of the last interview. Such planful behaviour contrasted with her early child-bearing habits: 'An absolute shambles in those days. No, we didn't plan anything like that then.' Undoubtedly this woman had developed a plan in the context of a work career. However, this plan had emerged out of recognition of the opportunities which came her way, which meant that she had to reorganize her domestic life in order to exploit them. She was then able to contrast her strategic behaviour at the time of the interview with the self-proclaimed 'shambles' of her early child-bearing days. Hers is a good example of retrospection which allowed her to see her current career in the context of a relatively unplanned past. There may well be some rationalization on the part of the respondent here, but it is self-consciously done to highlight the contrast between the past and the present/future.

FALLING PREGNANT: PLANNING THE FAMILY

Having children is probably the central life event for most of the households in the intensive survey. Many spoke of 'falling pregnant'; very few of 'getting pregnant', as if there were limits to planning. As we pointed out earlier, one respondent corrected the interviewer: 'I planned to have children', rather than 'planned the children'. This point is reinforced frequently throughout the interviews in comments like: 'We didnae say "let's go and have a baby", or any'hin' like that. And once we had the right number we decided that's enough' or 'I think the time was right to have family and that was it, ye ken.'

Having children was undoubtedly planned, but the timing and number were often a matter of some happenstance. One woman had a fairly complicated contingency plan for having a third child if her parents moved away from the area once her father retired. Her mother currently looked after her two children while she worked as a radiographer, and might be no longer available to do child-minding thereafter. If the respondent was then unable to find alternative child-minding arrangements and had to look after the children herself, she considered that having a third child might not add significantly to the task, despite prolonging her absence from the labour market. Similar sentiments were expressed by a female teacher who moved to a new town and found it difficult to get a job immediately 'Well,' she thought, 'if I'm not working . . .'.

In practice, most couples had two or three children within the first few years of marriage, in the words of one woman to 'get it over kind o' quickly'. Most children were spaced two years apart, indicating a degree of planning and just enough for a breathing space but not too far apart to lose the habit of child-rearing. Most preferred a boy and a girl, and many who tried for three spoke of their desire for whichever gender was missing. Some drew back. Said one woman: 'I would have had three if I'd been guaranteed a son. I needed a guarantee, so I thought "Well, I'll no' bother." '

We see even more evidence of forethought in these comments by a husband and wife when asked about having children:

Mr F: We won't have any more than that. That's been sorted out. That's been planned, yes.

Mrs F: We decided after two, no more. We had bought our house, and that was a reason why we didn't want any more family.

The linking of family, work, and housing is also seen in the following comment which conveys an even stronger sense of strategy:

Mr A: No, I think the time was right to have a family and that was it, ye ken. I felt we had gotten oorselves enough money and enough possessions at that time that we could sort o' afford to have a family and put oor money oot on that family and then by that time we could come back tae oorsels.

Interviewer: You were on your feet enough?

Mr A: That's right.

Interviewer: You had worked all these things out?

Mr A: Oh aye, I'm a planner.

Interviewer: In terms of marriage, family, and the house, it was all very much something that you had in mind and worked towards it?

Mr A: That's right.

These two couples are good examples of households whose 'making out' involves the planning of children, and they are prepared to acknowledge this. More commonly, many respondents drew back from such explicit claims about family planning. Such comments as this were not uncommon: 'We didnae plan no'tae have a family, y'know. We jist took it as it come along.' Another woman who had three sons in four and a half years explained it as follows. Asked about planning the family, she had replied: 'Not really. We had planned t'have a family reasonably soon, but we didn't think we were those sort o' people to whom it just happens quickly, but it did.'

Those respondents who were more concerned with getting by than making out more often had no family plans. One woman, when asked whether she and her husband had planned the family (she had two children), replied: 'It jist came. I cannae think aboot that, it was jist one o' those things.' Another, who had four children at intervals of 2, 3 and 8 years, said: 'Nothing was planned really. It was jist how it happened. No, we hadn't planned.' Plainly, while having children is not an activity many people care to articulate as 'planned' behaviour, we can nevertheless see within our sample how those concerned with 'making out' treat family planning as an important part of their strategies, while those settling for 'getting by' are more inclined to refer to it as 'just one of those things'.

ORGANIZING DOMESTIC LIFE

Getting by and making out are reflected in the ways in which child care and household tasks are managed within the household. Inevitably, much is shrouded in taken-for-granted assumptions about what is 'natural' concerning the allocation of domestic tasks, particularly among those who are primarily concerned with day-to-day living, with 'getting by'. Tradition, what has 'aye been', is invoked to justify how domestic life should be organized, especially where it has been inherited from parents' way of doing things. Take, for example, this exchange between a husband and wife:

MRS A: He's the one that does a' the managin', and it's not that I ever wanted t' dae it . . . It's jist happened like that, eh?
MR A: It jist comes fae the olden days. It's bred intae ye.

Another man justifies the segregated roles in the household in terms of his superior power as a breadwinner: 'It's because I've had maist money comin' intae the hoose, I think. Anyway, she gets the housekeepin' fur messages [shopping], food, an' the like. I keep the money fur coal.'

As we might expect, those concerned simply with getting by are more likely to adopt traditional social roles within the household. One woman put it this way:

He's always had a reasonably good job, 'n he liked to have me at home. His idea was that a woman's place is in the home and especially if you have children that's where they're supposed to be, otherwise don't have children. He's very set in his ways which is quite a good idea because why have children if y'don't want t' spend time with them?

However, this woman has in fact found a way round the problem (and incidentally provided a basis for wider opportunities in the future) by starting a course in nursing—not a 'job' as such, she says—and by having her in-laws staying with her to help run the house. Here, she had traded-off the undoubted inconvenience of an overcrowded house for the opportunity to take a course and have someone care for her children and do the cooking. In other words, having her in-laws to stay provides the opportunity for her to begin a nursing course which satisfies her husband's demands that she does not 'work' and that the domestic arrangements are taken care of. It was clear in the course of the interview that she had not invited her in-laws to stay with this in mind, but that their presence provided the opportunity for her to embark on the course. We might infer, then, that an embryonic strategy on her part was beginning to emerge. Her case makes the important point that strategies are not blueprints, but are born out of the opportunities and resources which become available to households and individuals in the course of their lives.

More commonly and more reactively, women find it more difficult to formulate their own strategies because they are required to fit in with household arrangements. Hence many women will take part-time jobs with hours which fit in with school times. Thus one took a job as a school-crossing attendant, having had to give up part-time work when the job was rationalized into a full-time one which she could not accommodate to her family's needs. The shift from part-time to full-time working is more likely to require a substantial reorganization of domestic life and its division of labour.

Where getting by is the aim, drawing back from change often makes sense. On the other hand, those with longer-term perspectives are more likely to accept the need to reorganize their domestic lives if and when the need arises and as opportunities present themselves. This is nicely articulated by one woman who had found a part-time job through a friend, and then was confronted with going full-time. Here we can see how opportunity requires innovation if it is to be exploited, for the purely reactive response would be to decline the offer.

MRS Y: A year after it, the powers that be decided that they would like somebody full-time. They needed somebody full-time instead o' part-time, and would I like t' do? Big deal. I got the first chance, and I thought 'What am I gonna do wi' the kids?' I mean, 9 o'clock to 4 o'clock. However, ma friend would see to them. . . . Yeh, I left at half past eight, y'see, 'n' they used t'go up t'Myra's till ten to nine, till it was time t'go t'school, 'n' then a quarter past three when they come out, they went up there. I was home at quarter past four.

INTERVIEWER: Did you pay her for that or not?

MRS Y: No.

INTERVIEWER: She just did it for a favour?

MRS Y: Yeh. Uh-uh.

INTERVIEWER: Was that a big decision, then, to go full-time?

MRS Y: Oh yes. Well, I mean, they [the children] were gonna have t'be seen tae, 'n' if they couldna be seen tae, then I couldna be the work.

We see here a more proactive and strategic perspective in action, one which involves a willingness to re-examine the existing, settled ways of organizing domestic life. 'Making out' seems to require a break with the past, rather than simply conforming to the way that it has 'aye been'. There is recognition that much greater openness is desirable, as this comment from a male respondent who was brought up by his grandmother makes plain:

She was exactly the same, like, she ran the show, and ma gran'faither, he just earned. I didna think that was right. Mainly because of the burden it put on ma mother and ma grandmother, like. They had a' the worries aboot finance, an' ma faither and gran'faither, they were ignorant.

Such sentiments contrast with a more traditionalist attitude to the domestic division of labour: 'It was jist the same; ma dad handed his wages over, and ma mum worked it all out as well.'

While we cannot claim that expressions of strategy always imply a break with old ways of doing things, we would expect that those seeking to 'make out' might wish to break with the past and develop their lives along new directions of their own making.

BUDGETING AND MAKING ENDS MEET

Issues of family budgeting are crucial to getting by. On the face of it, much has changed in so far as income seems to be handled as a joint asset rather than as the property of the male 'breadwinner' who hands over the 'housekeeping' each week. One of the reasons this appears to have changed (leaving aside the fact that many women are wage earners in their own right) is that earnings are increasingly paid directly into bank accounts or indirectly via cheques. This has meant that virtually all the households in the sample now have bank accounts. Banks are frequently being used in much the same way as traditional methods, namely, to smooth out demands on household income. Hence, systems of bank budgeting have developed whereby customers calculate annual expenditure on bills and these are spread throughout the year. In many ways, this system is the direct successor to the 'biscuit-tin accounting' we mentioned previously, and as practised by one (female) respondent:

I used to have a wee box, an old fashioned cash box, 'n' that was so much for the rent. Then sometimes I would have t'take money out again 'n' put IOU two pounds, this sort o' thing. They didna do standing orders then really. Ach, we find it works, works fine.

The extension of banking into working-class households has permitted new versions of old practices whereby expenditure is calculated in fine detail. These are little more than new devices for the old problem of making ends meet and getting by. While joint bank accounts might seem to indicate a more egalitarian approach, often all is not quite what it seems. For example, while separate incomes are usually described as 'ours', it is much more likely that the woman's money is used for items of household expenditure such as furniture which are deemed to 'belong' to her because they come within the domestic domain. It is much more unlikely that the woman will have 'pocket money' as the man has. In the words of one man, 'I get pocket money, of course, but that's after she's had the money'. Another male respondent pointed out: 'My wife has a wee account of her own, I think. I think she has, aye, I mean it's her money, it's right, ye know. I never had an account of ma own. I jist keep everythin' in the joint account.' However, this respondent received pocket money from the joint account, and his wife did not. A similar issue of control relates to who actually is responsible for the household money. In many cases, it is still the female partner who 'manages' the money, as in these cases:

Everything's done jointly. She deals with finance, she tends to look after that a lot more than I do. I just go out and earn the wage, y'know.

What happens after that I don't really know. As long as the bills are paid. (Male)

I do the budgetin'. I wouldnae say so much the brain, but I'm the financial one. It's always been like that. Bill hands over his wages to me, and I sort o' pay the rent, the insurance and milk, an' get the shoppin' in every week. (Female)

What these and other cases are indicating is not so much financial power as financial responsibility. When male respondents claim, as this one does, that 'She's the financial controller in the house', he gives the game away by adding: 'Let's face it, it's the wife who goes out and buys the shopping.' Another woman gave a nice illustration of this: 'Most other decisions he leaves t'me, usually the boring things like how t'pay the gas bill or something, but now and again he makes a decision and once he's set his mind on something there's no changing it, so.'

This chapter has tried to show that in the main households pay particular attention to devices for 'getting by' so as to reduce the financial risks they confront. Most would share the assessment of one man. 'After all,' he said, 'it wouldn't take much to put us under.' The main task undoubtedly is to make ends meet. Virtually all households which were interviewed had struggled to get by in the last few years. In the words of one male respondent: 'Out of all the years, the last twenty years, we've been sort o' conditioned on survival, and when things get tight we just tighten our belts.'

Belt-tightening consists of excising 'luxuries', holidays, clothes, and social activities. Once these have been reduced, 'necessities' are reduced (eating cheaper food, for example), and, where appropriate, the man works more overtime and the woman goes back to work, or moves to a better-paid job. This is one explanation of the fragmented job histories of most women in our sample, particularly those who work part-time. Once the economics of the household are stabilized, then the female partner's income can again be used to buy holidays, clothes, and so on. Her income becomes not simply a vital ingredient of 'getting by', but of improving the quality of life of the household.

In this process of adjusting to the vagaries of life, most households avoid debt, whether it be borrowing from family (very rare) or from banks. Simply borrowing to get by is judged to be bad economics, whatever the source. Help from kin is overwhelmingly in kind rather than cash, notably in the form of help with child care which can at least be passed off as an enjoyable activity for the carer (usually the mother or mother-in-law).

While borrowing money might seem a logical way of developing longer-term aims, respondents express a strong fear of debt, especially that which results from defaulting on bank loans or running up large credit card debts. Bank loans are used, usually for car purchases, but most households would echo the view of one respondent: 'I'd rather pay for it if I have the money. That way, we're in control.' Banks are used to smooth out lumpy debts for essentials such as heating, phone-bills and lighting. Not borrowing money has a practical aim for most households. As one woman described it: 'We never take anything we can't pay for because we can't afford to. We always save fur holidays 'n' things like that. We don't sort o' save t'have money in the bank. We just can't do it.'

This avoidance of debt is largely learned from the experience of getting by in a fairly uncertain economic climate. It may well be a function also of the stage these households have reached in the life cycle, in mid-career, as it were, as well as the economic and social conditions which these respondents have encountered during their lives. It might rest too on deeper cultural beliefs about paying for what you get, and does not seem to be class-specific. Here is a comment from the GP who comes, as his wife does, from a local middle-class family:

I suppose it's how we've both been brought up, and the sort of basic attitudes that have always been imprinted on us. Certainly, from my family point of view I can never remember us doing anything—I don't think there was any question of credit or whatever it was called in those days, borrowing involved.

The main fear among the households we interviewed, however, related to credit cards. These were almost seen to have a pernicious life of their own, as if simply owning one was courting debt (and family destruction). Those who had them used them for 'emergencies'—petrol on holiday, for example, and only one household used them systematically as a means of obtaining extended credit, clearing the debt month by month. These comments were typical.

I don't like them, never use them. It's jist mair debt.
I dinna believe in them actually. I think you would run up a lot o' debt

with thae credit cards. We always try and say that if you're wanting any'hing, buy it or save up till you have enough to get it rather than take it on the credit.

As if proof of the danger of credit, our sample contained two families in which the man's wages went entirely on trying to reduce substantial credit card interest. One man had used such credit to set up his house when he was discharged from the army, and was clearly in deep debt, and consoled himself with the thought that there had 'never been court proceedings or anything like that'. In the other household, the female partner was working full-time to keep the house and the man had taken two jobs to make ends meet.

The fear of debt, then, is pervasive among those interviewed, to such an extent that plans are often short-term and cautious, but none the less exist. We would plainly be mistaken to think that, on the whole, our sample had no broader plans or strategies; our respondents are, by and large, concerned with reducing risks and planning for contingencies in what is undoubtedly a fairly volatile labour market both locally (in Kirkcaldy) and nationally (in Scotland).

FUTURE ASPIRATIONS

If 'making ends meet' highlights the conservative and largely non-strategic aspects of our respondents' lives, then asking about plans and dreams seems to elicit comment about broader strategies, or, indeed, their absence. These perspectives are perhaps best articulated through comparisons across the generations. Those who appear to operate more strategically are, to put it simply, more likely to contrast their own position with that of their family of origin, and to have further aspirations for their children. Compare, for example, these two comments.

The first respondent, while making a contrast with her family of origin, expresses doubt that she will achieve as much as they have: 'I don't really think about it [the future] much. I wonder, I often wonder, will I be as well off as my mum and dad when we're their age?' (This woman's husband had similarly conservative views about his own future: 'It's hard to say. I'm quite happy at my work, and hopefully I'll be able to stay there till I retire.')

The second respondent deliberately uses the contrast with her parents to stress how her aspirations are different from (and, by implication, better than) theirs: 'I never wanted to be like ma mum and dad's situation, where sort of—council house and everybody's got brown furniture. I never had ideas like that at all.' (This woman had also broken with the financial division of labour of her parents: 'I never thought that was fair—never. Just because he works, it shouldn't really just be his money.')

We see similar contrasts with regard to children between those seeking simply to get by and those with aspirations to make out. One rather extreme conservative attitude is well expressed by this respondent: 'Plans? Jist let them get a job and get them oot o' ma road. And to bring mair money intae me instead o' me gie'in' it tae them.' On the other hand, those more strategically minded are more likely to express sentiments such as these: 'The ambition is to keep goin' forward, and for the kids, I would like both my kids to go through college.'

Among such respondents, the future aspirations for the children are positive if rather vague, such as 'I want them to have somethin' behind them, definitely.' In this regard, planning for their future will involve taking out insurance policies ('for their education, or in case something happens to me'), or in buying 'educational' toys like home computers at Christmas.

HOUSING: STRATEGIES AND ASPIRATIONS

Undoubtedly one of the most important spheres involved in 'making out' is housing, in the sense both of the capital gains to be made out of it, and the contribution it may make to the quality of life of the household, its consumption potential. Sometimes, children are deemed to be the main beneficiaries, as in this comment by the woman who disliked council housing and brown furniture. For her, housing is an important means of capital accumulation which she can pass on to her children: 'It's mainly for the kids: When you buy a house it's somethin' that you've, ken, it's money in the bank, somethin' for them in the future.'

More generally, the importance of housing in our respondents' plans and dreams is a striking feature of the study. In response to the questions in the Household survey: 'Do you have any plans for yourself and your household at the present time?' 'Could you tell me about them?', virtually all those with plans of some sort mentioned housing (fifteen out of the seventeen mentioning 'plans' of any kind). In the main, they mentioned home improvements, putting in a new kitchen, bathroom, double glazing, central heating and the like. The uniformity of these responses is quite remarkable given that respondents were not directed to think of 'plans' in any specific way (interviewers were instructed to say, if respondents asked what kind of plans, 'Anything you like').

Our intensive interviews confirmed the importance of housing in people's plans, and even among the 50% claiming in the Household survey that they had no plans to speak of, at least four out of this seventeen mentioned housing plans in the course of the intensive interviews.

The commitment to housing is further reflected in the high levels of owner-occupation among the thirty-four households interviewed, levels well above the 50% in the Kirkcaldy sample who were owner-occupiers. Fully twenty-eight (or 82%) are owner-occupiers, and of these, thirteen have bought their council houses. Further, of the remaining council tenants, four out of the six mention house purchase when talking about their plans. The attractions of owner-occupation are, above all, financial, with twenty-three out of twenty-eight owner-occupiers mentioning 'good investment' in the survey as the most important reason for owning, with half indicating that they 'liked the idea of owning their own property'.

Of course, we cannot conclude that all those who have bought their houses are concerned with 'making out'. There are financial and practical benefits too, yet even these are concerned with creating future opportunities, as reflected in this observation: 'It was jist that I wanted ma ain hoose so that if I wanted t' dae anythin' to it, I could do it, ye see.'

Contrast this with the equally vague, but sociologically significant observation: 'It's the only way to advance, I feel, really.' This comment contains the sense of a future aspiration, and implies a more strategic orientation than the previous comment. The husband of this respondent had used a small legacy (received after his father was killed in a mining accident) to buy a small flat in the area with the express intention of moving up the housing ladder.

In some cases, the commitment to owning is long-standing and premeditated. At least two households in our sample bought their houses before they married, and one couple had even moved to Kirkcaldy from Edinburgh thirty miles away for that purpose because property was cheaper there. They had subsequently been involved in a series of house moves with clear strategic intent—to improve the size and quality of houses, to shift neighbourhoods—and had aspirations to build their own house, and/or to buy a property in France to retire to.

At the same time, housing aspirations are realistic and carefully constructed. One man who had built his own house (he was an electrician to trade) and who was investigating the purchase of a similar project in Spain to retire to, was the one who made the revealing statement that 'We don't plan, but we're careful.' This sense that households are involved in incremental planning—in adapting life plans to unforeseen circumstances—rather than in grandiose 'Plans' is nicely expressed by the man who had used his father's small legacy to buy a house before he married:

We've no great life plan in front of us—relatively unimportant things like houses and things are priorities. If somebody says 'What's your future plan?', well, we've no' got ony. We've no' made ony. There's no great plan to do this or that by 1995, so it's jist short-term things. Everythin' seems to be goin' a'right the now, right enough.

These denials of 'planning' seem to be semantic rather than conceptual, and underlying both comments is a sense of strategy. This sense which the latter respondent conveys of trying to reduce uncertainties and contingencies (such as investing in your own house, thereby giving greater freedom over where you live) while claiming not to plan is a not uncommon response. One woman commented: 'We're not terribly good planners; we sort o'just wait 'n' see how things work oot.' However, she also has detailed plans for extending her house in a big way, premised on giving the household more control over its quality of life.

'Taking things as they come', then, is not simply an expression of fatalistic values, but a recognition that life's exigencies, particularly as they are manifest in Kirkcaldy, are frequently unpredictable and volatile. Hence, having 'plans' especially to do with housing the family is a perfectly rational means of making out through the housing market. When households have so little control over the local labour market, housing does afford a greater possibility of improving living conditions and even economic life chances. In the words of the ex-serviceman who bought a house prior to leaving the RAF: 'If you've bought a house, you're half-way there'; while in the next sentence saying: 'I never really expect anything. I always take things as they come.' Such sentiments are not necessarily contradictory. They reveal the desire to control at least some of life's uncertainties while acknowledging that one can do little about many of them. Frequently, this is a risky business, as one man who had bought his house indicated: 'It wouldnae take much to put us under. But what we feel is that we've got tae put up wi'that. We've jumped in at the deep end for havin' a decent hoose in a decent area. We're daein' no' bad.'

Where households do go under, as in the case of the ex-serviceman who has run up substantial credit card debts despite his considerable attempts to adjust to life outside the army, economic conditions make 'planning' in the sense we have used it here, namely, to control incrementally life's exigencies with a view to future goals, quite impractical: 'Once upon a time we used to plan, but we can't plan for anything now.' His view of the future is vague and bleak: 'Well, everybody wishes they had better things. That's why everybody fills in the coupon [pools].' In other words, for this respondent progress can only come about through a financial windfall, rather than by means of achievable goals in one's lifetime. Those who preface their remarks on their future plans with comments like 'Well, if I won the pools . . .' are unlikely to be those with the most strategically developed ideas as to their future.

What our interviews show very clearly is that the propensity to plan is not necessarily, as some sociologists and politicians would have it, an automatic outcome of stable and deep-seated social and cultural values, but can also be a practical response to a recognition that life is very uncertain, particularly in a labour market like Kirkcaldy which has undergone considerable economic and industrial change in the last thirty years. Consequently, 'plans' have to be rational adaptations to life's demands, often clearly articulated and precise as are those relating to housing, for example, and quite consistent with a recognition that 'whatever comes, comes'.

CONCLUSION

This chapter has sought to argue that individuals and households are involved in continuously adapting to changing circumstances, but generally not on an *ad hoc* basis. Instead, many people articulate plans and strategies within which they can make sense of events, and which express a desire to control the life course in an uncertain world.

We are fairly certain that these plans belong to households rather than to individuals, while recognizing that some life trajectories (such as the male career) are given prominence over those of others. We found few cases of competing trajectories among households and couples, probably the result of taken-for-granted assumptions about how the household should be organized, how children should be had and reared, and what mechanisms the household should employ to get by and make out.

Can we be sure, however, that, in setting out their ways of 'making out', many of our respondents are articulating strategies? Certainly, virtually all households operated in the grey area between acknowledging that everything 'just happened' and claiming that 'everything was planned'.

Nevertheless, if we treat strategies not as recipes for action, as blueprints, but as broad sets of ideas that people use to make sense of the future of their individual and collective lives, then strategies do seem to operate in many households. For much of the time (and perhaps largely reflecting our research design in selecting households in 'mid-career'), most were concerned with 'getting by', with short-term defensive strategies, 'with taking things as they come'. In the serious business of 'getting by' which all households confront, insecurity is not a deterrent to planning, but makes it even more vital if the household is to survive and prosper. That some households and individuals are involved, too, in 'making out' is a clear indication of a process of modification and negotiation which both allows household strategies to emerge out of individual goals and which in turn sets these goals in the context of household plans.

3

Working-Time Patterns, Constraints, and Preferences*

SARA HORRELL, JILL RUBERY,
AND BRENDAN BURCHELL

INTRODUCTION

One critical dimension in the interactions and interrelationships between social organization, social change and the structuring of labour demand is the organization of working time. Labour demand necessarily has a time pattern or structure, which is in part determined by technological and market forces but also by social and institutional forces, ranging from custom and practice and collective bargaining arrangements to systems of family organization and the domestic division of labour. Individuals not only have to accommodate their working-time patterns to their own domestic and leisure activities but also have to accommodate to the working-time patterns of other household members. All forms of social organization, from the domestic division of labour to leisure time activities, depend on the structure and intermeshing of working-time patterns, while social organization will in turn influence the structure of labour supply available to the economy.

These mutual interactions take on much greater interest at a time when there are significant pressures leading to changes in

* The authors were members of the Social Change and Economic Life Initiative team based at the Department of Applied Economics at Cambridge University. We are indebted to all the other participants in the Initiative who helped to develop the Work Attitudes and Household questionnaires. We would particularly like to acknowledge the work of Carolyn Vogler, who managed the surveys from the centre, and the work of the other members of the Cambridge team, both in developing the parts of these questionnaires which are specific to the work of the team and the follow-up Welfare survey, on which this paper largely draws, and for their intellectual support in developing these areas of analysis.

both the time structure of labour demand and in the system of social organization. The pressures towards more flexible work patterns within the industrial system (Hakim 1987; ACAS 1988; CBI 1989) can be expected to have significant repercussions on working-time patterns, including changes in average hours of work, changes in the predictability of working-time patterns, and changes in the spread of working time through the day, week and even the year. At the same time, changes in women's labour market participation patterns can be expected to have significant implications for social organization, with repercussions not only on such factors as the domestic division of labour but also on the interactions between household members, particularly partners, and their working-time patterns, their domestic responsibilities, and their leisure activities. Pressure for change in working time has also come from trade unions and government departments concerned with sharing out labour demand more evenly to reduce unemployment, and more recently with changing working-time requirements to alleviate emerging skill shortages, particularly in areas where women with children could be attracted back into work under part-time or job-sharing arrangements.

The importance of current pressures towards change in working-time arrangements is widely recognized but there has been little research which pays attention to the demographic and household dimensions of working time. Such surveys as have been undertaken tend to concentrate solely on the labour market aspects, whether based on surveys of firms or individuals. Thus we know a reasonable amount about the emergence and sectoral distribution of jobs with non-standard working-time patterns (Hakim 1987; Rubery 1989) but not a great deal about the social and demographic characteristics of those undertaking such jobs, or indeed how these patterns mesh with social organization at the household level. One main exception is the *Women and Employment* survey which looked in detail at women's hours of work and household arrangements (Martin and Roberts 1984) but could not carry out a complementary investigation of men's hours of work. Perceived ability or willingness to comply with different types of working-time regimes has been an even more neglected area of working-time research.

The emphasis on the labour market or demand-side perspective takes attention away from the repercussions of change in working-time practices on social organization and, in turn, on labour supply. It may in fact be the case that pressures for change emanating on the demand side for, for example, ever more variable working times, may ultimately prove to be incompatible with the system of social organization on the supply side, where the move towards two-earner families and more continuous female participation requires greater predictability of working time in order to facilitate the intermeshing of working-time patterns and domestic responsibilities.

Questions on working time included in the various surveys are analysed here in an attempt to remedy some of these gaps in existing research and to highlight aspects that might be fruitful areas of future research. However, even with these data we are not able to disentangle the processes by which working time has been determined, whether by employer dictate or employee preference. Nor do we have information on the range of working-time regimes that were available to employees when taking their current job. These data must be interpreted more as descriptions of current working-time arrangements and their implications for individuals and households and not as pure indicators of either demand- or supply-side preferences.

The first part of this paper is concerned with the working-time requirements of the survey respondents' current jobs, paying particular attention to the working-time patterns of individuals with specific demographic and social characteristics. The second section looks at how working-time patterns intermesh within households and the final section looks at attitudes towards potential working-time arrangements and desires for change in current working-time systems.

THE SURVEYS

The data used come from three surveys conducted under the Social Change and Economic Life project: the Work Attitudes/Work History survey, the Household and Community survey and a Welfare survey carried out by the Cambridge team alone. The data used from the two main surveys refer only to the Northampton area; the 300 respondents to the Household and Community survey were followed up by the Cambridge team in the Welfare survey. Although, in principle, working-time questions from the three surveys for the Welfare survey respondents alone could have been analysed, we dismissed such a strategy as the sample size would have been severely limited; well below 200 because of non-responses and the exclusion of households where changes in composition, work status, and jobs had occurred between interviews. Furthermore such a sample would have made breakdowns by social and demographic characteristics virtually impossible. We therefore consider results from each of the separate surveys, so using the largest available sample sizes at each stage in the analysis.

Again for reasons of sample size, complexity of information, and in keeping with our objective of looking at household interactions, we have only been able to include information on household and family types which constitute a reasonably sized subsection of the survey. Thus we concentrate on partnership households, often only those where the male partner is in full-time work or self-employment.[1]

In dividing the households by family-type we have used the following three-way classification throughout: partnerships with at least one child under 5; partnerships with at least one child aged 5 to 16, and none under 5; partnerships without any children aged under 16. This last category is the most heterogeneous in the sense that it includes households which have never had children and also households where the children are all over 16. However, sample numbers precluded any finer breakdown,[2] and this division enabled us to look at the current presence of children as a constraint instead of at how having children at sometime may affect subsequent behaviour.

WORKING-TIME REGIMES OF CURRENT JOBS

Knowledge of the characteristics of the labour supply of jobs with non-standard and flexible working times is important if the extent to which employers can expect existing workforces to work such regimes is to be understood. Through consideration of the survey data on basic and total hours worked, the times of day when work took place, the frequency of non-standard working (standard working assumed to be 9 a.m. to 5 p.m., Monday to Friday), and flexible working, we try to ascertain whether there are gender differences in the working-time regimes of the jobs undertaken and whether there are systematic differences in these for males and females according to their domestic situations, in particular the presence or absence of dependent children and the ages of children where present. That is, what are the characteristics of the labour supply providing working-time regimes such as unsocial hours working and flexibility?

Gender Differences in Working-Time Regimes

The usual starting point for any consideration of working-time regimes is the number of hours worked. As would be expected, our surveys found gender differences in the hours worked by full-timers; women tend to have shorter basic hours, and to do less overtime, than men (see Table 3.1).[3] Although non-manual workers are often observed to have shorter working weeks in collective agreements, these differences could not be accounted for by the different proportions of males and females involved in manual and non-manual work. Predictably, the main hours differences occurred between full- and part-time workers. Other working-time dimensions of jobs revealed more interesting and less predictable patterns.

Forms of non-standard working were quite common for all labour force groups (see Table 3.1); even frequent night work, which received the lowest percentage scores, applied to over 10% of respondents. Between 14% and 19% of respondents, including part-timers, worked shifts, and over half of the men and almost a quarter of the women worked frequent overtime. Gender differences in frequency of occurrence of overtime are significant but not of shiftwork or nightwork. Whereas women in full-time jobs were much more frequently involved in overtime than those in part-time jobs, this relationship was reversed for nightwork; the shares involved in shiftwork were much the same in the two groups. High involvement of females, particularly those working part-time, in evening and weekend work was also found (see Table 3.2). Thus these surveys suggest that neither gender nor full- or part-time working are factors that preclude the undertaking of jobs involving non-standard working times.[4]

Table 3.2 extends the exploration of working times using the

TABLE 3.1 *Basic hours, overtime, and involvement in non-standard working time practices*[a]

| | Whole sample | | | | Partnership households | | | | | |
| | | | | | Male respondent | | | Female respondent | | |
	MFT	FFT	FPT		Child <5	Child 5-16	Other	Child <5	Child 5-16	Other
Basic hours	40.4	35.8	19.5	FT	40.3	42.5	39.7	28.1	34.9	36.1
				PT	–	–	–	18.5	17.4	22.7
Overtime	3.8	0.7	0.4	FT	3.5	3.8	3.4	0.0	0.9	0.7
				PT	–	–	–	0.2	0.5	0.3
% whose job involves:										
Shiftwork	19	15	14	All	15	27	11	12	16	12
Frequent nightwork	12	10	16	All	13	14	13	26	12	10
Being on-call	30	15	14	All	36	38	30	21	13	11
Frequent overtime	53	28	16	All	51	51	45	13	16	26
Sample size	(282)	(155)	(138)	FT	(69)	(86)	(112)	(6)	(35)	(71)
				PT	–	–	–	(25)	(57)	(35)

Note: MFT = male full-time; FFT = female full-time; FPT = female part-time.
[a] By gender and family-type.

Source: Work Attitudes and Work Histories survey: employees only, excluding self-employed.

TABLE 3.2 *Working time arrangements*[a]

| | Whole sample | | | Partnership households | | | | | |
| | | | | Male respondent | | | Female respondent | | |
	MFT	FFT	FPT	Child <5	Child 5-16	Other	Child <5	Child 5-16	Other
% whose days worked vary:									
Frequently	13	13	27	20	7	10	10	12	28
Occasionally	12	4	11	–	13	15	–	8	16
Rarely	32	11	16	37	38	37	–	20	–
Never	44	73	46	43	43	37	90	61	57
% who in last week worked:									
<5 days	2	9	45	–	7	4	49	28	13
5 days	62	81	35	50	70	55	51	54	85
> 5 days	37	10	20	50	23	42	–	18	2
Saturday or Sunday	21	17	29	30	10	27	–	31	8
Saturday and Sunday	21	9	10	26	13	21	–	6	15
Neither Saturday nor Sunday	58	74	60	44	77	53	100	63	78

% who ever work								
Saturday or Sunday	81	64	53	77	94	80	17	61	56
% who work nights	5	–	8						
% who work evenings	4	7	14						
% who work late:									
Frequently	37	30	–	26	58	28	–	6	21
Sometimes	26	33	15	27	19	26	14	23	28
Rarely	24	15	21	13	19	35	21	25	15
Never	14	22	64	33	4	12	65	46	36
% who work longer than basic week:									
Regularly	67	45	11	67	77	69	20	23	28
Occasionally	18	26	33	13	17	17	13	23	43
Hardly ever or never	15	30	56	20	6	15	67	53	29
% who take work home:									
Frequently	25	28	2	31	45	20	20	18	11
Occasionally	17	19	14	–	12	34	26	–	31
Rarely or never	59	53	84	70	43	46	54	83	59
Sample size	(82)	(36)	(27)	(19)	(19)	(29)	(9)	(21)	(16)

Notes: In this table, percentages do not always match exactly to whole people from the surveys because of the weighting procedures used to correct for the initial over-sampling of the unemployed.

MFT = male full-time; FFT = female full-time; FPT = female part-time.

[a] By gender and family-type.

Source: Welfare survey, employees only.

Welfare survey and looks more specifically at the labour force groups providing flexibility in working time. It emerges that male, female, full-time and part-time workers all offer the employer considerable amounts of flexibility in both variability of working time and provision of non-standard hours, but the forms offered differ. Part-time workers are more likely to vary the days worked and to work evenings and weekends than full-timers, whilst full-timers are more likely to work extra hours occasionally and late at short notice if required.

The high percentage of part-timers whose days worked vary frequently (27%) seems to provide support for the view that part-time work adds an important dimension of flexibility into the firm's employment arrangements. In contrast, female full-timers tend to have the least flexible working-day schedules with 73% saying the days worked never vary. Part-timers can offer the opportunity to firms to change manning levels during the Monday to Friday week, which cannot be achieved with full-timers on a standard week, and also the opportunity to use variable days to provide weekend cover, when full-timers may only work weekends on an overtime basis.

Working of non-standard hours also shows a contrast between women working full- and part-time, with the percentage of female part-timers working at least one day at the weekend in the week prior to the survey being comparable with that of male full-timers and considerably higher than that of female full-timers. However, for all groups a higher percentage occasionally work a day at the weekend although there is a lower percentage of part-timers who 'ever' work weekends compared to full-time workers. This may suggest that part-time jobs are strongly polarized into those that do involve weekend working and those that do not, while female full-timers may be less likely to work weekends regularly but a higher share may be expected to help out at weekends under exceptional circumstances. Areas where part-timers appear to offer less flexibility than their full-time counterparts are in 'working later than expected' and 'working longer than their basic week'. No part-timers reported that their work involved them in 'frequently' working later than expected and few reported 'regularly' working longer than their basic week; this compares with over a third and nearly a half, respectively, of both male and female full-timers. Moreover 64% of part-timers 'never' worked later than expected compared to only 22% of female and 14% of male full-time workers. This lends further support to the suggestion that full-timers may be more likely to help out as and when necessary while part-time involvement in non-standard and flexible working may be organized on a more formal basis.

The overall picture to emerge, therefore, is one where both part-time and full-time work can involve a large degree of non-standard hours working but are associated with different types of flexibility. Part-time work offers flexibility in the days worked, but not all part-timers offer this flexibility; instead it appears that part-time jobs may be polarized into those which have fixed and those which offer flexible working-time schedules. Full-time jobs tend to involve the employee in working flexible hours (weekends, late or longer than basic week) at least occasionally and keeping strictly to fixed days or hours may not be an option even in jobs where working time is stable most of the time. Men in full-time jobs are more likely to vary days and work overtime, but, with the exception of total hours worked, the gender difference in working-time patterns within full-time jobs are perhaps more remarkable for being relatively small, with women registering similar tendencies to work late and to take work home and for the majority to work more than basic hours and overtime on occasion.

Family-Type and Working-Time Regimes

The relationship between working time and family-type was found to be less clear cut than that between gender, hours, and working time. Female working times are often significantly related to the presence and ages of dependent children but aspects of male working times have a less pronounced relationship with household structure.

Male hours of work show an insignificant difference in basic and total hours by family-type in partnership households. Although men were more likely to work overtime if there were children in the household (see Table 3.1) questions in the Welfare survey revealed that this overtime was less likely to be paid for than it was for men with no dependent children, thus lending little support to the hypothesis that men work additional hours to make up household income at certain stages in the life cycle. For women, family-type does affect hours even when the higher proportions working part-time with young and dependent children are accounted for. Average hours for both female full-timers and part-timers tend to increase systematically as dependency levels decrease (giving a significant relationship when all women in partnership households are taken together). Thus there is fairly strong evidence to suggest that the presence of dependent children for women not only influences participation decisions, and decisions to work full- or part-time, but also the hours that are worked within these categories. These influences are not, of course, sequential and decisions to participate may be influenced by the existence of opportunities to work a shorter week in particular occupations or firms.

There were few differences in non-standard hours working for men by household type; only shiftwork was found to be more common for those with dependents, particularly those men without very young children. For women, however, there were again much clearer differences by family circumstances. Those with a child under 5 years of age were more likely to be involved in nightwork and to be on-call. This evidence suggests that not all forms of non-standard working are necessarily less desirable than standard working patterns for women with children, although longer hours in the form of overtime appears to be a working-time pattern which is relatively unpopular with women with dependents. Shiftworking did not vary strongly with family circumstances.

The earlier suggestion that there is polarization in the flexibility provided within the part-time jobs category is given further support from the analysis of days worked by household type (see Table 3.2). While the share of part-time jobs is highest among women with children under 5, this is the family-type where days worked are least likely to vary and, among these nine women, no weekend working took place in the week prior to the survey. Furthermore only two of the nine said they 'ever' worked weekends compared to 61% of those with children over 5 and 56% of those without dependent children. Thus flexibility in days of working which part-timers appear to provide may be limited to those part-time jobs filled by women without very young dependents. The vast majority (85%) of women without dependents worked five days in the previous week whereas the pattern for women with older dependents was polarized. On the one hand, women with children of 5 to 16 years old were more likely to have worked *fewer* than five days than women without dependents and less likely to have worked both Saturday and Sunday, but, on the other, they were also more likely to have worked *more* than five days and at least Saturday or Sunday in the previous week. Involvement in 'long week' working and in weekend working is thus definitely not confined to women without dependents. Not working late and not working longer than basic hours also appear to be associated with the presence of dependents, and working late 'frequently' was almost exclusively confined to women not in partnership households and those in partnerships without dependents.

Therefore disaggregation by family-type reveals fairly systematic tendencies for women with young dependents to have much less variable work patterns than women with older or no dependents. No systematic pattern of working time by family-type was found for men, and thus no evidence to support a life-cycle hypothesis of men's overtime and other working-time patterns.

Summary of Current Working-Time Regimes

Table 3.3 brings together the main findings on working-time regimes in current jobs described in this section through the construction of three indices to reflect working-time constraints and commitments. The time commitment index was constructed from the Work Attitudes and Work Histories survey. The level of time commitment is said to be higher (in the sense of it placing more constraints on other activities) if it involves long hours, overtime, shiftworking, nightwork or being on-call. Each of these elements have been added together to score an index with a maximum value of 6.5.[5] There are quite large and statistically significant differences in the value of the index between female full-timers and female part-timers (not a surprising result given the importance of basic hours in the index) and, more importantly, between male and female full-timers. The index rose with decreasing levels of dependency for women, while for men those without dependents scored lowest. The difference was statistically significant in both cases.

TABLE 3.3 Indices of job requirements

	Whole sample			Partnership households					
				Male respondent			Female respondent		
	MFT	FFT	FPT	Child <5	Child 5–16	Other	Child <5	Child 5–16	Other
Work Attitudes and Work Histories survey									
Index of time commitment	2.75	2.14	1.29	2.76	2.95	2.56	1.45	1.53	1.86
Welfare survey									
Index of work involvement	14.2	12.1	8.1	14.9	14.3	13.9	7.4	9.5	11.1
Index of unsociability	2.42	1.51	1.85	3.04	2.32	1.92	1.15	1.48	1.44

Note: MFT = male full-time; FFT = female full-time; FPT = female part-time.

χ^2 significant at 1% for MFT/FFT/FPT for all three indices; for males by family-type significant at 3% for time-commitment index; for females by family-type significant at 3% for time-commitment index and 2% for work-involvement index.

A similar index of work involvement was calculated for the respondents to the Welfare survey. This index not only took into account basic hours but also numbers of extra hours usually worked, frequency of working extra hours, frequency of taking work home and number of days worked, including weekend working, giving a maximum score of 22.5.[6] This more comprehensive index revealed a similar pattern to the time-commitment index with gender differences again being significant. The differences by family-type are more marked for women, although for men there is a smaller, and this time non-significant, difference between those with and without dependent children, and here men with children under 5 are the most involved with work.

The unsociability index selects out those aspects of working time associated with non-standard or unsocial hours. Scores are given for weekend, night, and evening working, frequent variation in days worked, frequently working later than expected, and unsocial start or finish times, giving a maximum score of 13.[7] This index gives some quite different results from those found for the work-involvement and time-commitment indices; women in part-time jobs score higher on the unsociability index than do women in full-time jobs, although men still have the highest score. For men, those without dependents have the lowest score, followed by those with 5 to 16 year olds, with those with under-5 year olds scoring highest. For women, having children under 5 again leads to a low score, but this time there is little difference between women with 5 to 16 year olds and women without dependents. However, these differences are not statistically significant for men or women.

These indices summarize the overall findings on the working-time regimes of current jobs. They highlight the principal differences between full- and part-time workers in terms of commitment and involvement and show the smaller but still significant differences that exist between male and female full-timers. Time commitment and work involvement also relate in the expected manner to family-type for women but there is less evidence of any systematic relationship between men's working times and household structure. The unsociability index illustrates the need to separate this aspect of working time from general measures of work involvement; for female workers the pattern with respect to unsociability is different, with part-timers having on average higher scores but women with children under 5 having particularly low scores, although the magnitude of the scores for all groups suggest that non-standard hours working is not strictly confined to particular household types. Variability of hours worked is also not confined to specific labour force groups although the forms in which flexibility is offered tends to differ between full- and part-time workers. The suggestion that part-time jobs are polarized into those that have fixed and those that have flexible work schedules is corroborated in most of the survey questions and it would seem to be those part-timers with young dependents that are least likely to be accommodating working-time patterns that involve such flexibility.

WORKING TIME AND THE HOUSEHOLD

In the preceding section we have considered the relationship between family-type and working time with reference only to individuals. In this section we look more specifically at the household nature of working time, that is, the intermeshing of the days and times of day that partners worked and at the degree of variation in working time accommodated by the household for each partner.[8] The household intermeshing of working time is of considerable importance if we assume it is at the level of the household, rather than of the individual, that decisions about labour supply, feasible hours of work for each partner, and household income requirements are made. In an environment with greater demand for flexible and non-standard working-time arrangements some understanding of the extent to which the household can accommodate such regimes for one or both of the partners is needed, particularly as the nature of the household and its role in social reproduction must, in the final analysis, put limits on the number of household members that can supply their labour in this way.

Table 3.4 looks at hours worked by family-type within partnerships. Similar patterns to those found for the individual are revealed but, in addition, we can see how hours vary according to whether or not the partner is in work and by partner's hours. A tendency for men's hours to be lower where the female partner is not in work can be observed, again giving little support for a

TABLE 3.4 *Average hours in employment*[a]

Female partner	Men's average hours			
	Child <5	Child 5–16	Other	All
Working	43.1	42.3	41.2	41.3
Not working	42.3	40.0	38.7	40.6
Sample size:				
Working	(78)	(174)	(200)	(451)
Not working	(109)	(75)	(73)	(258)

Male partner's hours[c]	Women's average hours[b]				
	Child <5	Child 5–16	Other	All	Sample size
1–35	18.2	24.9	33.9	28.3	(38)
36–45	19.2	22.7	32.9	26.7	(270)
46–55	22.4	26.0	32.1	28.0	(74)
56–65	18.3	27.6	32.0	27.8	(29)
66+	20.5	38.3	30.8	31.7	(19)

[a] By family-type and partner's hours.
[b] Women working only.
[c] Men employed full-time or self-employed only.
Source: Work Attitudes and Work Histories survey: partnership households.

hypothesis that men's hours will vary negatively with the female partner's hours to maintain family income. Equally there is relatively little variation in working women's hours by partner's hours. However, there is a systematic variation by family-type within each of the male partners' hour bands; women work longer hours as dependency decreases. We can conclude that female activity patterns are more determined by the presence of dependents than by partners' hours.

Partners' working patterns over the week might be expected to have more of an influence on the other partner's activity patterns than simply total hours of work. One of the important questions relating to the impact of increased labour force participation on household organization is whether this increased participation is associated with partners having similar work schedules so that their time available for home and leisure activities coincide or whether it is associated with adoption of a pattern of working analogous to shiftworking in factories, where one goes to work whilst the other stays at home and vice versa.

Table 3.5 shows the number of days worked by female partners in households where the male partner worked five, six, or seven days over the last week. Here there is some evidence of a trade-off between partners' working-time patterns; a higher percentage of female partners did not work at all in households where the male partner worked seven days. However, there is clearly no straightforward trade-off pattern as fewer female partners worked for six or seven days in households where the male partner worked only five days. Indeed these results suggest that there may be a subset of households where both partners aim to work only a standard week and to maintain certain parts of the week free for social or family life.

Table 3.6 provides some further information on the extent of overlap of working schedules of partners. The first point to note is that in 45% of all households both partners were working on the same five or more days per week, suggesting that, for at least

TABLE 3.5 *Percentage distribution of number of days worked by women by number of days worked by male partners (%)*

Number of days worked by female partner	Number of days worked by male partner		
	5 days	6 days	7 days
0 days	33	25	49
1–4 days	15	17	7
5 days	48	42	38
6 and 7 days	5	16	7
Total	100	100	100
Sample size	(74)	(23)	(19)

Note: χ^2 significant at 1%.
Source: Welfare survey.

TABLE 3.6 *Overlap of working days and arriving and leaving times of male and female partners*

	All	Child <5	Child 5–16	Other
% men and women working:[a]				
0 days the same	33	65	18	21
1–4 days the same	22	25	21	21
5 days the same	41	10	54	54
6 or 7 days the same	4	–	8	4
Number of same days worked by both partners as % of number worked by man:[b]				
Average %	83	73	84	86
Sample size	(82)	(14)	(35)	(34)
% households where:[c]				
M leaves home 1 hour + before F	33	18	52	19
M leaves home 1 hour + after F	6	8	7	4
M arrives home 1 hour + before F	11	16	14	4
M arrives home 1 hour + after F	18	16	24	11
F arrives home before M leaves and/or M arrives home before F leaves	6	16	4	4
Sample size	(81)	(15)	(36)	(30)

[a] Including where neither partner is in work.
[b] Both partners worked last week.
[c] Those who gave usual arriving and leaving times only and where man works full-time or is self-employed and where the woman is in employment.

Source: Welfare survey: partnership households.

a large share of households, working-time schedules overlap considerably, at least on a days basis. Breaking this down further by family-type revealed a much lower degree of overlap in days worked in households with children under 5. This is illustrated further by taking the average degree of overlap of days worked in households where both partners worked in the last week; the overlap is 83% for all households but only 73% in households with children under 5.

A 'shift' system of household working time could involve either completely non-overlapping work schedules or simply 'staggered' systems of start and finish times so that one partner is available to deal with household responsibilities at either end of the day. Only 6% of households were found to have non-overlapping types of work schedules in the sense that the female partner usually arrives home from work before the male partner leaves and the male partner arrives home before the female partner leaves (see Table 3.6). However, this proportion rises to 16% in households where both partners are in work and where there is a child under 5. Possibly because of the small sample numbers involved this relationship with household type is not statistically significant. A much higher percentage of households had staggered start and finish times, defined here by reference to their implications for the household; thus a staggered start is where one partner leaves home at least one hour before the other partner and a staggered finish is when they arrive home at least one hour afterwards. 39% of households had a staggered start but of these, 33% involved the man leaving at least one hour before the woman and only 6% involved the man leaving at least one hour after the woman. A smaller share of households, 29%, had staggered finishing times and again there was an unequal, if less pronounced, division by sex with the man arriving home at least one hour after the woman in 18% of households but in 11% the man arriving home at least one hour before the woman. Men were particularly likely to leave home earlier or arrive home later than their partner in households with children over 5, but, in contrast, men in households with children of all ages were more likely to arrive home before their female partner than in households without children. Thus although, by and large, the effect of staggered start and finish times was likely to be to reinforce women's responsibilities for domestic life, particularly in the morning, there was evidence of a sizeable minority of men in families with children who arrived home significantly before their female partners and thus could be involved in assuming some domestic responsibilities.

It would be expected that such 'shift' or 'staggered' working patterns may involve the male partner in taking at least some responsibilities for child care after school or in the school holidays. This is supported by responses to questions on child care in the surveys; 25% of men in households with children were involved in looking after them during the school holidays, the same percentage whether their partner worked full- or part-time. Of men, 36% were involved in looking after children after school in households where the female partner worked part-time and 20% where she worked full-time. The higher share of male partner involvement where women work part-time may be related to a higher incidence of part-time evening work, and thus be supportive of a view that the 'shift' pattern of household arrangements may be more common where women work part-time.

A further aspect of household working-time patterns is the degree of flexibility or variation that can be accommodated. The pattern of variation in days worked within partnerships (see Table 3.7) suggests that there are two main types of partnership: those where both partners work to strict schedules (days worked varied rarely or never for 58% of households) and those where days varied for one partner but the other kept to a strict schedule (35% of households). Variation in days for both partners was relatively rare. While the 35% of households where there was an apparent trade-off between one partner working variable days and the other fixed days split evenly into those with a male partner or a female partner having variable schedules, it is likely that these two types of household operate rather differently. Most of the women who worked variable days were part-timers, so that in most of these households the man would be working a fixed full-time schedule and the female a variable part-time schedule. However, we have already seen that part-timers are more likely to work part of the weekend than full-timers, so that the variation in days worked may still affect the male partner's domestic and social life.

The information on weekend working provides some support for the idea that there is a subset of households where both partners have fairly fixed work schedules which minimize interference with domestic or social life. In half the partnership households neither partner worked any weekend day in the previous week and in only 9% of households did both partners work at least one day at the weekend. However, overall, 50% of households had been required to make some accommodation to weekend working by at least one of the partners; this was generally the male partner but in a not insignificant minority of cases it involved the female partner.

Variations in hours worked on a daily basis can also cause

TABLE 3.7 *Distributions of partners' variation in days worked, in working later than expected, and in weekend work*

	% distribution of partnerships
Variation of days worked within partnerships:	
Both partners rarely or never	58
One partner occasionally/other rarely	5
Female frequent/male rarely or never, or female occasional/male never	17
Male frequent/female rarely or never, or male occasional/female never	17
Both partners frequent or occasional	4
Pattern of weekend working during previous week:	
Neither partner worked Saturday nor Sunday	50
Female worked at least one weekend day/ male neither	10
Male worked at least one weekend day/ female neither	31
Both partners worked at least one weekend day	9
Frequency of working late within partnerships:	
Both rarely or never work late	35
One partner sometimes/other rarely	10
Female frequently/male rarely or female sometimes/male never	4
Male frequently/female rarely or never, or male sometimes/female never	32
Both frequently or sometimes work late	20

Source: Welfare survey: both partners working.

problems for households in scheduling working time with other domestic responsibilities and social activities. The share of households where both partners are involved frequently or sometimes in working later than expected is, however, higher, at 20%, than the share of households where both partners experienced variations in the days worked or where both had worked weekends. At the other extreme the share of households which rarely or never have to cope with one member working variable hours is lower, at 35%, than the share where neither experienced variations in days or worked weekends. There is still a large share of households, 32%, where the pattern appears to be for the female partner to work regular hours and the male partner variable hours, but the share of households where the reverse was true was negligible (4%). Thus the households mainly split into three categories: those where both were liable to work late; those where the male partner only was likely to work late; and those where neither worked late.

This investigation of working-time arrangements within partnerships has provided some indication that a range of ways of accommodating the increasingly complex patterns of labour market participation are to be found within households. Some may involve a 'shift' system within households, others a 'trade-off' where one partner works fixed hours so as to accommodate to their partner's more variable working time and yet others appear to aim for maximum co-ordination of both partner's working time. All the systems adopted will affect the attitudes of labour towards different working-time regimes which employers may seek to introduce, and may thus restrict or encourage the search by industry for new forms of working-time arrangements. These issues can be investigated by looking at respondents' preferences for different forms of working-time regimes.

WORKING-TIME PREFERENCES

In a climate where demands for non-standard working times and a shorter working week by employers and unions are becoming commonplace, it is important to have information on employees' preferences for various regimes. The surveys therefore included questions on: the willingness of the respondent to consider a job offering certain non-standard working times; respondents' desired changes to working time, provided the total number of hours worked remained the same; and desired changes to the total number of hours worked, given that the hourly wage rate remained the same as currently.

In the Household and Community survey respondents were asked about their willingness to accept a job involving working-time requirements which might be expected to deter certain labour force groups, particularly women. The working-time

TABLE 3.8 Attitudes to jobs with different working-time arrangements[a]

| | Whole sample | | | Partnership households | | | | | |
| | | | | Male respondent | | | Female respondent | | |
	MFT	FFT	FPT	Child <5	Child 5–16	Other	Child <5	Child 5–16	Other
Household and Community survey									
% willing to consider taking a job involving:									
Periods away from home	45	25	9	54	49	36	4	15	22
Regular overtime	69	42	30	79	61	67	21	41	35
Taking work home	45	63	44	59	40	43	47	54	55
Working late when necessary	87	79	58	93	92	79	65	75	65
Sample size	(151)	(69)	(67)	(43)	(53)	(58)	(16)	(53)	(67)
Welfare survey									
% who would find it difficult to work:									
Weekends	43	54	59	50	62	29	94	52	41
Nights	62	65	65	50	74	68	94	54	64
Evenings	49	44	43	44	58	49	45	49	28
Late at short notice	31	41	52	40	52	15	65	54	16
Five hours more than currently	19	36	26	20	19	17	45	32	28
Sample size	(82)	(36)	(27)	(19)	(19)	(29)	(9)	(21)	(16)

Note: MFT = male full-time; FFT = female full-time; FPT = female part-time.

regime that was most unpopular with women was a job which required periods away from home (see Table 3.8), with women with children under 5 being particularly likely to rule out such a job. Amongst men those jobs involving being away from home were also among the most unpopular; a higher proportion of men than women were willing to consider taking them, but it still amounted to less than half the sample, the same proportion who would consider jobs involving taking work home. Women were on average more willing to take work home, particularly female full-timers, but were much less willing than men to work regular overtime. The working-time characteristic that was least likely to deter men and women was that of having to work late when necessary, although women working part-time were least likely to consider a job with this characteristic (58%). However, overall, relatively small differences were found by family-type, suggesting that these preferences are not solely related to the presence of children in the household.

The Welfare survey pursued this line of investigation in more detail, with respondents being asked to say whether they would consider it very or quite difficult, neither easy nor difficult, or quite or very easy to take a job with specific working-time requirements, and, if they would find it difficult, the reason for this. The least popular working-time regimes were working nights for men and women, followed by working weekends for women and working evenings for men (see Table 3.8). Men were less likely to consider it to be difficult to work late at short notice or to work five hours more in their current job than were women. Differences between women in full- and part-time jobs were relatively small; women part-timers were more likely to find working late at short notice difficult but were less likely to consider it difficult to work five hours more than at present. Part-timers are thus not necessarily working their maximum hours but need time to adjust to a longer working schedule. Men without dependents were less likely to find it difficult to work weekends or late at short notice; but they were just as likely not to want to work nights or evenings. Among men with dependents, those with 5 to 16 year olds were the most likely to see problems working weekends, nights, evenings, and late at short notice. For women those without dependents were the least likely to find all the different regimes difficult, except for working nights, and women with children under 5 were the most likely to find the regimes difficult except for working evenings, where a slightly smaller percentage than those with 5 to 16 year olds would find it difficult.

The reasons given for finding these regimes difficult showed much greater variation than the percentages who would find them difficult. Child care was the main reason given in each case for part-timers, but for full-timers, both male and female, social life was the most popular reason given for finding weekends, nights or evenings difficult. Only for working late at short notice was child care the most frequent response for female full-timers. For men child care was given as the main reason by a significant proportion of men for each working-time regime, except working five hours more, and time with family was also a popular response in all questions. However, partner's hours hardly ever appeared as a factor for men while it was a relatively frequent factor for women in part-time jobs. Further disaggregation revealed that despite apparently strong gender and full-/part-time differences, family-type has a substantial impact on the pattern of reasons given. For men with dependents under 5 child care becomes the most popular factor given ahead of social life for almost all of the working-time regimes. For women child care is also more commonly given for those with under-5 year olds than for all family types, but here the main differences are with those with no dependents; child care is also the most common reason given by women with 5 to 16 year olds for not working nights, evenings, or late at short notice, while for men with 5 to 16 year olds disruption of social life is still the most popular reason for finding each regime difficult.

When asked about changes respondents would like to make to their working time, well over half of both full- and part-timers said they would not want to make any change (see Table 3.9). More flexibility in hours and changes to start and finish times were the most common changes desired by both male and female full-timers; female part-timers most frequently mentioned changes which allowed them to work within normal hours, followed by changes to fit in with school hours, including school holidays, and more flexibility. Female full-timers were the most anxious to stop working weekends. It is worth noting that none of the respondents articulated a desire for radical change in their working hours along the lines of, for example, the annualized-hours schemes promoted in the personnel management and industrial relations press. This implies that pressure for such changes does not seem to be coming from individuals and their aspirations for different working-time patterns. Indeed these results indicate that individual aspirations may be highly constrained and influenced by current practices.

Disaggregation by family-type showed more flexibility to be the most frequently sought change by both men and women with children under 5. Men with children aged 5 to 16 were the least likely to wish for any changes, but women with 5 to 16 year olds were the most likely to specify some change, with changes to start and finish times and fitting in with school hours being the most frequently mentioned. Desire for change in working-time patterns can be expected to be related at least in part to the 'unsociability' of current working-time arrangements. Analysis of the unsociability index (see p. 113) by desired change (see Table 3.9) did indeed reveal that those expressing a wish to stop working weekends or to move to more standard hours usually had higher average unsociability index scores than those wishing for no change, but those wishing for more flexibility or changes in start and finish times had similar or even lower unsociability index scores than those wishing for no change.

Responses to the number of hours people would ideally like to work revealed that the proportions of men who wished to reduce and who wished to increase hours were relatively evenly balanced, at 30% and 24% respectively. Over half of female full-timers wished to reduce hours but a significant proportion of part-timers wished to increase hours, suggesting that there may be strong demand for 'short full-time' working. It is men with children under 5 who most wish to reduce hours but men with children 5 to 16 who would most like to increase hours. For women it is those without dependents who would most like to reduce hours, followed by those with children under 5. Children both demand more domestic time and more wage income and these conflicting pressures may explain the different responses by age of children.

Converting the desired changes into actual change in average basic hours we find that men on average would like to reduce hours by half an hour per week, women full-timers would like to reduce hours by 6.5 hours, but women part-timers would like to

TABLE 3.9 Desired changes to pattern of working time[a] and to hours worked per week[b]

| | Whole sample | | | Partnership households | | | | | |
| | | | | Male respondent | | | Female respondent | | |
	MFT	FFT	FPT	Child <5	Child 5–16	Other	Child <5	Child 5–16	Other
Changes to pattern of working time % distribution:									
no change	57	53	54	51	68	52	50	42	71
more flexibility	14	14	9	28	12	13	23	8	8
not working weekends	5	11	5	7	–	11	–	6	8
work standard hours	4	5	17	7	–	5	14	9	7
fit school hours	–	–	11	–	–	–	–	13	–
change start or finish times	15	17	5	7	19	9	14	23	6
other	5	–	–	–	–	9	–	–	–
Change to pattern of working time by unsociability index:									
no change	2.6	1.5	1.7	3.1	2.6	2.1	1.5	1.8	1.2
more flexibility	1.3	1.3	0.7	1.2	1.2	1.4	0.6	0.2	0.0
not work weekends	3.2	2.7	3.0	3.0	–	3.5	–	1.0	4.0
work standard hours	3.7	3.5	2.5	6.0	–	3.0	0.0	2.6	4.0
fit school hours	–	–	2.3	–	–	–	–	2.3	–
change start or finish times	2.4	0.7	1.0	7.0	2.0	0.5	1.5	0.5	1.0
other	1.0	–	–	–	–	1.0	–	–	–

Changes to hours worked per week:

% who would like to:

reduce hours	30	52	10	37	27	25	42	18	62
keep them the same	46	40	69	50	36	55	45	69	38
increase hours	24	8	21	13	37	20	13	13	–
Average change to basic hours by current basic hours:									
<30 hours	-5.7	-7.2	+1.5	–	+6.0	-6.9	+0.7	-0.5	-3.4
31–45 hours	+1.3	-6.6	+7.7	-0.9	+0.6	+2.5	-4.3	-2.8	-7.7
46+ hours	-12.2	0.0	–	-17.7	0.0	-8.3	–	–	–
All	-0.5	-6.5	+1.6	-4.3	+0.9	+1.3	-0.4	-1.3	-7.1
Sample size	(79)	(34)	(27)	(19)	(17)	(29)	(9)	(21)	(16)

Note: MFT = male full-time; FFT = female full-time; FPT = female part-time.

[a] Given no change in average hours.
[b] Hourly wage remaining constant.

Source: Welfare survey.

increase hours by 1.6 hours per week. Although the average change is therefore clearly towards an overall reduction in hours, for men, however, the average negative result arises from a desire by men working very long hours to cut them substantially. In fact, the desired average change for men with basic hours between 31 and 45 hours per week was an addition of 1.3 hours per week, so that it is only in the case of women full-timers that we can say that on average, for those currently working standard hours, there is a desire to reduce the standard week.

SUMMARY AND IMPLICATIONS

Three main lines of argument have been developed from the survey results reported here. First, there is evidence of extensive and highly variable involvement in flexible and non-standard working in all types of jobs. Men and women may be involved in jobs requiring different types and degrees of flexibility but there is widespread involvement of both sexes in weekend, evening, shift-work, overtime, and working later than expected. Furthermore, differences in types of flexibility are usually stronger between full- and part-time jobs than by gender, with the main difference by gender relating to total number of hours worked. Part-time jobs also appear to be polarized between those with fixed and standard work schedules and those with flexible or non-standard hours.

The second finding is that there is evidence of relationships between working-time patterns and household circumstances, from partner's working time to the presence of children. These relationships are much stronger for women than for men and relate particularly to the presence of children. Women with under-5 year olds appear to see predictability and regularity as prime determinants of work time, while those with 5 to 16 year olds are more involved in flexible working patterns and forms of non-standard working such as weekends. Nevertheless there are indications that the presence of children does affect both the working-time patterns and preferences of a significant proportion of men. There are problems in identifying these influences from the data as the effects seem to work in different directions, as hinted at by some of the results. In some cases men seem to be seeking to work fewer hours or to organize working time around their families in a more convenient way, but in others the influence may be to add working hours because of income needs, although the overall results provide relatively poor evidence for the income-needs hypothesis.

Looking more specifically at the interactions within households revealed that a range of systems of accommodating to partners' working time could be detected, from those which aimed to synchronize work and leisure times, those that operated some form of 'shift system', alternating waged work and family responsibilities, to those where the female partner provided the family backup to a male partner involved in long or variable working hours. The first and third forms of household organization were most common, but particularly among those with under-5 year olds some evidence of the alternating pattern of domestic and family responsibilities could be found. These results suggest the need for further research into how families accommodate to different working-time schedules, to identify whether a typology of types of household system is emerging and to what extent there may be a relationship between these typologies and life-cycle factors on the one hand, and occupational status on the other.

The third finding is that, from the evidence relating to preferences for working-time patterns, there may well be considerable 'supply-side' resistance to employers' plans to increase the use of flexible and non-standard forms of working. This resistance to flexibility is not found across the board, nor is it resistance to flexibility *per se*; indeed the most frequent change that men and women wished to see was an increase in flexibility, but under their control not the employer's. There is evidence to suggest that it is the unpredictability of working time under more 'flexible' arrangements that is likely to cause problems, particularly for women; it is in preferences concerning working late at short notice that one of the main gender differences occurs. Compatibility between domestic arrangements and working time may require at the minimum at least reasonable notice of change. While weekend and night working are among the least popular options, a high proportion are already involved in such work, and others appeared willing to give them a try. It is thus probable that employers will find some individuals and families willing to accommodate to non-standard working, and these patterns may even suit families operating a type of shift system for domestic responsibilities, but it is also clear that the majority still oppose these forms of working. Evidence from current practice suggests that some households do try to synchronize their working time around standard weeks and it is likely that the emerging labour supply may become increasingly polarized into those where certain forms of flexible working are acceptable and those where standard and predictable hours are preferred; moreover these preferences do not necessarily relate to individuals but to household systems of organization (which in turn cannot be simply predicted from demographic variables such as the presence of children). The lessons of this finding, if it is borne out by further research, may be that rather than imposing flexible working patterns on all current employees within an occupation, a range of different types of working regime should be allowed to exist side by side, wherever that is technically possible, to provide opportunities for individuals to choose those which suit their own preferences and household circumstances.

The evidence from this survey also counsels against dividing working-time regimes by simple demographic variables, such as gender or presence of children; women are currently heavily involved in various forms of non-standard working practices, and for many, such working-time arrangements are likely to be essential to meet their income and domestic requirements. Any arrangement of working time by demographic characteristics is likely simply to reinforce stereotypes which do not fit with preferences and practices, even given current arrangements for domestic responsibilities. According to such stereotypes women may not be viewed as 'committed' workers who could be relied upon to take responsibility for their work outside normal working hours, by working late or taking work home, but this image of women workers does not square with the information on female full-timers in the surveys, many of whom are involved in such activities. Nevertheless some women, and indeed some men, will not be able or willing to extend their commitment to their work beyond their basic working week or to vary their working-time patterns.

A further conclusion that can be drawn from the evidence of both a wide range of working practices and a relatively limited desire for change in working-time arrangements is that there is likely to be a high degree of inertia built up around existing arrangements, not simply because of 'custom and practice' but because individuals have had to make complex arrangements to fit their current working time to their social and family arrangements and any disruption to working time will have significant effects on other aspects of their life and family members. Taking this last point together with our earlier finding on diversity in working-time practices and preferences, we can see that while there is an extensive share of the labour force of both sexes currently working non-standard hours and willing to take jobs with demanding working-time schedules, the assumption cannot be made that all individuals are flexible or that one system is likely to be preferable to another. As the share of families trying to accommodate working-time patterns of more than one member increases, the main expectation must be an increase in the strength with which household members hold their working-time preferences.

NOTES

1. We have considered breakdowns by manual/non-manual and full-time/part-time work for all individuals, whether or not they were in partnerships, but for reasons of space few of these results are reported here.
2. Small sample numbers have generally inhibited the use of significance tests and much of the discussion relates to differences in percentages that are not necessarily statistically significant. Results of significance tests have therefore not been systematically reported throughout but are mentioned where the relationships have been found to be strongly significant, or where apparently wide differences in percentages have still been found not to be significant.
3. The data on hours was derived from information provided by respondents relating to their last pay cheque, the number of hours this payment covered, and how many of these were basic and how many were overtime hours. The full-/part-time categorization was not based on some standard cut-off point but on the respondent's self-definition except in the cases where the respondent was self-employed, in which case a cut-off point of 30 hours was used.
4. For further evidence on the extensive involvement of both men and women in non-standard hours regimes from a survey of employers' working-time strategies, see Horrell and Rubery (1991).

5. The index was computed as follows: basic hours: 0–20 0.5 points, 21–30 1 point, 31–40 1.5 points, 41–50 2 points, 50+ 2.5 points; frequent overtime 1 point; shiftworking 1 point; frequent nightwork 1 point; being on-call 1 point.

6. The work involvement index was computed as follows: number of days worked last week, 0–7 points; worked Saturday or Sunday 1 point; worked Saturday and Sunday 1.5 points; ever worked Saturday or Sunday 1 point; take work home frequently 1 point; work longer than basic week regularly 2 points, occasionally 1 point (if neither but frequently work later than expected 1 point); basic hours 1 point for every 10 hours (or part thereof) up to 6 points for over 50 hours; extra hours 1 point per 5 hours (or part thereof) up to 4 points for over 15 hours.

7. The unsociability index was constructed as follows: frequent variation in days worked 1 point; every Saturday or Sunday 1 point; worked Saturday or Sunday the previous week 1 point; frequently work later than expected 1 point; work nights 2 points; work evenings 1 point; usually start work between 9 p.m. and 6 a.m. 2 points; usually start between 6 a.m. and 8 a.m. 1 point; usually finish between 6 p.m. and 8 p.m. 1 point; usually finish between 8 p.m. and 6 a.m. 1 point. Half the points are awarded if these start and finish times are given as occasional rather than usual.

8. The analysis of individuals used information from one respondent per household (respondents being chosen through a randomizing procedure known as a Kish grid). The surveys also collected information on the working time of the partner of the respondent, in the case of the household survey by interviewing the partner. In this section we utilize this information in conjunction with the questions already analysed for the respondent.

4

The Labour Market: Friend or Foe?*

BRIAN G. M. MAIN

INTRODUCTION

Standard economic theory portrays economic agents as experiencing a life cycle of consumption expenditures which are out of phase with income flows. The corresponding income flows, principally from earnings, are seen as lagging behind consumption expenditures but as reaching a peak in excess of consumption sometime in the later part of the life cycle. Eventually, on retirement, income once again falls below consumption outgoings. The pattern of consumption expenditures is much smoother than that of income flows. The two streams of outgoings and income are reconciled by recourse to the capital markets, that is, by borrowing and lending (saving). Recent developments in economic theory, particularly under the 'new classical school',[1] place considerable emphasis on the disconnectedness of consumption from labour supply. Subject to a need to 'balance the books' over the full life cycle, agents are regarded as phasing their labour supply in a way that reflects the labour market rewards available at any time.

As an hour of labour supply can be thought of as the sacrifice of an hour of leisure, then the wage rate reflects what is given up for every extra hour of leisure consumed, that is, for every hour not supplied to the labour market. From this perspective, the wage rate can be viewed as the price of leisure. The logic behind the new classical school's approach is that economic agents will consume more leisure (supply less labour) when the price of leisure (wage rate) is low and will consume less leisure (supply more labour) when the price of leisure (wage rate) is high. This

* I am particularly grateful for the support of the University of Edinburgh team. Remaining errors are my own.

hypothesis can be developed into a theory of the business cycle.[2] The essential thrust of the theory is that the labour market does not so much thwart the plans or desires of individuals as rather present individuals with a range of opportunities which they exploit to their maximum advantage.

It is the purpose of this paper to deploy some of the data from the Kirkcaldy part of the Social Change and Economic Life Initiative data set to throw light on the extent to which individuals find themselves able to exist in harmony with the labour market, and the extent to which individuals find themselves either victims of the labour market or, at least, unable to utilize the labour market as they might wish. This will be done by focusing on two particular phenomena, namely, the time when individuals felt themselves to have had the most difficulty in making ends meet, and, for women, the experience in returning to the labour market after the birth of the most recent child. It is possible to probe these aspects of life experience through sets of questions asked only of respondents in Kirkcaldy. These asked respondents to identify the time in their lives when they experienced the most difficulty in making ends meet and also inquired as to the causes of, and reaction to, this circumstance. Additionally, women who had returned to the labour market after having had children were asked about their resulting labour market experience. This information will be used in conjunction with the detailed work and life history data that were collected on all Social Change and Economic Life Initiative respondents.

The next section of the chapter investigates the time of economic crisis in people's lives, and the subsequent section discusses the experience of women returning to the labour market. A summary and some tentative conclusions are offered in the final section.

HARD TIMES

Some 463 women and 338 men in the Kirkcaldy sample were able to identify a time in their lives that they could say was the time that they had the most difficulty making ends meet. For 100 of the women and 67 of the men that time was 'now' (i.e. at the time of the interview). One difficulty in examining the timing of

such an event is that a respondent of age 30 is essentially constrained in identifying this event to a range of years far narrower
than faced by someone aged 50. Table 4.1, therefore, presents the
frequency distribution of this time of economic crisis broken
down by current age.[3]

The lack of any clear pattern in the results of Table 4.1 is surprising. According to the standard life-cycle theory of consumption,[4] one would expect the late twenties and early thirties to be
identified most frequently as hard times, as it is then that the
demands of children are generally placing a severe burden on
household income. Table 4.1 reveals that, for both genders, the
forties are certainly less marked by such traumas than earlier
years, but a general life-cycle pattern does not stand out in any
clear way. Table 4.2 examines these same data from a different
perspective by presenting the average age at which various age
groups of respondents had the most trouble making ends meet.

From Table 4.2 it can be seen that, for women, the average
reported age of crisis does not increase to any great extent after
the age of 40 when they report an age of 32. This does lend some
support to the notion of a life-cycle pattern of consumption with
particularly high needs relative to income as children grow up.
The pattern for males reveals a much less marked pattern. Due
to the average age gap between husbands and wives one would
expect the male profile to plateau at a slightly higher age than
that for females. But no plateau is discernible. The evidence of
the life-cycle pattern of consumption leading to difficulties in
making ends meet is, therefore, far from persuasive and one is
left with the possibility that such crises are somewhat random
and, possibly, outwith the control of the individual.

Table 4.3 examines the stated causes of these crises in making
ends meet. It is worthwhile commenting on some gender differences apparent in these responses, before turning to their particular content. It can be seen that the fortunes of a female's partner
are more likely to be identified as the cause of the problem than
are the fortunes of a male's partner. For the majority of individuals throughout this period of study, the contribution of the
male's earning power to the household has undoubtedly dominated that of the female. Similarly, low pay, while more common
among women, is a problem for the household when it is experienced by a male partner, due to the generally longer hours of

TABLE 4.1 *Age at which respondents had most trouble making ends meet by current age*

Current age	Age at which had most trouble making ends meet (% of row)									Row %
	15–19	20–24	25–29	30–34	35–39	40–44	45–49	50–54	55–59	
Females										
20–24	39	61								12
25–29	15	41	44							15
30–34	18	20	35	27						13
35–39	15	25	16	21	23					16
40–44	3	22	19	6	19	32				15
45–49	11	20	16	16	18	4	16			10
50–54	7	23	18	14	7	5	5	23		10
55–59	6	29	15	17	4	4	0	4	21	10
Column %	14	30	21	12	9	6	2	3	2	100
Number[a] = (463)										
Males										
20–24	50	50								11
25–29	10	45	45							12
30–34	16	26	30	28						13
35–39	11	35	6	26	24					16
40–44	5	23	21	21	10	21				12
45–49	3	15	28	13	8	13	21			12
50–54	5	18	13	15	10	3	10	28		12
55–59	7	16	9	11	11	9	0	5	32	13
Column %	13	28	19	15	9	5	4	4	4	100
Number[a] = (338)										

[a] The total number of respondents.

work he supplies to the labour market. In terms of household-originating causes, it is interesting to note that males give relatively more importance to 'setting up home' than to 'children' as a cause of financial crisis. The ranking is reversed for women, perhaps reflecting the different spheres of responsibility existing within the household. Lastly, marital breakup is more likely to be identified by women than men as a cause of financial crisis. This may well reflect the asymmetric financial impact of divorce and separation, including the responsibility for any children.

It is clear from the detail of Table 4.3, that the impact of the labour market through unemployment, low pay, or industrial action, is a dominant influence on the financial balance of economic well-being. These, of course, affect the income side of the household's budget. Also seen to be important, but affecting the expenditure side, are setting up home and family formation (children). It is of interest to see how the labour market was utilized by the household in responding to these crises.

Evidence on the role of the labour market can be gleaned from Table 4.4, which presents the strategies that individuals mentioned deploying in order to cope with the difficulty they experienced in making ends meet. In terms of labour market strategies it is notable that females are as likely to identify their partner's

TABLE 4.2 *Average age at which respondents had most trouble making ends meet by current age*

Current age group	Average age at which had most difficulty making ends meet financially	
	Females	Males
20–24	20.1	19.4
25–29	24.0	23.9
30–34	25.3	25.2
35–39	27.7	27.6
40–44	32.5	30.5
45–49	31.3	33.1
50–54	33.5	36.6
55–59	34.1	39.1
Number [a]	(463)	(338)

[a] The total number of respondents.

TABLE 4.3 *Reasons why respondents had most difficulty making ends meet financially*

Reason given	% who gave this reason	
	Females	Males
Unemployed/stopped working	24.2	29.9
Partner stopped working	14.9	9.8
Low pay or on grant	13.0	21.3
Partner low pay or on grant	7.6	0.3
Industrial action	1.1	3.6
Partner industrial action	3.9	0.3
Setting up home	14.3	22.2
Bought home/mortgage increase	7.6	6.2
Children	24.7	16.9
Illness	3.2	4.1
Marital breakup	7.4	1.8
Death of partner	1.7	0.0
Cost of living	19.9	16.9
Number[a]	(462)	(338)
Non-response (excluded)	(1)	(0)

[a] Number of respondents.

activities as they are their own, while males mention their partner's labour market response much less frequently. The exception to this observation is in the case of starting or returning to work which, because of the domestic division of labour, is an option more likely to be open to women. But in terms of working overtime or taking a second job, these labour market options seem to be more open to men than to women. That said, however, Table 4.4 provides a vivid measure of the relative flexibility or otherwise of the labour market in terms of offering individuals freedom of action. While the most frequently mentioned labour market strategy is by the 11.8% of males who report working overtime, this is completely dominated by strategies that involve the expenditure side of the financial balance. Thus 58.5% of men and 56.5% of women mention cutting back on luxuries. Similarly, cutting back on necessities is mentioned by 35.5% of men and 41.9% of women. Indeed, it is interesting to note the degree of concurrence between male and female responses on these dimensions. Use of the capital market whether formally, through credit, or informally, through family and friends, is much less common than adjustments to consumption.

Some further insight into these coping strategies and the influence of the labour market can be gained by re-examining the responses of Table 4.4 but restricting the sample to those who claim that the cause of their financial crisis originated in the labour market.[5] The responses are further broken down by whether the problems were in the first place the respondent's own or the partner's. These results are presented in Table 4.5. It is worthwhile noting that while a majority of women attribute this period of crisis to their own experience in the labour market, very few men identify the female side of their partnership as being the source of their crisis. Once again, it is non-labour-market coping strategies that are most frequently mentioned. And once again there is a remarkable degree of similarity across groups in the frequency with which each is mentioned. Labour market responses are much less frequently mentioned, and the

TABLE 4.4 *How respondents coped when they had most difficulty making ends meet financially*

Strategy mentioned	% who mentioned this strategy	
	Females	Males
Worked overtime	2.5	11.8
Partner worked overtime	3.8	1.2
Took second job	2.7	4.5
Partner took second job	2.5	0.9
Started/went back to work	11.2	2.7
Partner started work	0.9	4.8
Gave up holidays	23.3	23.3
Cut back on other luxuries	56.5	58.5
Cut back on necessities	41.9	35.5
Recourse to credit	7.6	5.8
Financial help from family and/or friends	14.6	13.0
Number[a]	(446)	(328)
Non-response (excluded)	(17)	(10)

[a] Number of respondents.

frequency of their mention varies markedly with the group in question. It is clear from Table 4.5 that whereas some men have the option of working overtime, this is extremely rare for women. Additionally, males seem more likely to take a second job as a means of coping with difficulties in making ends meet. Males report this as a relatively important labour market strategy irrespective of whether the problem originates with themselves or their partner. Females themselves record a modest propensity to take a second job if the problem is their own. In general, however, labour-market-based strategies appear to be relatively infrequent, particularly in comparison with strategies affecting expenditures.

As a final check on labour market experience around the time of crisis in making ends meet, some of the work history data are utilized[6] to provide details on the labour market experience of the respondents one year on either side of the year identified as

TABLE 4.5 *How respondents coped when they had most difficulty making ends meet as a result of a labour market problem[a]*

Labour market strategy mentioned	% who mentioned this strategy			
	Females		Males	
	Own problem	Partner's problem	Own problem	Partner's problem
Worked overtime	1.2	0.0	5.7	12.1
Partner worked overtime	4.2	2.6	1.6	0.0
Took second job	2.4	0.9	5.3	12.1
Partner took second job	1.2	5.2	0.5	0.0
Started/went back to work	9.0	12.9	4.8	3.0
Partner started work	1.8	4.3	4.2	6.1
Gave up holidays	23.5	23.3	26.5	30.3
Cut back on other luxuries	59.6	56.9	60.3	63.6
Cut back on necessities	41.6	48.3	38.6	45.5
Recourse to credit	7.2	7.8	5.3	0.0
Financial help from family and/or friends	21.1	15.5	19.0	6.1
Number[a]	(166)	(116)	(189)	(33)

[a] Number of respondents.

the crisis year.[7] To simplify interpretation of these data, the analysis is restricted to those who report either stopping work or unemployment as a reason for their difficulty in making ends meet. The actual unemployment in question may, of course, have occurred some time before things came to a crisis. Thus of the fifty-two men covered, eleven were already unemployed and one permanently sick one year before things reached their worst.

In terms of labour market flexibility, however, it is interesting to note (see Table 4.6, part A) that twenty-nine men were in full-time employment and one in part-time employment one year afterwards. For females there are two significant differences in employment profile. First, recourse to part-time employment appears much easier than for men. Thus although full-time employees dropped from twenty-nine to ten, the number of part-time employees rose from five to eleven. The second notable difference is in the 'housewife' labour market status. The thirty-one women classified as such one year before the crisis had probably left employment for family formation reasons and, indeed, the number rises to forty-three one year later. This makes an exact interpretation of the labour market transition more difficult than in the case of men.

Part B of Table 4.6 concentrates on those in employment at the two times and records the hours per week that were being worked. Thus, even for those who had managed to find employment again, it can be seen that it is generally at reduced hours. Of the fourteen men working fifty hours or more in the year before the crisis, only five are doing so in the year after. The trickle downwards in hours is also seen in the hours worked by women where there is a virtual collapse of full-time hours, offset in part by an increase in part-time hours. Part C of Table 4.6 confirms that for many of those who find employment again it is, initially at least, at a level of pay that compares unfavourably with previous experience. This trend is most marked among females, and indeed among males around half those in work are in better paid jobs. Part D of Table 4.6 demonstrates the move out of trade union membership into non-membership. One implication that can be drawn from this finding is that when jobs are found again they are likely to be in the non-union sector.

In general, this subset of labour market transitions suggests that for some individuals recovery through the labour market

TABLE 4.6 *Labour market transitions around the time of most difficulty making ends meet due to loss of job*

	Females		Males	
	Year before	Year after	Year before	Year after
(A) Employment status				
Full-time	29	10	40	29
Part-time	5	11	0	1
On scheme	1	0	0	0
Unemployed	6	11	11	19
Permanently sick	1	1	1	1
Student	2	0	0	2
Housewife	31	43	0	0
Maternity leave	3	2	0	0
Number[a]	(78)	(78)	(52)	(52)
(B) Hours of work				
8–15	1	1	1	0
16–22	3	7	0	0
23–30	0	2	0	0
31–35	5	1	2	0
36–40	23	9	15	17
41–45	3	1	5	6
46–49	0	0	3	2
50+	0	0	14	5
Number[a]	(35)	(21)	(40)	(30)
(C) Level of pay compared to last job				
Better	20	8	26	15
Similar	8	4	9	6
Worse	4	9	3	9
Not applicable	3	0	2	0
Number[a]	(35)	(21)	(40)	(30)
(D) Trade union status				
Member	14	7	31	15
Non-member	21	14	9	14
Number[a]	(35)	(21)	(40)	(29)

[a] Number of respondents.

from labour-market-related difficulties (loss of employment) is possible. Some individuals even end up in better-paid jobs. For many, however, recovery is slow and when it occurs it may involve lower hours than being in financial difficulties would suggest as desirable. It may also involve the loss of trade union protection. This analysis remains somewhat speculative, however, as the time identified with having most difficulty making ends meet is not necessarily contemporary with the incident that causes this difficulty: for example, job loss could occur two years before things get really desperate.

But taken overall, Table 4.1 through Table 4.6 suggest that financial crises are not concentrated at one point of the life cycle; that they are quite likely to arise from events in the labour market such as unemployment or low wages; that strategies which emerge to cope with these crises are less likely to be centred on the labour market or income-generating side of the household's activities than on the expenditure side; that there is some conflict in the views held by men and women about the relative importance of each other's labour market activity in coping with crisis; and that, in the case of employment cessation, the labour market offers a relatively slow-acting range of strategies for recovery that seem quite limited in their scope.

RETURNING TO PAID EMPLOYMENT AFTER CHILDREN

The second area where we can gain some insight into the flexibility of the labour market is the experience of women in returning to paid employment after a period out of the labour market to have children. Women in the Kirkcaldy part of the Social Change and Economic Life Initiative were asked a series of questions about their employment experience after the most recent child. Table 4.7 maps out that general attitude to paid employment. Just over one-third had returned to paid employment with over one-half showing no interest at all in such a return. Such responses will, of course, be influenced by whether or not further children are planned. There is no control for this factor here. This table therefore is difficult to interpret. The women involved may have had their most recent child some thirty years ago or

TABLE 4.7 *Employment experience after most recent child*[a]

Action taken	(%)
Did paid work	36.0
Tried to find paid work but were unsuccessful	3.4
Saw no point in trying to find paid work	8.2
Did not want paid work	52.4
Number[b]	(464)

[a] % of women who had at least one child by action taken after most recent child.
[b] Number of respondents.

TABLE 4.8 *How respondents found work after most recent child*

Method	(%)
In same job or firm as before	11.4
Adverts in local press	25.2
Adverts in national press	3.3
Applied on speculation	14.6
Through Job Centre	10.6
Private job agency	3.3
Heard through family	9.8
Heard from friends	28.5
Number[a]	(123)
Not responding (excluded)	(20)

[a] Number of respondents.

only some 30 days ago. Consequently, it was decided, to focus on those women who had actually returned to paid employment and for whom there was a complete life and work history. This resulted in a sample of 143 women.

Table 4.8 demonstrates the ways in which these women found their way back to paid employment. For around 11%, this seems to have been a straightforward procedure of returning to work in the same job or firm as before, possibly under the auspices of the maternity leave provisions of the Employment Protection Act.

The remainder used a traditional range of search channels. It is interesting to note the relatively modest contribution made by Job Centres, with only 10.6% of the women indicating successful use of this channel.

Table 4.9 looks specifically at the declared problems experienced by these women in starting work after their most recent child. Unsurprisingly, a large number, 21.5%, mention the problems of finding child care. This has long been a critical problem for women in the British labour market and, as Dex and Shaw (1988) have made clear, it is not helped by the lack of tax relief on child-care payments. More surprising, perhaps, is the fact that 57% of women declare themselves to have experienced no problems in starting work after the last child.

As a check on this apparent ease of re-entry to paid employment, a comparison was performed on the length of time each woman declared that she would have preferred to lapse between having her most recent child and returning to paid employment and the time that actually did lapse. The first piece of information is found in response to a direct question on the subject, while the second datum is derived by examination of the detailed life and work history obtained for each respondent in the Social Change and Economic Life Initiative. The information so derived is presented in Table 4.10. Looking first at the marginals, it is clear that women do not find it easy to attain the optimal timing

TABLE 4.9 *Problems experienced in starting work after last child*

Problems experienced	(%)
No problems	57.0
Hours of work	4.1
Finding child care	21.5
Time involved and the strain of coping	3.3
Not a family-related matter	4.1
Had to be near home	0.8
Missed the child	2.5
Other	6.5
Number[a]	(123)
Not responding (excluded)	(20)

[a] Number of respondents.

TABLE 4.10 *Preferred time and actual time from last birth to starting work*

Preferred time from birth to start work	Actual time from last birth to start work (years)							Row (%)
	<1	1–2	2–3	3–4	4–5	5–6	6 or more	
less than 1 yr	9	4	0	2	1	0	2	12.6
1–2 yrs	6	6	6	1	0	0	1	14.0
2–3 yrs	1	0	7	1	1	0	1	7.7
3–4 yrs	1	2	1	3	2	1	0	7.0
4–5 yrs	0	0	1	1	2	2	2	5.6
5–6 yrs	13	7	9	7	5	4	10	38.5
6 or more yrs	5	1	2	3	5	3	2	14.7
Column (%)	24.5	14.0	18.2	12.6	11.2	7.0	12.6	
Number[a] = (143)								

[a] Number of respondents.

of their return to the labour market. Some 24.5% were back in paid employment in less than one year but only 12.6% would have found this desirable. Over one-third (38.5%) of these women thought that a period of around 5 to 6 years was desirable, but only 7.0% of women returned to employment after such a gap.

The detail of Table 4.10 is even more revealing. It is obvious that while some women return to the labour market sooner than they would prefer (seventy-three out of 143),[8] others (thirty-seven out of 143) return later than they would have desired. Thus, although 12.6% of these women declared that they would have desired to return to the labour market within 1 year, nine out of these eighteen actually returned later than 1 year, with two actually taking longer than 6 years to return. In terms of returning at or around the desired time only thirty-three of the 143 women in this table returned at what they regarded as their preferred time.[9]

The picture that emerges in Tables 4.9 and 4.10 is one of a labour market in which women do not find it possible to time their participation to coincide with their desires. It does not follow, of course, that all of the fault lies in the labour market. Domestic pressures may oblige women to return to paid employment sooner than they might otherwise choose. But the 26% of women who return to the labour market later than they think optimal may well have been restrained by the lack of employment opportunities and, as Table 4.9 suggests, by the lack of child care.

CONCLUSION

This paper has attempted to examine the flexibility of the labour market as experienced from the supply side by focusing on two particular events in people's lives. The first of these events is what might be labelled a financial crisis—the time when individuals report experiencing the most difficulty making ends meet. This is found to vary substantially from individual to individual. There is some tendency for it to occur when individuals are in their twenties to early thirties but there is really no marked life-cycle pattern. The evidence from the recollections of the respondents involved in such crises, and the evidence gathered from their work histories around that time of crisis all suggest that while the labour market could be the cause of the problem, it was far from being a commonly available answer to the problem. And, when it was used, there seemed to be limitations on the extent or speed with which it could be utilized. The much stronger tendency to implement expenditure adjustments rather than labour-supply adjustments must at least call into question some of the more sweeping generalities of the new classical economics. What is going on in the labour market seems to be much less controlled than would be suggested by ideas of optimal timing.

The second life event studied in this paper is the return to paid employment by women who have had children. Here the evidence on the role of the labour market in restricting behaviour was more ambivalent. This is not altogether surprising as the growth of employment of married women, and in particular the growth of part-time jobs, has been one of the distinguishing features of labour market change over the past three decades. The problems regarding child-care provision noted above are well known. What is, perhaps, less well known is that over a quarter of the women studied had returned to the labour market later than they thought optimal. In addition, it has been well documented (Greenhalgh and Stewart 1985; Main and Elias 1987) that among all returners, and almost certainly among the 51% who return to paid employment earlier than they think optimal, there will be severe problems of occupational downgrading and mismatching between the individual's skills and experience and the job to which they return.

Most of the analysis in this paper has been exploratory in nature and it would, therefore, be imprudent to draw any firm conclusions. But at the very least, the results presented above must give some cause to question models of the labour market which rest on the assumption that adjustments in labour market activity can be effected in a relatively painless manner to fine tune the consumption of leisure and market purchased goods—a question of optimal timing. In fact, individuals experience crises in making ends meet, and experience difficulties in achieving desired labour market transactions. There is a clear suggestion in some of the findings presented above that it would be inappropriate to classify such difficulties merely as transitory frictions. Individuals do seem to spend considerable periods of time out of equilibrium—finding the labour market less of a friend than a foe.

NOTES

1. A standard representation of these views can be found in Barro (1984).
2. See Lucas and Rapping (1969) for an early version of this approach and Clark and Summers (1982) for empirical tests.
3. For the purposes of this paper, any reports of severe financial difficulty earlier than the minimum school-leaving age relevant to the respondent are ignored. Some half-dozen responses are lost in this way.
4. For example, Modigliani and Brumberg (1954).
5. Originating in the labour market is taken to cover job loss, low pay, or industrial action affecting self or partner.
6. Computer programme for data analysis were originally developed by Peter Elias and Christine Jones, Institute for Employment Research, University of Warwick.
7. In each case, what is reported is the labour market state or characteristic that was most prevalent during the year in question.
8. Calculated from those lying below the diagonal of Table 4.10.
9. Calculated from those lying on the diagonal of Table 4.10.

PART II

Patterns of Change in the Domestic Division of Labour

5

The Domestic Labour Revolution: a Process of Lagged Adaptation?

JONATHAN GERSHUNY, MICHAEL GODWIN, AND
SALLY JONES

TWO MODELS OF THE HOUSEHOLD DIVISION OF LABOUR

We find, in the 1970s and some of the 1980s literature on the division of domestic labour, two contrasting views of the nature of the household's response to changes in its relationship to the formal labour market. We might summarize these crudely as follows:

1. *Adaptive partnership (AP)* The division of domestic labour reflects changes in the pattern of participation of household members in the formal economy. If the wife gets a paid job, the employed husband does a higher proportion of the household's domestic work than previously, to compensate for the wife's new work responsibilities outside the household.
2. *Dependent Labour* (DL) Women's labour is 'secondary'. Social structures define women's role as that of reproducing and maintaining men as the primary labour force, and so women's proportion of the couple's domestic labour is insensitive to change in her commitments outside the household.

We will suggest what comes to a third view, in which adjustment of work roles takes place, not through a short-term redistribution of responsibilities, but through an extended process of household negotiation (and perhaps reconstitution), extending over a period of many years, and indeed across generations. We will refer to this process as one of *lagged adaptation.*

There is a considerable body of empirical evidence which has been interpreted as supporting the Dependent Labour view.

Studies of domestic work-time allocation show that the reduction in the wife's proportion of the household's domestic work following her entry into the workforce is insufficient to compensate for her increase in paid work. Married women in employment bear a disproportionate 'dual burden' of paid and unpaid work. This empirical finding is confirmed by the evidence that we draw from the Social Change and Economic Life Initiative data.

However, in what follows we question the interpretation of this finding. The most persuasive of the 1970s arguments (which is discussed in the next section) relied on empirical descriptions of the current practices of particular households (as indicated by time-budget studies of married couples). It was essentially cross-sectional, in so far as it was concerned entirely with differences between husbands and wives, and between couples with various combinations of employment statuses. The recent research (an example of which is also discussed in more detail in the next section) has been by contrast much less static in its approach, and more concerned with the processes through which households develop their domestic work practices. Detailed semi-structured interviews with small samples of husbands and wives establish the complex interplay of calculation and belief which underlie the changes in the distribution of domestic responsibilities through the course of the marriage.

We will demonstrate that the 'dual burden' evidence is paradoxically quite consistent with a version of the adaptive partnership view. Women's participation in paid employment has been increasing continuously for the last thirty years. New work opportunities mean that women who did not have jobs, now have them, and that men who had not previously thought of themselves as husbands of employed wives, now become such husbands. Once we apply the processual approach used in the recent 'qualitative' studies of couples to the survey evidence, we immediately realize that the cross-sectional 'dual burden' evidence may be interpreted as an average across households in varying stages of adaptation to these changing circumstances. We will use a combination of retrospective, longitudinal, and cross-national comparative survey data to show that the division of domestic labour does indeed, albeit over an extended period, adapt to (or, since these household practices in turn have employment consequences, with) changing employment patterns.

FROM THE 'DUAL BURDEN' TO THE 'SECOND SHIFT'; A STALLED REVOLUTION

The starkest expression of the dual burden, dependent labour argument (and indeed the articulation of the AP/DL divide as summarized in the previous section) comes from Meissner *et al.* (1975). They present evidence from a substantial Canadian time-budget survey of couples. They show that the paid work time of employed husbands of non-employed wives approximately balances their wives' unpaid work time. But those employed men with employed partners have unpaid work times, and totals of paid plus unpaid work time, which are substantially less than their partners' equivalents. The two-job couples are much less equal in their division of work than the one-job couples. Now assume that the cross-sectional difference between the one-job and two-job couples represents the longitudinal consequences of a transformation of a one-job household into a two-job household, and the conclusion is clear: the increasing rate of women's participation in paid work leads to a growth in their 'dual burden'.

The evidential basis of this argument is not at all in doubt. Very similar results from time-budget data had been previously reported by Young and Willmott (1973)—though inexplicably, given that they collected data from couples, they compare men with employed women rather than employed men with their employed wives. Ann Oakley (1974) and others (e.g. Baruch and Barnett 1983) have reported similar results from questionnaire evidence. And the multinational collection of time-budget evidence maintained by the present authors and discussed in the penultimate section of this chapter (which currently consists of thirty-three national-scale surveys from seventeen developed countries covering the period 1961 to 1987) shows the same disproportion between employed men's and employed women's work in every survey without exception.

Our objections are, rather, to the nature of the inference from this evidence. The most important problem is the shift from cross-sectional evidence to a conclusion about historical or longitudinal processes. But first, consider an issue of principle: the Canadian argument belongs to an essentialist or 'as if' school of political economy. The researchers are plainly much too sophisticated to believe that the individual members of each household all carry around miniature versions of the dependent labour theory, and organize their time on this basis. But nevertheless, the implication of their argument is that the outcome of the household decision making is 'as if' all the members of the society had such beliefs.

It seems reasonable to assume that in reality different people believe different things. The justification for the more intensive, small-scale and ethnographic style methodology employed in Hochschild (1990), is the need to investigate the nature of the various beliefs and strategems that determine household behaviour. Hochschild reconstructs, using evidence from lengthy household contacts, a number of very different processes through which households' domestic practices emerge.

Perhaps the central element in her account is the notion of the 'gender strategy':

a plan of action through which a person tries to solve problems at hand, given the cultural notions of gender at play. To pursue a gender strategy, a man draws on his ideas about manhood and womanhood, beliefs that are forged in early childhood and thus anchored to deep emotions. He makes a connection between how he thinks about his manhood, what he feels about it and what he does. It works the same way for a woman. (Hochschild 1990: 15)

She identifies two 'pure' polar types of gender strategy: the 'traditional' ('breadwinner' for men, 'homemaker' for women) and the 'egalitarian' (where both partners identify equally with the workplace and the home). Between the two pure types she places the 'transitional' type which consists of a number of different combinations of the two pure types. 'Most men and women I encountered were transitional,' she tells us, and then, with an intentional irony, 'At least, transitional ideas were what came out when I asked people directly what they believed.' In some cases there were contradictions between what people said they believed and what they actually did. And in some cases there were differences between husbands' and wives' beliefs. To resolve these intra- and interpersonal contradictions and differences, households develop 'family myths'—beliefs (or at least conventional statements) about the individuals' or households' behaviour which are at odds with Hochschild's own observations of them.

Her case studies exhibit a tremendous variety of combinations of overt and covert gender strategies. In some cases both partners in a two-job couple may adopt overtly 'egalitarian' strategies, while actually maintaining 'traditional' patterns of work responsibilities, using the 'myth' that the husband's responsibilities for 'odd jobs' and car repair balance the wife's routine domestic work. But in other cases, both partners in a two-job marriage may assert overtly traditional gender ideologies, deploying a family mythology which radically understates the husband's domestic contribution.

At the heart of her book is the disjunction between beliefs and behaviour. 'Though many couples now believe in sharing, at this point in history few do share.' (p. 203) Fewer than one-fifth of her respondents even claim actually to be sharing domestic work equally. She describes the current state of American society as the 'stalled revolution—when women have gone to work, but the workplace, the culture, and most of all, the men, have not adjusted themselves to the new reality'.

But accepting both her processual approach to the analysis, and her evidence, we might still question whether the revolution she describes is in fact stalled, or just slow. Consider: all the couples she interviews are made up of people (in their twenties or thirties in the late 1970s or early 1980s) who were brought up in the early stages of her revolution. So her respondents' own gender ideologies ('formed in early childhood') stem from a period in which 'traditional' strategies went virtually unquestioned. She observes, amongst her interview subjects, a universal anguish about the distribution of domestic work. This presumably reflects the fact that almost the whole of the generation that she is observing (together with the previous and subsequent generations) must confront and uproot the emotionally charged gender images of their childhood. The very fact that the anguish is so palpable, alike to Hochschild as a professional researcher in this field and to every casual reader of her book, is itself evidence that this process of confronting and uprooting inherited gender ideologies is really taking place. The process is certainly very far from complete and still very painful; but, following Hochschild's argument, we could only expect it to be complete and painless once all adult members of households were themselves children in households with unchallenged egalitarian gender models—that is, a very long time into the future.

Which brings us back to the central problem with the Canadians' analysis. They argue directly from the fact that one-job couples divide work more equally than do two-job couples, to the proposition that the historical entry of the wife into the workplace does not lead to any adaptation in the fundamental principles of gender responsibilities underlying the domestic division of labour. An alternative interpretation of the 'dual burden' evidence is that many or most households currently consist of people with gender strategies which are to some degree intermediate between the two pure types. That is, adaptation takes place, but happens gradually: most couples are at present only partially or imperfectly or incompletely adapted. And this is precisely what Hochschild's detailed observations show.

Our task in what follows, is to take the argument a stage forward by establishing a link from the important 'processual' findings from Hochschild's small-scale and non-representative 'qualitative' data, to larger-scale sample evidence. The survey-derived evidence which we present contains of necessity (since it derives from a fully structured interview schedule covering many topics other than the domestic division of labour) much less detail about beliefs and processes than Hochschild derived from her detailed household interviews. But we can use the historical evidence it contains (about parents' domestic work practices and about the couples' own work histories) to make more general and generalizable statements about the longitudinal processes of change. And on the basis of the processual model which emerges from our evidence, we can suggest precisely why Hochschild's revolution may be expected to be a slow one.

But before we move to the substantive discussion, we have two preliminaries: a methodological discussion of different sorts of evidence about what actually happens in households; and (since ultimately the whole argument turns on the question of the fairness of the distribution of work in a household) a consideration of what exactly work consists of.

MYTHS AND METHODS

We must address one particularly acute methodological problem which stems directly from the foregoing theoretical discussion.

Hochschild tells us that one mechanism for managing the pressures of adaptation to changed circumstances is the 'family myth'—systematic misrepresentations of household practice, which allow arguments about who does or should do what to be disguised from the protagonists. Hochschild is present in the household and can observe directly any mismatch between the couples' accounts of their activity and what they actually do. This, of course, poses a serious problem for quantitative research: how can a structured survey instrument distinguish between the myth and the underlying actuality of household activity patterns.

Our proposed answer to this question goes back to the roots of the standard methodology for the analysis of the division of domestic labour, the time-budget survey. It is in fact rather difficult to establish individuals' time allocation patterns, for a quite straightforward reason: people do not know how they allocate their time (Robinson 1976, chapter 1). We have (in general) no reason to know the quanta of time we devote to particular activities. Such knowledge is (in general) of no practical use in daily life. With some very specific exceptions, neither we ourselves nor anyone else needs to know the total of hours devoted to particular purposes over a given period. Nor would it be very easy for us to maintain such running total estimates of time use. For precisely which categories of activity would we maintain the totals? Over what sort of period? There are, of course, particular circumstances in which we do know how much time we devote to particular activities. If we are paid by the hour at the end of each week, for instance, we may keep a running total of our paid work on a weekly basis. But this is not the general case. Simply: time allocation is not a natural category of self-knowledge.

And it is precisely this lack of self-knowledge that allows the 'family myth' to develop. Since we do not in fact know how much time we really devote to our activities, we are free to invent whatever time-use estimates are consistent with our overt gender strategies. If the couple's shared ideology is that housework is divided equally, it does little violence to its members' senses of reality if both represent their total time devoted to the activity as equivalent, irrespective of the actual hours spent by the two partners. (Such myths will be facilitated, incidentally, if the partners' domestic work is done at different times in the day.)

But though we do not know how much time we spend in

particular activities we do still know what we have done. We can normally reconstruct the sequence of the day's activities, and recount this sequence to an observer. We will (often if not necessarily for every element in the daily sequence) be able to give a reasonably accurate time at which particular activities started or finished (perhaps because of personal or institutional conventions—'lunch at 1', 'clock-on at 8.30'—or because of a coincident event such as a television programme or factory hooter). We are trained from childhood to give sequential accounts of our days: we are regularly asked, by parents and friends, to give such accounts, and we are accustomed to giving them. These sequential representations of the day (or the week) really are natural categories of human self-knowledge.

It is this contrast between our ignorance of our own aggregate time allocation and our knowledge of our activity sequences, that explains the use of the diary in time-budget research. Time-use researchers cannot ask people how much time they spent washing up last week. But if people are asked to describe what they did yesterday in as much detail as they can provide, researchers can then calculate how much time is devoted to the various activities. Time-budget analysts thus know something about their respondents that their respondents do not in general know about themselves (and indeed they can only know what the researchers know by going through precisely the same process—first establishing the activity sequence, then summing the durations of each instance of a particular category of activity—that the researchers follow).

In the Social Change and Economic Life Initiative we collected two different sorts of information about domestic division of labour. First, in the course of the Household questionnaire, we asked husbands and wives independently about how various categories of unpaid work (cooking, washing up, house cleaning, clothes cleaning, house painting, gardening, car maintenance) are divided between the husband and wife. Second, at the conclusion of the interview, we asked both husband and wife to keep a detailed activity diary for a week.

We would expect these two sorts of evidence to cast light on two separate phenomena. The questionnaire-derived evidence will certainly bear some relation to the actual division of labour: couples in which the husband in fact does none of a particular category of work will hardly be likely to claim that he does all of it. But since, as we argue, neither husband nor wife really know how much time they devote to each activity, the answers will be strongly affected by the prevailing family myth—without there being any particular intention or effort to mislead the researchers. The diary evidence, by contrast, relates to a natural category of self-knowledge, and while there may at the margin be some influence from prevailing myths, for this to have any substantial effect would require a sustained effort to mislead the researcher by systematic falsification of the sequential record. So, we might say that, to the extent that they differ, the questionnaire-derived information is likely to be more representative of the 'family myth' about the division of domestic labour, and the diary-derived information be more representative of the actuality.

(We should note at this point a systematic bias in the data-collection method. Most diary respondents with jobs class all the time spent at the workplace as 'time at work' in their diaries: they tend not to distinguish short rest-breaks. By contrast people recording unpaid work at home tend to record short breaks for, say, a hot drink or a smoke. As a result time-budget data will tend to overestimate the amount of time devoted to paid work as against unpaid. And since women do more unpaid work than men, and more men than women have paid jobs, and those women with paid jobs work in general shorter hours, and the number of rest-breaks is proportional to hours of paid work, so this sort of data will have a systematic tendency to underestimate women's work time relative to men's.)

How do the divisions of domestic work emerging from the questionnaire relate to the diary evidence? We have in fact to consider three kinds of evidence on the distribution of domestic tasks: the man's questionnaire responses (in which he tells us his view of how much housework he does and how much his wife does), the woman's view (in which she gives her views on the same subject), and the diary data (his and hers). Table 5.1 gives the means of the men's and the women's questionnaire responses to questions on the distribution of various domestic tasks (scoring 'female partner does it all' as 1, 'female partner mainly' as 0.5, 'both equally' as 0, 'male mainly' as −0.5 and 'male does it all' as −1). The men's and women's responses are very similar on average. Table 5.1 also gives diary estimates of the men's and

TABLE 5.1 *Division of various household tasks*

	Mean contributions[a]		Diary estimates[b]		Mean contribution
	Male answers	Female answers	Men	Women	
Cooking	0.62	0.62	14.3	55.9	0.59
Washing up	0.41	0.41	8.2	24.2	0.49
Cleaning	0.61	0.61	5.0	26.2	0.68
Clothes washing	0.80	0.80	0.9	13.3	0.87
DIY	−0.28	−0.27	12.6	4.6	−0.46
Gardening	−0.12	−0.11	24.6	10.6	−0.40
Car maintenance	−0.64	−0.63	8.0	1.0	−0.79

[a] −1 = all male; +1 = all female.
[b] Minutes per average day.

women's mean allocation of time, on an average day, to these tasks. The final column in the table calculates the gender balance of contributions of time to the various tasks on the same −1 to +1 scale used for the questionnaire data (see the appendix to this chapter). Considering the very rough nature of the questionnaire scales, they show a quite remarkably close aggregate correspondence with the diary results.

But this merely compares the aggregate scores from the various different sorts of indicators. We have the three different sorts of evidence: we need to compare the picture of each household's division of domestic labour (dodl) scores from each of these sources. So we have derived three different indices which summarize the division of the four stereotypically female unpaid-work categories: cooking, washing up, house and clothes cleaning. We derive separate summary indices from the male and from the female questionnaire data simply by averaging the scores (as described in the previous paragraph) for each of the activities. And we make a similar index from the diary data by similarly averaging the male/female time division. So we end up with three distinct accounts of the household division of labour: two drawn respectively from the husband's and the wife's responses to questions about how they distribute domestic work ('questionnaire-derived dodl indices'), and a third constructed by putting together the diaries, kept by each spouse, of their own domestic work. How do these accounts, of the same phenomenon, drawn from three separate sources, compare with each other?

The associations among these three variously derived dodl indices are really not particularly strong. The husbands' and wives' dodl indices have a raw correlation coefficient of 0.71 (i.e. half the variation in one is 'explained' by variation in the other). And the correlations between the male- and female-derived dodl indices and the diary-derived indices are respectively 0.43 and 0.37. (The appendix to this chapter provides a more extensive discussion of these results.) Husbands and wives are telling somewhat different stories in their interviews; but their stories are more similar to each others' than they are to the account that emerges from their diaries.

The results are at least consistent with our suggestion that the questionnaires reflect some sort of negotiated consensual myth which lies at some distance from the actual division of labour. In what follows we will first discuss the results from the questionnaire data, using a simple average of the spouses' questionnaire-derived dodl indices ('Q-dodl') with the range 0 to 1 (where 0 means that the wife does none of the work, and 1 means that she does all of it), and then we turn to consider the time-budget evidence. But first we must consider the question of 'work'.

WHAT IS 'WORK'?

So far in this chapter we have concentrated on domestic labour within the household. But the AP and DL hypotheses relate, as we have seen, to a concern about a broader concept of work which embraces activities in 'the economy' and in the household: is 'work' equitably divided between husbands and wives? This is an old sociological chestnut. The problem is that everyone uses the word 'work' in multiple senses which are dependent on context. So we cannot just ask people 'What do you consider as work?' The respondent has to make inferences about what the questioner means; different respondents will have different notions; respondents may not even have any explicit notion of 'work' that is used in considerations of appropriate division of household work.

We could sidestep the issue here, and simply assert the

standard economists' operationalization for the broad notion of work. This may be derived from the broad concept of 'economic activity': 'An economic activity of an individual is one which may be done by a third person (generally hired at a market price) without affecting the utility value returned to the individual' (Hawrylyshyn 1977). In this view 'work' includes all activities connected with paid employment, and in addition, all domestic production activities, some child-care activities, and some shopping.

But alternatively, there is a sort of empirical test we can adopt, which relies on a somewhat recursive use of the Hawrylyshyn definition. It examines simultaneously, indeed, both the definition of work used by the survey respondents and a weak version of the AP hypothesis itself. Consider: the 'domestic division of labour' describes the allocation of 'work' among household members (and for the purposes of the present discussion, between spouses in a couple). If there is some mutual adaptation of husbands' and wives' 'work' to wives' changing employment situation, as the AP hypothesis has it, there must be some statistical association between the husbands' and the wives' total of 'work' time. Hawrylyshyn defines the broadest set of activities that could be included in a definition of work so the actual notion of work employed within any particular household will be either the whole of Hawrylyshyn's list or some proper subset of it. If there are significant AP-type associations between husbands' and wives' work totals, that association will be strongest for that set of activities that constitutes the sample's generally accepted notion of 'work'. And if there is no such significant association between any of the alternative possible notions of 'work', then we must accept a rather strong version of the DL hypothesis.

So, take the Social Change and Economic Life Initiative time-budget 'couples' data set (which is combined, as we shall explain in a moment, with a similar 'couples' data set from 1974/5). Calculate, for the husband and wife in each case, the various different possible 'work' totals, as the various different subsets of the Hawrylyshyn categories. Generate a matrix of correlations, between each of the various husbands' totals and each of the wives'.

There are two possible alternative outcomes:

1. None of the totals show any very substantial correlations. In this case, irrespective of the particular definition of work, differ-

ences in wives' work totals are not associated with differences in husbands', there is no adaptation, and we get no guidance as to the choice of activities to include in the category 'work'.

2. Some categories do show substantial correlations, in which case, we may reject the strong DL hypothesis. Here we do get some guidance as to the nature of 'work', since, if couples are redistributing unpaid work to compensate for changes in time spent in paid work, the most strongly correlated totals will indicate the underlying definitions used by the couple in deciding how much compensation is needed. So by inspecting the size of the correlation coefficients, we may infer the appropriate definition or definitions of work to take forward into an investigation of the weaker versions of DL and AP.

The evidence that emerges from Figure 5.1 places us very clearly in the second category. The full Hawrylyshyn set in fact performs quite well. But clearly the Hawrylyshyn set minus commuting time dominates the alternative definitions. And there is plainly a consistent two-dimensional space defined by the alternative possible definitions; within this space, the further we get from Hawrylyshyn-minus-commuting, the lower is the correlation between the husband's and wife's total. The spatial consistency may be interpreted as indicating (1) that husband and wife agree on a definition of 'work' that includes paid work, routine housework, odd jobs, child care and shopping, and (2) there is some mutual adjustment in the total of work so defined. There is an obvious potential for circularity in this argument. It could have resulted simply in picking that adventitious subset of the Hawrylyshyn categories that best fits our arguments. But the combination of the spatial consistency of the results with the fact that the strongest association is between the husband's and the wife's totals of all the substantive Hawrylyshyn categories, serves to confirm the appropriateness of Hawrylyshyn's definition. Hawrylyshyn-minus-commuting is plainly the appropriate broad definition of work upon which to base our analysis. In the next section we shall concentrate on just the unpaid part of work (i.e. the division of domestic labour) for which we can concentrate on the questionnaire-derived evidence, and then return to the broader question of the total work time, as estimated from the diaries, in the following section of the paper.

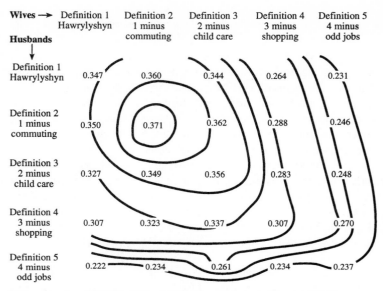

(970 couples, from UK 1974, 1975 and 1987. All coefficients significant at 0.0005)

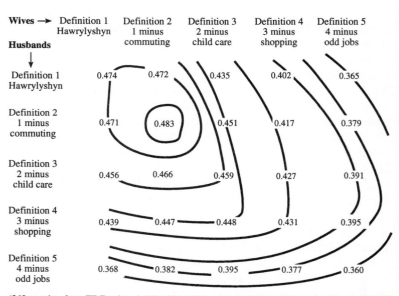

(262 couples, from FT Employed, UK 1974, 1975 and 1987. All coefficients significant at 0.0005)

FIG. 5.1 Correlations between husbands' and wives' work totals (various definitions of 'work')

DIVISION OF DOMESTIC WORK: AN APPLICATION
OF THE Q-DODL INDEX

The Q-dodl index might seem to suggest a quite straightforward way of choosing between the AP and DL hypotheses. The hypotheses turn on the responsiveness of the household division of labour to the wife's employment status. We have demonstrated that the questionnaire contains cross-sectional evidence about the household's division of domestic responsibility. Can we not therefore simply choose between the two by comparing the Q-dodl indices of households in which the wife has varying employment statuses?

The evidence that emerges seems quite clear. Table 5.2 gives estimates of the household division of labour from three different sources: from the diary evidence (D-dodl), from questionnaire evidence for the full sample (Q-dodl), and from questionnaire evidence from just that part of the sample in which both husband and wife completed full diaries for the entire week. The table gives mean dodl scores and 'treatment effects'; the dodl score for a particular demographic or employment category is given by the sum of the mean and the appropriate treatment effects (the means and effects come from *Multiple Classification Analysis*, Andrews *et al.* 1973). The D-dodl and Q-dodl 'treatment effects' of the couple's joint employment status are (given the very different techniques used in deriving them) really quite strikingly similar. And they do provide some evidence of an effect of employment status on the division of domestic labour. Non-employed wives with full-time employed husbands appear to do (from the Q-dodl index in Table 5.2) approximately 83% of the total of unpaid household work (i.e. the mean of 0.78 plus the treatment effect 0.05). Full-time employed wives of full-time employed husbands do 73% of the housework. Part-time employed wives do 82%—hardly less than the non-employed. There is some limited adaptation, but even full-time employed wives do nearly three-quarters of all housework. It would appear from this cross-sectional comparison that housework remains the wife's responsibility irrespective of her employment status.

The problem is, however, a little more complicated than this. Clearly the AP hypothesis concerns the full range of work

TABLE 5.2 *Comparison of diary and questionnaire estimates of division of domestic labour (dodl), indicating the woman's proportion of couple's domestic work[a]*

	Diarists		Whole sample
	Diary (D-dodl)	Questionnaire (Q-dodl)	Questionnaire (Q-dodl)
Number[b]	(392)	(392)	(1 199)
Grand mean	0.809	0.786	0.784
Young, no kids	–0.03	–0.02	–0.03
Younger kids	–0.01	–0.00	–0.00
Older kids	0.02	0.02	0.01
Old, no kids	–0.01	–0.03	–0.01
Both FT	–0.04	–0.05	–0.05
Male FT, wife PT	0.03	0.03	0.03
Male FT, wife NE	0.04	0.05	0.05
Other	–0.03	–0.04	–0.02
R-squared	0.048	0.117	0.080

Note: FT = full-time employment; PT = part-time employment; NE = not employed.
[a] 0 = all male; 1 = all female.
[b] Number of respondents.

activities, including both unpaid and paid work, and asserts that the domestic division of labour adapts in a compensatory way for the wife's changing employment status. It certainly does not imply that husbands of employed wives do 50% of the domestic labour—since paid jobs vary in their weekly hours. The adaptive partnership model would certainly expect a 35-hours-per-week full-time clerk married to a 50-hours-per-week manufacturing-process worker to do more housework than his/her spouse. In the next section we will turn to time-budget evidence of the overall balance between the total work of husbands and wives.

But though the question ultimately turns on the division of the broader notion of work, we do still have to consider the question of variation in the housework component of this. We have found four groups of characteristics with significant associations with the Q-dodl index: the couples' employment and family status; the couples' expressed attitudes about household division of labour;

the details of the wives' work histories; and (rather to our surprise) couples' reports of their parents' domestic division of
labour. The influences of these four sets of characteristics on the
Q-dodl index relate together in a rather complex way. But we
first consider these independently.

Table 5.3 sets out the results of an analysis of variance of the
Q-dodl index (equivalent to the final column of Table 5.2) by the
couples' employment and family status. The couples' joint
employment status variable does, as we have already suggested,
imply a certain limited adaptation (though only 7% of the variance in Q-dodl is explained). Husbands with (at least full-time)
employed wives certainly do substantially more of their housework than those with non-employed wives. As we see from the
same table, the age of the couples' youngest child (which is
strongly associated with the wives' employment statuses) explains
about 3% of the variance in Q-dodl, and the two status variables
jointly explain 8% of the variance.

This evidence provides us with material for a very simple sort
of causal modelling. Let us assume that family status is causally
prior to employment status (specifically, that the strong association between the age of the youngest child and the wife's employment status is explained by the wife taking primary responsibility

TABLE 5.3 *Q-dodl by family and employment status*

	Q-dodl
Family status:	
Aged 20–40, no children	0.73
Youngest child < school age	0.80
Youngest child > school age	0.80
Aged 41–60, no children	0.74
Eta-squared (=R^2)	0.028
Employment status	
Both full-time	0.73
Man full-time, woman part-time	0.82
Man full-time, woman non-employed	0.83
Other	0.78
Eta-squared (=R^2)	0.067
R-squared for both variables	0.080

for child care). From this assumption, we could infer that of the 8% of the variance in Q-dodl explained by the two variables, child status explains 3% of the variance, and that couples' employment status itself explains the remaining 5% of the variance on Q-dodl. However, as we shall see in a moment, once we construct a rather more specific model, employment status emerges as rather more important than the evidence in Table 5.3 would suggest.

Table 5.4 sets out some estimates of the influence of the parents' domestic work practices (as recollected by couples). Again, a modest but significant effect. Q-dodl is calculated from the couples' description of their own patterns of division of the cooking, washing up, the cleaning, and the laundry. The questionnaire asked both spouses about their parents' division of these same four activities. We have thus been able to construct a Q-dodl index for each of their parents; as we see from the regression in Table 5.4, the parents' indices explain around 5% of the variation in the couples' Q-dodl. Table 5.4 also gives a simpler way of visualizing the effect. Couples whose parents were both reportedly below the mean of the parents' Q-dodl, have themselves a mean Q-dodl of 0.77; couples whose parents both lay above the mean have a Q-dodl of 0.83.

This is not in itself such a striking result: we tend to reconstruct our worlds so as to make them consistent with our current practices. Our recollections of what our parents were accustomed to do when we were children must inevitably be

TABLE 5.4 *Q-dodl by parent dodl indices*

Where: WPDODL is wife's parents' dodl
HPDODL is husband's parents' dodl

Q-dodl = 0.5417 + 0.1119 * WPDODL + 0.1713 * HPDODL

R-squared = 0.047   significance = 0.0000

Q-dodl broken down by HPDODL and WPDODL

WPDODL	HPDODL	
	Above mean	Below mean
Above mean	0.83	0.78
Below mean	0.79	0.77

coloured by what we now do, or feel we ought to do. So the causal connection may go in an apparently anti-historical direction.

Table 5.5 indicates the influence of perceptions of who ought to be responsible for domestic work on Q-dodl. Where both members of the couple say that ultimate responsibility should be shared, Q-dodl is 0.69; where they both consider it to lie with the wife, Q-dodl is 0.83. Again, this relationship is not in itself necessarily very interesting. Quite possibly, our respondents construct their views of proper behaviour from what they actually do. But we can use these views, however they may be derived, to investigate the relationship between the recollected parents' division of domestic labour and the respondents' own.

TABLE 5.5 *Q-dodl by 'Who should have ultimate responsibility for housework?'*

Woman's answer	Man's answer	
	Shared or man	Woman
Shared or man	0.69	0.77
Woman	0.78	0.83
Eta-squared = 0.135		

Note: If the two parents' dodl indices are entered in the ANOVA, the R-squared rises to 0.173 implying that 3.8% of the variance in Q-dodl may be attributed to the parents' dodl once all the variance associated with the 'who ought?' question has been accounted for.

Simply, if our respondents are reconstructing their parents' behaviour according to what our respondents currently view as proper, then the association between the parents' and the current Q-dodl should disappear once we control for their current views. This is, of course, a very conservative test, since the current views may themselves be derived from parents' practices. But Table 5.5 shows that, even when the variance associated with current views is extracted first, parents' Q-dodl still explains nearly 4% of the variance in the current respondents' Q-dodl.

Table 5.6 shows the influence of the wife's employment history on current Q-dodl. We have constructed two indicators from the

TABLE 5.6 *Q-dodl by wife's work-history variables*

Wife's years of work experience	Q-dodl[a]
None	0.84
up to 1	0.84
1–2	0.78
2–3	0.79
3–4	0.80
4–5	0.80
5–6	0.81
6–7	0.80
7–8	0.80
8–9	0.76
9–10	0.75
10+	0.76

Wife's work sequence	Q-dodl[b]
Not currently employed	0.82
Currently FT, no PT history	0.73
Currently FT, some PT history	0.72
Currently PT, no FT history	0.81
Currently PT, some FT history	0.78
R-squared	0.090

Note: FT = full-time employment; PT = part-time employment.

[a] Controlling for work sequence.
[b] Controlling for work experience.

work-history records. The first counts the wife's total years of employment (whether full- or part-time) over the last twelve years; we see that there is a general tendency for the husband's proportion of domestic work to increase (i.e. Q-dodl gets smaller) with the wife's years of work experience (and this tendency remains when we control for respondents' age—older people are, if anything, less inclined to divide domestic work). The second characterizes her employment status, distinguishing also between those who are currently full-time employed who have previously been part-time employees, and those who are currently part-time and were previously full-time. We might note particularly that currently part-time employees who have some history of full-time work have a rather lower Q-dodl than those with none. These two variables jointly explain 9% of the overall variance in Q-dodl.

The pattern of associations among these 'independent' variables, and between them and the Q-dodl index is of course very complex. In particular, the employment, family status, and 'ought' variables are, we presume, all strongly associated with an unmeasured 'woman's proper economic role' variable. And in some cases, the causal connection may well be as much from the dodl index to the other variables (we expect in particular the 'ought' attitudes to be strongly influenced by current practices). So we do not seek to do any very sophisticated causal modelling. So far in this section (in Tables 5.2 to 5.6) we have established a number of pairwise relationships between Q-dodl and the various explanatory variables; we now simply put all of these explanatory variables together into a single analysis of variance, and consider how the total of variance in Q-dodl may be apportioned amongst the various explanatory factors.

The procedure we adopt is very straightforward and can be explained quite simply (it uses part correlations as an indicator of the scale of the effect of one independent variable controlling for others). Consider, a variable C, 50% of whose variation may be explained by the three category variables L, M and N. How much of the explained variation may be attributed to each of the category variables? Let us say that each of them individually explains 30% of the variation in C, so, plainly, some part of the variation in C could be explained by more than one of the independents: call this the 'shared' variation. Conversely, some part of the variation in C may be explainable uniquely by one or other of the independents. We can calculate the size of this unique variation very simply. We know that the analysis-of-variance model including L, M, and N explains 50% of the variation in C; if we now estimate a second model including just L and M as independents and find that 40% of the variation in C is explained, we will have established that the unique effect of N must be to explain 10% of the variation C. We can treat L and M similarly: so we need four analysis-of-variance models (i.e. one including all the variates, and three which exclude in turn one of the three variates) to estimate the unique effects of three independent variables.

Table 5.7 carries out this sort of calculation for the variables we have been discussing in this section. Let us initially concentrate on the three groups of variables concerned in models 1 to 4 in the table, and look at the second column of the upper part of the table, labelled (for reasons that will soon be apparent) 'without interactions'.

If we want to assess the unique effect of the 'Who ought to have ultimate responsibility for domestic work?' ('norms') variables on Q-dodl, then, following our very simple procedure, we subtract the proportion of variance explained by work histories and parents' dodl (model 4) from the proportion explained by all three variables (model 1). The difference between them (i.e. 0.223 − 0.143 = 0.080) is simply the additional variance explanation we get by adding in 'norms' to the analysis of variance—'norms', we might say 'uniquely explain 8% of the variation in Q-dodl'. The

TABLE 5.7 *Variance decomposition: Q-dodl–woman's proportion of couples' domestic work*

		Proportional reduction of total sum of squares	
		With interactions[a]	Without interactions[a]
Models:			
(1) Norms, work history, parents' dodl		0.385	0.223
(2) Norms and parents' dodl		0.236	0.173
(3) Norms and work history		0.318	0.183
(4) Work history and parents' dodl		0.277	0.143
(5) Employment status			0.029
(6) Employment and family status			0.056
	Total	Interactive	Direct
Individual effects:			
Norms	0.108	0.029	0.080
Work history	0.148	0.098	0.050
Parents' dodl index	0.067	0.027	0.039
Joint effects	0.062	0.008	0.054
Total variance explained	0.385	0.154	0.223

[a] Family and employment interactions.

effects so derived are set out in the second half of Table 5.7, in the column labelled 'direct'. We see that the unique (or individual) effects of the three variables sum to 16.9% of the variance in Q-dodl, the joint effects come to 5.4%, giving a total explanation of 22.3% of the variance in Q-dodl.

So far we have not included the employment and life/family status indicators in the models. These are not in themselves very highly correlated with Q-dodl. We have seen (Table 5.3) that a full breakdown of Q-dodl by these two variables serves to explain only 8% of the variance. And in the slightly reduced form used in Table 5.7 (classified as in Table 5.3, but joining together the 'man full-time employed, woman non-employed' and 'other' categories) employment status alone explains 2.9% (model 5), and adding family status to this only increases variance explained by these two variables, jointly and severally, to 5.6% (model 6).

Our investigations, however, reveal that the effect of parents' dodl in particular seem to differ for the various life-cycle and employment categories. For example—and not unexpectedly—parents' domestic labour practices seem to have rather less influence on the division of domestic labour in households with children and two full-time jobs, than in similar households in which the wife is non-employed. Thus in addition to any direct effect of parents' practices on the current division of domestic labour, there is also an effect that comes from the interaction between parents' practices and the household's current family and employment status. We must now do something just slightly more complicated to take account of these interactions.

If we simply add in the other variables included in Table 5.7, the direct or unique effect of employment and family status (i.e. that part of the effect of status which is not correlated with that of any of the other independent variables) falls to around 1% of the total variance in Q-dodl. This, however, is radically to underestimate the contribution of the status variables. Rather than treating them as simple independent variables, we could look separately at each of the effects of these variables for each of the combined family and employment status groups. The column labelled 'with family and employment interactions' is calculated in this way; the overall proportion of variance in Q-dodl explained rises to 38.5%. The difference between these two estimates is the effect of the interaction between status and the other variables: so we can plausibly attribute about 15% of the variance in Q-dodl to the interactive influence of family and employment status with the other variables. (The column labelled 'interactive' is calculated straightforwardly by subtracting the 'direct' from the 'total' effects.)

We should stress that the interaction effects are quite distinct from the joint effect. We find a total joint effect of 6.2%; this is simply shared variation amongst the various independent variables in the analysis which cannot at this stage be portioned amongst them, but which may as a result of more sophisticated analysis emerge as being specifically associated with one or another of them. The interaction effect by contrast is genuinely a consequence of the combined influence of the set of variables, in which the influence of one independent variable on the dependent variable is modified by that of another independent variable.

The overall 39% of variance explained may appear to be somewhat disappointingly low. But consider: we have previously concluded that the Q-dodl index relates more to 'family myth' than the actuality of the division of domestic labour. It is constructed as the average of the male- and female-derived dodl indices, which, though they purport to describe the same reality, have a correlation of only 0.7.

'Explanation' is of course used loosely here. The part played by the 'norms' variables is in itself particularly questionable (on the previously mentioned concern that it may be no more than a rationalization of current practices). But they are nevertheless important as a control for the retrospective 'parents' practice' variables. As we calculate the 'parents' effect' controlling for the current views of what is proper, we arrive at a conservative minimum estimate of the impact of parents' patterns of behaviour on Q-dodl. Given also that some portion of the joint effects must be attributed to the parents, we conclude that the couples' parents' patterns of dodl account for around one-fifth of all the explained variance in the couples' own account of the division of domestic labour. This is not an entirely surprising result. It parallels, for example, the well-known influence of parents' party political allegiance on current behaviour and attitudes. It is nevertheless a striking result, and, as far as we are aware, not previously remarked upon.

In sum, then, we have around 8% of the variance in Q-dodl directly associated with current 'norms', 4% directly related to parents' dodl, 6% in various joint effects, 5% directly associated with the wives' work histories, and about 15% with various interactions between employment and family status and the other variables. These last two elements account for 20% of the variation in Q-dodl, and more than half of the total variance explained. Clearly Q-dodl is sensitive to the wife's employment status and history.

Q-dodl is as likely to reflect myth as reality. But even if it does reflect myth, these results are consistent with household's overt intention to modify their divisions of labour (or at the very least an awareness of what is now considered to be a politically acceptable answer). This evidence we have discussed in the section is, of course, entirely cross-sectional. But it is really quite a small inferential step to move from evidence that longer histories or longer hours of women's paid work are associated with a more equal division of domestic work between spouses to the longitudinal proposition of, at the very least, a progressive shifting of couples into Hochschild's 'intermediate' categories (whose members acknowledge the desirability of moving away from traditional gendered work patterns). And since there is a substantial association between the questionnaire and diary evidence, we must not reject out of hand the possibility that this cross-sectional result also reflects some historical shift in the actual division of domestic labour; the following discussion of the diary material will in fact show this to be the case. Our findings so far are themselves at the least consistent with the 'adaptive partnership' view: the division of domestic labour appears to be to some degree responsive to variation in the wife's employment history and status. Does this have any implications for the overall distribution of work in the broad sense between husbands and wives?

HUSBANDS' PROPORTION OF TOTAL WORK TIME

The Dependent Labour hypothesis rests heavily on one single empirical observation—one repeated with great regularity, however, wherever appropriate time-budget data are available. Employed husbands of employed women work in total significantly less time than their wives. We find (e.g. Young and Willmott 1973; Meissner *et al.* 1975) a gradient: full-time employed husbands of non-employed women have about the same work-time total as their wives; if their wives are part-time employed their total is a little smaller; if their wives are full-time employed, they do substantially less work. Plainly the inference to be drawn is that, as women increasingly enter the formal economy on a full-time basis, so the overall household division of labour will become increasingly unequal.

However, the evidence, in these and other studies, is wholly cross-sectional. They seek to generalize from sets of observations of differences between households at a single point in history, to changes over historical time. The cross-sectional evidence from the Social Change and Economic Life Initiative time-budget data set produces a cross-sectional gradient which corresponds to these results. Our 1987 data also shows the regular gradient from the higher proportion of household work done by husbands with 'non-working' wives, to the much lower proportion done by husbands of wives with full-time jobs.

But one of the great advantages of this data set (and indeed one of the main reasons for collecting the data) is the possibility of linking it with earlier UK time-budget surveys of couples. (There are in fact two such, dating from 1974/5 and 1983/4; we have so far only made use of the earlier of these.) Figure 5.2 compares the two surveys. Both exhibit the gradient, and in both cases the gradients correspond to the pattern expected from the previous research. But here, for the first time, we are able to look at change over historical time.

For each of the three categories of household, the husband's proportion of the household's work is higher in 1987 than in 1975. The mean proportions in this figure derive from a multiple classification analysis, in which we have controlled for historical differences in household composition: so, in particular, we can be certain that this does not reflect the increasing tendency of mothers with small children to take paid employment. Nor does it appear, as has sometimes been asserted, that any growth in men's household work is exclusively in the non-routine category: Figure 5.3 (which deals only with households with full-time employed wives) shows that while women's work has contracted fastest in the area of cooking and routine housework, it is precisely in these areas that their husbands' work has grown fastest (though 'odd jobs', including gardening and car maintenance, remains the

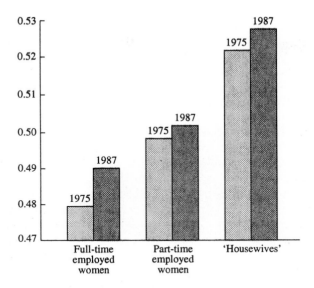

FIG. 5.2 Husbands' proportion of all household work time

largest single category, it constitutes hardly more than one-third of the husbands' total in 1987). Figure 5.4 shows that irrespective of the household employment status, the husbands' domestic work time has grown substantially, and that in each case 'cooking and routine housework' is proportionately the fastest-growing subcategory of domestic work, and 'odd jobs' the slowest.

There are two implications from these results. First, though more women are in employment now than formerly, and employed women do in general more work in total than their husbands, this does not necessarily mean that the overall division of work between husbands and wives is getting less equal, since the cross-sectional gradients are shifting upwards, and men in each category of household do an increasing proportion of household work over time.

Second, though the historical change is greatest in the case of husbands with full-time employed wives, it is present in all three types of household. It is, in other words, a general social trend. It may take its origin from women's increasing presence in paid work. But its impact is experienced irrespective of the wife's

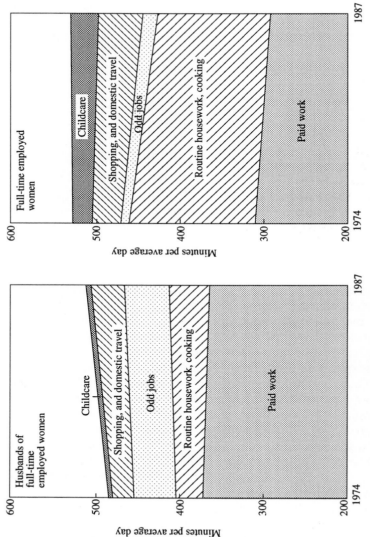

FIG. 5.3 Change in unpaid work time in households with full-time employed wives, 1974/75 to 1987

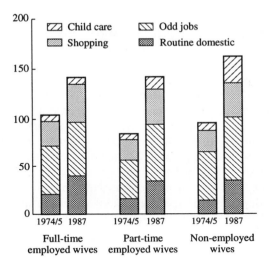

FIG. 5.4 Husbands' unpaid work, 1974/5 and 1987

current location in or out of the labour market. The mechanisms involved may well be susceptible to empirical analysis taking advantage of the link between the Social Change and Economic Life Initiative time-budget sample and the work and life histories. But for the moment we may simply speculate that the process may take its origin from pressures caused within particular households by the wife's re-entry into employment, which leads in turn to general public debate that influences other sorts of households.

The results in Figure 5.2 take us some way towards an 'adaptive partnership' conclusion. But they still leave us with a puzzle: why the gradient? If couples do indeed adapt their distributions of domestic work to compensate for changes in the patterns of paid work, why is it that husbands of full-time employed women still do a substantially smaller proportion of the total work of the household?

One simple answer may be that households adapt gradually. The explanation for the gradient may lie in the mechanics of change. Households do not necessarily concentrate a great deal of attention on the issue of the division of labour within the

household. When the wife first enters paid employment there may
be no discussion of domestic work patterns; in some cases the
wife may do her new job and also carry her previous load of
domestic responsibility. But inevitably in such cases the extra
work must put some considerable pressure on the wife. Attention
is therefore drawn towards the issue of the division of domestic
work, and consequently the couple may gradually modify their
practices so as to reduce the pressure. Even where the couple
have formally or informally negotiated changes, it may be difficult to establish an equitable partnership; just as we have suggested that they may not know how much work they themselves
do, they may similarly not know how much work their partners
do. The adaptation of the division of domestic labour may, in
short, lag behind the change in paid work patterns.

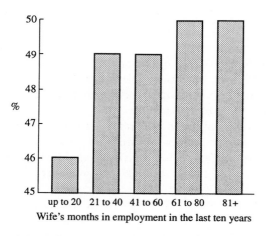

Fig. 5.5 Husbands' proportion of total household work

We can test this hypothesis quite simply, by linking the time-
budget data with the work-history material. Figure 5.5 shows the
husband's proportion of the household's total work in various
types of household distinguished by length of the wife's experience of employment over the last ten years. In households where
the wife has twenty months or less in employment, the total of

the couple's work is divided in the ratio 46 : 54 between the husband and wife; over the range of twenty-one to sixty months the total of work is divided 48 : 52; and where the wife has more than five years' work experience, the total work is evenly divided. These results (which correspond closely to those derived from the Q-dodl index shown in Table 5.6) are clearly consistent with the hypothesis of lagged adaptation.

They are also, of course, consistent with another process, a sort of sample selection. The very same pressure of work on women entering paid employment, which by our hypothesis leads to a process of renegotiation of the household division of labour, may also lead to the dissolution of the household. In our data we have only those households which have survived. The regular trend illustrated by Figure 5.5 presumably reflects a combination of the renegotiation of work practices in surviving households, and the dissolution (and hence for the purposes of our analysis, the loss) of some at least of those households in which domestic division of labour is not successfully renegotiated. (Also, some women may preserve their partnership but reduce or abandon paid work.) We cannot disentangle these effects except by further work on life-history data.

But the important point that emerges here is quite unexceptionable. The gradient, far from proving the dependent labour hypothesis, may in fact prove to be a consequence of adaptive partnership—though perhaps a more gradual, and conflictual, process of adaptation than proposed by the early 'adaptation' theorists such as Young and Willmott.

INTERNATIONAL COMPARISONS

We should immediately admit that the historical changes in the balance of work in the UK are very small when considered as a proportion of the total of work time for the husband and wife. If these small longitudinal shifts were all we had to go on, we might perhaps feel that this time-budget information added little to the questionnaire-derived evidence. But, as we shall see, this relatively small UK historical shift fits neatly into a very clear and regular cross-national pattern. A result that, considered in isolation, might possibly be a random fluctuation, emerges in the multinational comparative context as a part of a regular, indeed rather dramatic, historical trend.

Unfortunately there is no comparable material which gives cross-time estimates for couples (there is some French data from the mid-1980s which has one single day for each spouse, but there is no other national collection with week-long evidence on activities of both spouses, and certainly none with historically comparative material of this type). There are, however, other countries with cross-time comparative time-budget statistics. So, for our international comparisons we must fall back on aggregate statistics which look separately at the evolution of the activities of married men and of married women. In the UK 'couple' statistics we see wives increasingly likely to have jobs, and the husbands of employed women taking on more of the unpaid household work. The reflection of this phenomenon in the aggregate statistics, would be a straightforward historical convergence between married men's and women's time devoted to the various types of work.

In fact, evidence of this sort of convergence has been emerging from individual countries' longitudinal evidence (though to a puzzling degree these results have gone unnoticed by the proponents of the more pessimistic arguments about the division of domestic labour). Amongst these are Norwegian evidence covering the period 1971 to 1980 (Gronmo and Lingsom 1986), a comparison of trends in the US from 1965 to 1985 and the UK from 1961 to 1984 (Gershuny and Robinson 1988), and more recently comparative material on trends in Finland (Niemi and Paakkonen 1990). In these and other studies, we find clear evidence of regular and substantial shifts of work time: through successive decades, men do more unpaid work and less paid, women, less unpaid and more paid.

The present authors have been for some years constructing a multinational longitudinal comparative data file (by taking time-budget data sets from the original researchers, and recoding them into a common comparable activity format—the same activity schema as that used for the Social Change and Economic Life Initiative time-budget data set). We now have material from nineteen countries, amounting in all to nearly a quarter of a million days of diary material (an earlier version of this collection is discussed in Gershuny 1990). Eight of the countries represented in our collection have suitable cross-time comparative material for our current purpose.

Table 5.8 selects just the married (and regularly cohabiting or 'living as married') men and women between the ages of 20 and 60 from these countries. The table makes two quite clear points.

First, there is a regular, steady, and substantial growth in men's proportional contribution to the unpaid work total. The scale of change is reasonably consistent across periods and countries. The data from the mid-1960s shows men doing around one-quarter of the total of unpaid work, that from the 1970s shows men's proportion to lie around 30%, and the 1980s proportions reach or approach 40%. Each country without exception shows a rise in the men's proportion in each successive survey. In most of the countries at least since the early 1970s, men's unpaid work time has been increasing; in most, women's has been decreasing. (The picture is somewhat confused by the very substantial rise over this period in the total of both men's and women's time devoted to child care and shopping. If we look just at the core 'cooking and cleaning' component of housework we find evidence of this transfer of domestic work from women to men in every case that we have comparative evidence for the 1970s and the 1980s.)

Second, we see that the men's proportion of the total of work is in general decreasing. The table, perhaps misleadingly, suggests that the aggregate of work time is substantially higher for men than for women (reflecting the previously mentioned tendency of time-budget evidence to overestimate paid work time). But holding the absolute level on one side, women's proportion of work is certainly increasing in seven out of the eight countries. (The eighth country (Finland) shows a small increase in the men's proportion, from 51% to 52% of the total: given the bias in the data-collection method, we might expect that 52% represents something like equality of total work time between the sexes.)

These two points together add up to a clear case for a model of gradual or lagged adaptation. With women's increasing entry into paid employment, so their total workload increases, as the DL hypothesis would predict. But the increase is moderated, though not entirely offset, by the substitution of some male unpaid work for some female. The compensation is not complete, the women's paid work increases faster than the men's substitution of unpaid

TABLE 5.8 Change in work time in eight countries[a]

| | Men's time as a % of men's plus women's | | | | | | | |
| | All work-related activities excluding commuting | | | | All unpaid work activities | | | |
	1961–70	1971–77	1978–82	1983–90	1961–70	1971–77	1978–82	1983–90
Canada	54	missing	57	—	—	34	37	—
France	—	52	—	—	25	28	—	—
Netherlands	—	59	57	51	—	28	31	41
Norway	—	60	57	—	—	34	39	—
UK	—	57	—	54	—	26	—	37
USA	56	55	—	54	26	32	—	35
Hungary	52	51	—	—	25	28	—	—
Finland	—	—	51	52	—	—	35	39

Note: Paid work time includes work breaks, unpaid work time excludes breaks, so men's total work is overestimated.

[a] Married men and women only.

for paid work, but nevertheless a process of adaptation is clearly under way.

CONCLUSIONS

We have used the Social Change and Economic Life Initiative data to produce some striking substantive results.

1. A careful analysis of the sources of explanation of variation in Q-dodl, shows a substantial sensitivity to women's current employment status and work histories. So (to the extent that it is proper to draw such an inference from cross-sectional evidence), the questionnaire data do not support the view that domestic division of labour fails to respond to changes in women's employment. (In the course of this analysis we discovered, somewhat to our surprise, that a not-insignificant proportion of the variance in couples' present division of domestic labour may be explained by practices recollected from their parents' households.

2. The combination of the couples' diary data with previous diary samples produces evidence of some historical change. The Social Change and Economic Life Initiative couples reproduce cross-sectional results found in other diary studies, which seem initially to support a pessimistic view of domestic division of labour. But when we compare these data from 1987 with earlier (1973 and 1974) cross-sectional evidence from matched time-budget surveys, we find evidence of increasing equality within households.

3. Linking diary data to work history material enables us to start to examine the process and mechanism of distribution. The hypothesis of lagged or gradual adaptation emerges from this evidence. We suggest, on the basis of this linked material, that domestic practices may change gradually through an extended period after a wife's entry into paid work, as the household adjusts to the implications of the new job.

4. Comparison of the British time-budget data with evidence from seven other developed countries shows strikingly consistent patterns of change. Married men's proportion of the total of domestic work time has a regular and substantial growth, over the last three decades, and in all eight countries. However, the women's proportion of the total of paid and unpaid work

increases in most countries over this period, so the process of adaptation to women's increased rates of participation in paid work is only partially achieved.

We have been able to establish some of the crucial elements of a 'lagged adaptation' model of change in the domestic division of labour (see Figure 5.6). The couple's division of domestic labour is a function of both the early socialization of the partners, and of the wife's employment experience. Starting from an initial position where the husband is generally employed and the wife generally non-employed, both partners may have a traditional gender strategy and the household has a stable and non-conflictual division of domestic labour. Women start to enter the workforce, and the influences of socialization and employment experience at first push in different directions: socialization tending to maintain traditional female responsibilities for unpaid work, but the time-use consequences of the woman's job leading to a 'dual burden', and hence pressure for change. The consequence of the pressure may be to produce a 'family myth' that is at odds with the actual division of labour, but this merely transfers overt interpersonal conflict into an intrapersonal tension, which presumably leads to subsequent problems. Or it may lead to a genuine, if partial, shift in the burden of responsibilities.

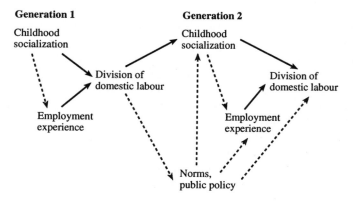

FIG. 5.6 Slow change in the domestic division of labour

The new myths, and changed patterns of domestic labour, must then feed back into the socialization of the next generation. Children growing up in an environment that has been affected by these processes, observe patterns of behaviour which are less encouraging to the traditional gender strategies: their socialization will encourage more of them towards intermediate or egalitarian gender strategies. So in this generation the influences of early socialization and the consequences of work experience will be less opposed, and change in the domestic division of labour will thus be easier.

This pattern of change is demonstrated by the Social Change and Economic Life Initiative retrospective data and the cross-time comparison of time-budget surveys, and is clearly consistent with the multinational comparative evidence. One further step in the analysis, which concerns the part played by household formation and dissolution in this process, really requires panel-type survey data: we must presumably wait until the Essex Panel Survey begins to yield longitudinal data before completing this argument for the UK.

But there are some further links in Figure 5.6 that we have not properly discussed. There are other influences on the pattern of domestic work than just the beliefs of the members of the household, ranging from the public regulation of employment (part-time work, parental leave allowances, and so on) through to the provision of services to the household (e.g. child care and maintenance). Actual changes in the division of domestic labour, as well as the unresolved contradictions between gender images and actual employment patterns, lead to changes in the general environment within which the household operates. And these other influences in turn feed back into the division of labour. The full model must take account of these environmental factors.

We should also add that while the total work time of full-time employed husbands and full-time employed wives may be tending towards equality, still the mix between paid and unpaid activities is very different. This has substantial consequences, particularly for career progression. Women's remaining disproportionate responsibility for domestic work (60–40 in favour of men, according to Table 5.8), necessarily means less time, effort, and attention is available for paid work. This must in turn be reflected in women's accumulation of human capital, and hence be an important factor in the explanation of the continuing differential between men's and women's levels of pay and occupational attainment. So the argument shifts its base: even if lagged adaptation does lead to a 'symmetry' in the Young and Willmott sense that the total of work may in the longer term tend towards equality between the husband and wife, still the differential pattern of responsibilities for paid and unpaid work provides substantial advantages to the husband in terms of earnings and status.

One very important part of the environment is the general economic culture. Socialization, after all, relates to more than just the household. Norms are what is generally known to be normal. As what is normal changes, what is known to be normal changes—but with a certain lag. With public discussion of these issues, comes public awareness of change. The sociological study of the changing domestic division of labour is itself an agent in the process it studies. So perhaps there is a certain not-inappropriate exhortatory justification for Hochschild's claim that the revolution is 'stalled'. The model we have outlined suggests that the division of domestic labour does change, but only very slowly, over a period of generations. One regulator of the speed of change is the state of public awareness of the progress and problems of this process. So the very fact of claiming that the revolution is stalled, may speed its progress.

APPENDIX: AN INDEX OF THE DIVISION OF DOMESTIC LABOUR

There are things that only diary data can tell us. Diaries are the only source of information on the amounts of time devoted to particular activities. And we need this quantitative information if we are to assess the balance of activity within the household. But diary samples are costly and (despite the reassurance we may derive from research (Gershuny 1990) suggesting that this does not lead to relevant behavioural biases in the sample) they have low response rates. A particular worry for Social Change and Economic Life Initiative data is the loss of sample size: the 1,800 households yield approximately 1,200 'couples'. From these we obtain 520 couples (43%) who both returned diaries (a 50% individual response rate might well have produced a 25% couple response rate—but there does seem to be a process of mutual encouragement). And in the main text we have adopted the (perhaps overcautious) policy of only using the 390 couples whose diaries contain no missing data whatsoever. Thus, when we use the diary material, we lose between half and two-thirds of our sample. Our main substantive concern is with the division of domestic labour (dodl), and to investigate this we often need to control for the couple's employment, family, and other characteristics. Accordingly, cell-sizes rapidly fall below viability.

At the centre of our interest is the way the division of domestic labour alters (or fails to do so) with changes in household employment status. In principle, we need time-budget diary data to show aggregate quantitative balance between the amounts of different sorts of work done by the partners in a couple. The Household questionnaire does, however, contain some questions about division of household tasks. If we could somehow use this evidence, rather than time-budget data, we would immediately increase cell-sizes two- or three-fold, and enable much more sensitive analysis. In this Appendix, we investigate how well the questionnaire 'division' data serves as a substitute for time-budget material.

Our first question is: how does the questionnaire data perform as predictor of the diary results at an individual level? Table 5.A1 takes as its starting point the women's answers to the various questions about the division of domestic work. (So we read the first column of Table 5.A1 as '15 women said the man is almost entirely responsible for the cooking' and so on.) The next column gives mean scores for the same questions addressed to those women's partners. There are plainly some substantial differences between the men's and women's answers (if there were no differences, the mean score for the group of men whose partners answered 'man almost entirely responsible for the cooking' would be −1). But nevertheless the general trend of the results is correct.

Note that the men's and women's answers to the questions about the division of domestic tasks were collected independently. Each partner had a self-completion questionnaire, and the interviewer supervised the process to ensure that the couple did not discuss their answers. So it is not surprising that the same question should elicit somewhat different answers from the

TABLE 5.A1 *Comparison between various questionnaire and diary answers*

Women's answers	Whole sample			Both full-time employed	
	Number of women answering	Mean of men's answers	Mean from diaries	Number of women answering	Mean of men's answers
Who does the . . .					
Cooking for the family?					
–1.0 M almost entirely	15	–0.43	–0.25	3	–0.83
–0.5 M mainly	44	–0.19	–0.44	14	–0.28
0.0 shared equally	211	0.26	0.37	66	0.23
–0.5 F mainly	484	0.66	0.60	101	0.58
–1.0 F almost entirely	436	0.85	0.72	78	0.83
Washing up?					
–1.0 M almost entirely	21	–0.36	–0.13	5	–0.60
–0.5 M mainly	88	–0.24	0.01	32	0.21
0.0 shared equally	422	0.17	0.42	129	0.11
–0.5 F mainly	370	0.60	0.57	59	0.55
–1.0 F almost entirely	240	0.83	0.74	21	0.93
Hoovering, cleaning?					
–1.0 M almost entirely	13	–0.11	0.09	3	–0.33
–0.5 M mainly	45	–0.20	0.19	14	–0.03
0.0 shared equally	211	0.25	0.66	71	0.22
–0.5 F mainly	527	0.68	0.71	104	0.58
–1.0 F almost entirely	361	0.86	0.79	55	0.80
Clothes washing?					
–1.0 M almost entirely	3	0.00	—	5	–0.60
–0.5 M mainly	17	0.00	0.73	32	–0.22
0.0 shared equally	57	0.38	0.47	129	0.11
–0.5 F mainly	417	0.76	0.91	59	0.55
–1.0 F almost entirely	683	0.87	0.92	21	0.21
Painting and decorating?					
–1.0 M almost entirely	190	–0.67	–0.81	48	–0.63
–0.5 M mainly	485	–0.46	–0.64	101	–0.46
0.0 shared equally	306	–0.02	–0.47	67	0.02
–0.5 F mainly	65	0.45	–0.47	9	0.39
–1.0 F almost entirely	41	0.70	–0.10	11	0.68
Gardening?					
–1.0 M almost entirely	119	–0.63	–0.76	35	–0.61
–0.5 M mainly	402	–0.45	–0.67	96	–0.45
0.0 shared equally	349	0.06	–0.11	73	0.03
–0.5 F mainly	128	0.53	0.20	29	0.62
–1.0 F almost entirely	55	0.77	0.30	10	0.70

Women's answers	Whole sample			Both full-time employed	
	Number of women answering	Mean of men's answers	Mean from diaries	Number of women answering	Mean of men's answers
Car maintenance?					
–1.0 M almost entirely	402	–0.73	–0.73	93	–0.71
–0.5 M mainly	387	–0.65	–0.81	92	–0.64
0.0 shared equally	37	–0.18	–0.29	10	0.20
–0.5 F mainly	9	0.06	0.44	2	–0.50
–1.0 F almost entirely	13	0.42	0.00	5	–0.10

Note: M = male; F = female.

partners. The final two columns give the mean scores of the questionnaire returns from the subsample of men in households where partners both had full-time jobs: in this group the household activities correspond marginally better to the women's answers. Our hypothesis is that full-time employed couples are more constrained by their circumstances to discuss the division of domestic labour than other couples, and hence are more likely to arrive at explicit and mutually agreed accounts of how it is actually distributed in their own households.

The third column links the women's responses to the questionnaire items to the equivalent scores that emerge from their own households' diaries. The match is certainly less than satisfactory, but still the correct trend emerges. The preliminary conclusion that emerges from this table is that men's and women's questionnaire responses are reasonably well associated, and both are somewhat less well associated with time-budget data.

This informal analysis is borne out by the more formal statistics in Table 5.A2. As indicators of the association between the various measures of task distribution we use eta-squared statistics, which may be interpreted as proportions of variance explained. (These are equivalent to R-squared statistics, but relax the requirement that the independent variable be a continuous measure; the equivalent table of R-squared statistics produces very similar, though very slightly weaker, associations. All the associations in the table are significant at the 0.001 level.) Though Table 5.1 (in the main text) shows that the mean scores

TABLE 5.A2 *Associations between questionnaire and diary estimates*

	Whole sample		Both FTE	
	MQ/FQ	FQ/DP	MQ/FQ	FQ/DP
Cooking for the family	0.44	0.22	0.50	0.23
Washing up	0.47	0.16	0.50	0.17
Hoovering/cleaning	0.45	0.05	0.40	0.07
Clothes washing	0.23	0.06	0.17	0.26
Painting and decorating	0.48	0.06	0.46	0.07
Gardening	0.55	0.27	0.56	0.27
Car maintenance	0.22	0.15	0.21	0.07

Note: FTE = full-time employed; MQ/FQ = male questionnaire/female questionnaire; FQ/DP = female questionnaire/diary proportion.

from the male and female questionnaires correspond very closely, we see from Table 5.A2 that only around half of the variance in one set of answers is explained by the other. And though the questionnaire estimates of mean task divisions correspond well with means from the diary data set (which we assume to be a reasonably reliable estimator), the associations between the questionnaire items and equivalent diary activities are low.

What are we to make of these results? The differences between the male and female questionnaire responses will presumably relate in part to genuine differences in perception between the partners, and in part to the unavoidable vagueness of the question categories. (What exactly does 'almost entirely' mean?) The differences between the questionnaire and the diary estimates will in turn relate to both of these factors, to the nature of the prevailing 'family myth' concerning the division of domestic work, and additionally to the fact that while the questionnaire items refer to general practice, the diary describes the special activities of one particular week. But nevertheless, the mean estimates from the three sources do correspond quite closely. For the moment, therefore, we may tentatively and provisionally conclude that the questionnaire items on individual categories of domestic work may yield unbiased, but certainly very 'noisy', indicators of the division of responsibility for the tasks.

Our goal is to develop a single index of the division of domestic labour based on questionnaire data. Table 5.A3 shows corre-

TABLE 5.A3 *Indicators of domestic division of labour*

1: mean score of men's answers
2: mean score of women's answers
3: average of 1 and 2
4: division calculated from diary data

Correlation matrix for whole diary sample

	1	2	3	4
1	1			
2	0.7059	1		
3	0.9248	0.9223	1	
4	0.4287	0.3688	0.4320	1

Number [a] = (392)

All associations significant at 0.001

Correlation matrix for full-time employed diarist couples

	1	2	3	4
1	1			
2	0.7991	1		
3	0.9465	0.9504	1	
4	0.5845	0.4380	0.5376	1

Number [a] = (86)

All associations significant at 0.00

[a] Number of respondents.

lations among three alternative questionnaire division-of-domestic-labour indices (derived respectively from the men's responses, the women's and the mean of the two, each calculated by averaging the scores for the four 'female'-dominated domestic tasks in the previous tables) and a diary-based index calculated as the woman's proportion of total time devoted to the four tasks. We find a correlation of 0.71 between the male- and the female-answer-based indices (i.e. 50% of the variance in one is explained by the other) which approximately corresponds to the level of association between the alternative questionnaire indicators of the individual tasks. The third index, a simple average of the male and female scores, correlates, as we might expect, well with

both. The male-answer index is much better correlated with the
diary-based index than the female-based. And the combined
questionnaire-based index correlates slightly better with the diary
index than does the male.

Now, suppose we were to hold our worries about the low correlation between the diary- and questionnaire-based indices on
one side for a moment, and use the combined questionnaire-
based index as an indicator of the division of domestic labour:
would we be misrepresenting household practices as estimated
from the diary data? Figure 5.A1 compares the frequency distributions for the combined questionnaire and the diary division of
domestic labour indices. (We have transformed the scale to have
a range from 0 to 1, which may be interpreted as the wife's proportion of the couple's total of domestic work.) Both indices
show a similar broad dispersion. They have slightly different
modes, but the distributions nevertheless have very similar general shapes.

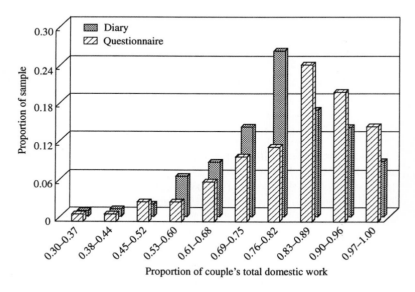

FIG. 5.A1 Wife's proportion of domestic work: frequency distributions
for the questionnaire-based and diary-based estimates of the division of
domestic labour indices

We have established that the mean estimates and the disper-
sions of the two indicators are broadly similar for the sample as
a whole. Does the same hold for subgroups of households in the
sample? Table 5.2 (in the main text) uses multiple classification
analysis to estimate the effects of belonging to various employment and family/life-cycle categories on the division of domestic
labour, as measured by the two indices. The grand mean as estimated from the diary indicator is 0.81 (which means, in terms of
the diary data, that the wife does 81% of the domestic work).
The corresponding estimate from the questionnaire-based indicator for the subsample of diarist couples is 0.79, and for the whole
questionnaire sample is 0.78. The following rows show the effect
of belonging to the employment and life/family-status subcate-
gories on these grand means (adjusted effects). The effect para-
meters for the diary and questionnaire-based indicators are very
closely matched: we conclude that substantially similar estimates
of means for the various subgroups emerge from the two sorts of
estimator. There are no evident biases, at least with respect to
these particular socio-demographic categories.

Figure 5.A2 compares the frequency distributions for the
employment subgroups from the questionnaire and diary measures. The distribution from the diary-based index is a little less
regular than that derived from the questionnaire, as we would
expect from the smaller number in the diary sample. But the
same pattern of change—a shifting of the distribution to the
right, as we move from couples with a full-time employed wife to
couples with a non-employed wife—emerges from the two indicators.

So our conclusion for the questionnaire-based division of
domestic labour index (henceforward Q-dodl) is similar to that
for the individual questionnaire division of labour items. A diary-
based index is greatly superior, since (we conclude on the basis of
comparisons of the answers given by the two partners in each
particular household) the questionnaire-based index contains a
lot of statistical noise. Nevertheless the questionnaire- and the
diary-based indices are very significantly correlated (though the
strength of the correlation is not as high as we might ideally
wish). The same results hold for subgroups: no evident bias has
emerged as resulting from the use of the questionnaire index.
And the four questionnaire items on which the Q-dodl index is

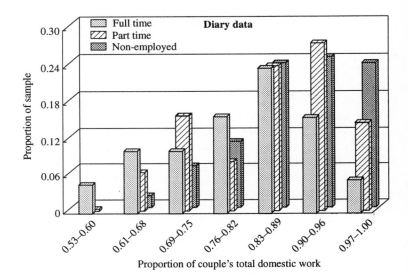

Fɪɢ. 5.A2 Wife's proportion of domestic work: frequency distributions
for the employment subgroups from the questionnaire and diary
measures

based require only a few seconds to administer. In short, for this
particular purpose, the cheap and undemanding nature of the
questionnaire-based index may greatly outweigh the technical
superiority of the diary-based index.

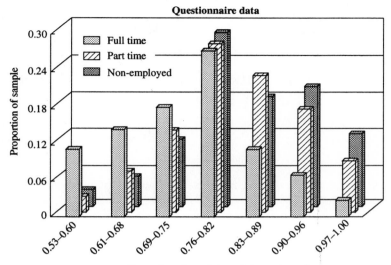

Proportion of couple's total domestic work

6

Household Time Allocation and Women's Labour Force Participation

SARA HORRELL

Home production time has been argued to play an important facilitating role in the historical increase in married women's labour force participation. The increased availability of market substitutes for home-produced commodities and domestic technology has reduced the time required by home production, so enabling women to supply labour to the market in response to real wage rises (Mincer 1962). Similar effects are predicted on a cross-section level (Becker 1965). Thus differences in time uses will be related to women's wage rates and, by implication, would be expected to be observed between working-wife and non-working-wife households. Changes in time use alter the structure of demand and have repercussions on the industrial structure and employment (Morgensen 1990). Therefore household time use becomes an integral part of the economic system and a change, such as the increased labour force participation of married women, has both expenditure and domestic production time counterparts. Thus explicit consideration of intrahousehold uses of time is needed if market time uses are to be linked to demand patterns and the consequences of future changes in time use predicted.

Economists acknowledge the importance of time use when analysing the choices made by households. The standard labour-supply literature has both time and money as scarce resources and these constrain choices over time spent in work and leisure. But this has been criticized for its assumption that all time spent outside paid work is leisure; home production is an important alternative use of time. The New Home Economics incorporates home production time into analyses of household behaviour. Becker (1965) argues that goods are not consumed for themselves, as is usually assumed, but are inputs into household production which, when combined with time inputs, create the commodities that households desire. Leisure does not exist as a separate time use. Acknowledgement of the use of time in household production provides additional insights into the goods demand and labour supply of households and links household production to labour supply. Becker (1965) predicts that a compensated rise in the woman's wage will imply an increase in the hours worked in the market, substitution between time and goods in the production of each commodity, and a switch from time-intensive to market-goods-intensive consumption.

However, Becker's model has been argued to be too general, and some recognition of the division of non-labour-market work time into household production and leisure is needed (Gronau 1977). Gronau shows that home production and leisure do not have the same relationships to socio-economic variables or constant relative prices, so these two uses of time cannot be treated as one entity. Different implications follow if home production, defined as having market substitutes, is differentiated from leisure, defined as having only poor market substitutes and which cannot be enjoyed through a surrogate. In particular, an increase in unearned income will leave the time spent in home production for the employed unchanged but will reduce the time spent in this activity by the non-employed. This result is considered to be the crucial test of the model as it is not predicted by Becker's model. But it can be shown that these results rely on one principal and rather implausible assumption: the perfect substitutability of home-produced goods and market goods. Without this assumption the model no longer yields tractable and easily interpreted results and the effect of wage rate changes on time use remains open.

Indeed the validity of price and income variables for explaining time use within the home has been questioned. Some studies of household time allocation show that wage rates have little effect on home production time (Gershuny 1983; Morgensen 1990) and indicate that traditional divisions of labour and cultural norms have greater explanatory power. In addition, substitution between market- and home-produced goods and the time-saving characteristics of domestic technology have been argued to be limited (Brown and Preece 1987). If housework time is relatively unresponsive to market variables, the consequences of increased female participation in the labour force on demand for these types of goods will be negligible. Instead, reduced leisure may be the cost of engaging in market work with consequences for related demands. Limited opportunities for reduction of housework time may also involve substitution of time between partners; where women work, a reduction in the woman's household time could be offset by increased inputs from the man. The standard literature tends to assume that only the woman is involved in home production (Gronau 1973, 1974) and empirical tests considering only the woman's time use (e.g. Gronau 1977) are not designed to expose such substitutions. Evidence of women's paid work being accommodated by reduced leisure and a greater involvement by men in housework would suggest that the neoclassical emphasis on time being saved in home production has been misplaced.

This chapter uses a small sample of time-budget diaries from the Social Change and Economic Life Initiative survey to investigate how time use in partnership households is affected by the woman's involvement in paid work. The first section critically examines Gronau's model of time use. It is shown that the model involves restrictive assumptions, leading to results that cannot be presumed to hold with a more general model, thus illustrating the need for empirical investigation. The second section reviews some results from existing time-use surveys. The survey and results from the time-budget diaries are then discussed. In particular, the responsiveness of household production time to wage rate changes is considered and the time devoted to household production and leisure by working-wife and non-working-wife households compared. The implications of these results for the validity of the neoclassical model and the links between working-wife households' time use and expenditure patterns are developed in the final section.

'LEISURE, HOME PRODUCTION, AND WORK'—GRONAU'S REFORMULATION OF THE THEORY OF THE ALLOCATION OF TIME REVISITED

Gronau's (1977) model of time use differentiates between leisure and home production time.[1] If the individual works, it predicts that an increase in the wage rate will reduce the time spent in home production but the effect on leisure will be indeterminate. An increase in the hours worked in the market will occur if leisure decreases or if any increase in leisure is less than the decrease in home production. Thus the effect of a rise in the wage rate on labour supply gives the conventional finding that it depends on the relative magnitudes of the income and substitution effects. The substitution effect is expected to dominate for women as the elasticity of women's labour supply relates to the scope to reduce hours in household production as well as take hours from leisure. The results are substantiated using data on time use in the three types of activity by white, married women. Essentially the same model is used to consider productivity in home production and attribute a value to home output (Gronau 1980).

However, the model suffers shortcomings. The treatment of the two-person household and possible substitution of time between partners is considered rather superficially in the text and it is only when one attempts to extend the model to the two-person case that its basic flaw is exposed. If market- and home-produced goods are perfect substitutes, specialization is precluded in the two-person household, so implying that the gains from marriage, in terms of increased output, are zero.[2] Becker's (1974) theory of marriage illustrates the fundamental importance of specialization in home production and market work by the partners in allowing there to be gains from marriage. To base predictions on a model which does not allow gains from marriage is in contradiction to the rest of the New Home Economics literature, if not intuitively implausible. But to drop the assumption of perfect substitutability of market and home-produced goods yields less tractable results about the uses of time, even in the single person case. Without perfect substitutability of goods, Gronau's model cannot be collapsed into the graphical representation widely used in the labour-supply literature (e.g. Fallon and Verry 1988) which allows the effect of changes in the wage rate on time use to be easily predicted. More importantly, the unrealistic equilibrium condition attained when no gains from marriage are possible is used as the basic condition to measure productivity and value home output (Gronau 1980). This must cast doubt on the estimates obtained.

In earlier models Gronau (1973, 1974) has not assumed that market and home-produced goods are perfect substitutes. Instead market goods are combined with time inputs to produce home goods, with leisure and other market goods being treated separately. With this model further predictions can be made about time allocation. For instance, if both partners are working, an increase in the husband's wage will cause the wife to allocate more time to household production and less time to market work. A rise in the wage of the wife will result in the husband taking more leisure and reducing his market work. However, it should be noted that the specification of this model does not allow the possibility of an increase in the husband's housework time as a response to an increase in the wife's wage. This is a consequence of Gronau's prior assumption that the husband will completely specialize in market work. Only two uses of time, work and leisure, enter his time constraint. This is not consistent with most evidence on time use; men generally do contribute some time to home production. Furthermore, substitution in housework time between partners must be feasible under the conditions required to maximize the gains from marriage (Becker 1974).[3]

Gains from marriage will be maximized if at least one of the two partners specializes completely in one sector, either home production or market work. However, involvement of both partners in both sectors is to be found in many households. This is explained by complementarity of partners in production reducing the sexual division of labour in the allocation of time (Becker 1981). Partners being complements rather than substitutes in the production process is also necessary to explain the predominance of marriage rather than single-sex, multiperson households, who would be equally capable of gaining from specialization (Becker 1974). Male and female time inputs are not perfectly substitutable and both are required for production of certain commodities, such as children, and this complementarity allows partners to be active in all time uses.

Gronau's models are therefore inappropriate for considering time allocation in the two-person household; if there are to be gains from marriage, market and home-produced goods cannot be perfect substitutes. Also substitution between partners in housework time should be allowed; as partners are required to be complements to explain marriage complete specialization is not implied. However, Gronau's modification of the Becker model where not all time is allocated to home production remains reasonable; leisure is a good which cannot be traded between the partners. This limits gains from specialization to tradeable goods.

A more realistic model of time allocation would therefore include all uses of time as possibilities for both partners and have complementary time uses in the production of one commodity, say children. In addition, market goods can be classified as substitutes for home-produced goods, as inputs to household production and as non-substitutable final goods, each with associated time uses (Chadeau and Roy 1981). Where both partners participate in the labour market and in home production a model incorporating these requirements yields complex results and the extent to which any particular household time use will respond to wage rate changes or be the domain of one partner remains a matter for empirical investigation.

TIME-USE STUDIES

Existing empirical studies have found varying degrees of responsiveness of time uses to wage rate variables, and differing effects of women's paid work on housework time; some cast doubt on the appropriateness of the neoclassical economic model for considering household time allocation.

Gronau (1977) finds working women's housework time[4] and leisure both decrease with increases in the female wage, although the decrease in leisure is four times that of the decrease in housework. Responses to an increase in the male wage vary; non-employed women increase housework time and reduce leisure, employed women decrease hours of paid work and increase leisure but the effect on housework time is insignificant. However, the effect of wage rate changes on housework time appear to be limited and leisure is the main activity from which time is reallocated to market work in response to an own wage increase for working women. More recent Danish time-use surveys (Pedersen 1990) find wages and income are only significant for paid work; these variables are insignificant when included as explanatory variables for other time uses. Instead household characteristics have the main explanatory power.

Other studies show working women spending less time on housework (Vanek 1974; Vickery 1979; Gershuny 1983) but this seems to arise from the reduction of time inputs into the non-physical care time for other family members (Vickery 1979) or is largely attributable to differences in child care requirements (Vanek 1974). Shopping time and behaviour is unaffected by the woman's work status (Strober and Weinberg 1980; Piachaud 1982) and there is little evidence of any differences in frequency or method of meal preparation once factors such as income and life-cycle phase have been accounted for (Strober and Weinberg 1980). Reductions in 'pure' housework time therefore appear to be limited for working women. This is supported by arguments that market substitutes for housework are limited, that market goods and home goods are not interchangeable, and the time spent in housework, which may be subject to socially defined minimum standards, cannot be significantly reduced to offset the woman's time spent in paid employment (Brown and Preece 1987). Certainly housework time has stood at 10% of individuals' total time for the last thirty years in Denmark, despite substantial changes in paid work time (Morgensen 1990), so it would appear that possibilities for substitution are limited.

Few of these studies consider whether any reduction in housework time that may be achieved by the woman is offset by increased inputs from the man, so maintaining the total time required. The standard argument is that, if housework time cannot significantly be reduced, the main substitution will be wife's leisure time for paid work. In fact, time budgets collected over a number of years show women's total work time increasing for the majority of the period and only recently beginning to fall (Gershuny 1983), so substantial redistribution of total work time between partners seems unlikely. Vickery (1979) discusses the Walker and Woods (1976) survey which shows that husbands do not put more time into household work when their wives are working. The increase in total work time for women with little offsetting participation in housework by men has been argued to suggest that households do not optimize in the economic sense, instead adopting traditional divisions of labour for household tasks which are not adjusted to any great extent even when there are major changes in the total work performed by individual family members (Gershuny 1983: 155). The neoclassical result of specialization according to relative wages is certainly not upheld by Danish data. Where women earn more than their male partners they still do two-thirds of the housework. The housework division of labour would therefore appear to be determined primarily by cultural norms (Komendi 1990) and these norms are sufficiently strong for households to allocate time in direct contradiction to economic specialization arguments.

However, more recent time-budget work offers an indication that men may be doing slightly more in the home (Dolan and Scannell 1987), although this has been suggested to result from responsibility for provision of some services being moved to the home from the market, rather than increased participation by men in traditionally female tasks (Komendi 1990). The possibility that men do more in the home when women work is therefore worthy of investigation with recent time-budget data. Such substitution occurring would imply that models of time allocation which do not enforce complete specialization are more appropriate. In addition, investigation of more finely subdivided time uses (covering paid work, housework, child care, other household production, necessary personal care, and leisure) allows closer examination of areas where time inputs may be reduced and possibilities for market substitution exist when women are working.

THE SURVEY

The data used for this analysis were from the time-budget diaries completed by those respondents to the Social Change and Economic Life Initiative Household survey who were willing to do so. They, and other members of the household over 14 years of age, were given diaries divided into fifteen-minute intervals covering seven consecutive days. In this, details of each person's main activity, other activities, and where and with whom the main activity was performed were to be recorded. The diaries necessarily took a self-completion format and were to be returned by post, although interviewers were instructed to do a limited amount of progress chasing. Such procedures for eliciting information invariably have relatively low response rates, although this is not thought to produce substantial biases in diary-based time-use estimates. The time budgets provide a valuable source of information on time use and in this survey were collected over a longer period and in more detail than is generally the case. They therefore make an ideal basis on which to compare time uses by working and non-working wives.[5] In addition, the household completion of diaries provides detailed information on partners' activities so allowing comparison of the man's use of time in the different types of household. The data used here are from the Northampton Household survey conducted in spring 1987 and from the time budgets collected for the same area.

The analysis has been confined to partnership households where there are a couple or couple and dependent children only in the household. In addition, only households where the male partner was self-employed or in full-time employment were selected. Of the 300 household interviews conducted 127 fall into this category and of these seventeen refused to give income data, leaving a final sample of 110. Of these households, thirty-six returned diaries completed by both partners. Fourteen were non-working wife households, fourteen were households in which the woman worked part-time and in the remaining eight the woman worked full-time. Thus there were sufficient numbers to make comparisons for the three types of household. The diaries were read and the main activity in every quarter-hour recorded so allowing average time spent in each activity over the week for both husband and wife for each type of household to be computed. Whilst the sample is small, the differences that arise in household time usage when the woman's work status is controlled are sufficiently large to give rise to some interesting implications for time-use strategies when women are working. Also, responsiveness of time use to wage and income variables for the twenty-two working-wife households is considered using regression analysis.

Information on participation in activities for both partners was collected in the Household survey. In a self-completion questionnaire administered during the interview, the respondent and his/her partner separately filled in details on how frequently they did each of nineteen activities and with whom the activity was normally done.[6] The activities covered a wide range and are here discussed in broad categories; social, home-based, and all.[7] By ascribing suitable values to the frequency with which an activity was done, an index of participation in each of the broad activity groups by husband and wife is calculated; the number of activities undertaken with another member of the household is also computed. The results for the sample of 110 households are reported and provide support for and additional information on some of the implications of the time-budget data. Analysis of variance, using the woman's work status, age of the youngest child, and disposable household income as explanatory variables, was used to indicate the statistical significance of the woman's work status in explaining activity participation of the man and the woman.

RESULTS

The analysis of the time-budget diaries (see Table 6.1) shows the average time spent on each activity by the man, the woman, and both partners taken together, according to the woman's work status. The time committed to work by the male partner is fairly constant for all groups.[8] Thus there appears to be little substitution between partners in paid-work activities and, given that such substitution may be expected, this suggests institutional rigidities in choice over hours of work, particularly for men. Working women spend less time sleeping than their non-working counterparts. Such a finding has been reported elsewhere (Strober and Weinberg 1980) and implies that this small sample of time budgets does not give rise to unreliable results.

Of primary interest is the time devoted to housework. Becker (1965) and Gronau (1977) suggest that working women will devote less time to housework by substituting either time-saving durables or market-produced goods, but the time-budget data emphasizes a rather different aspect. Women working part-time do spend slightly less time in housework activities, particularly meal preparation, washing up, and cleaning, than non-working women. However, the male partner puts more time into these areas of housework than his counterpart with a non-working wife. This results in half the woman's reduction in time spent in this activity being made up by her partner. In terms of household time allocation, households with women working part-time only save 1 hour 16 minutes in housework per week, less than 5% of total time spent in housework by non-working wife households,

TABLE 6.1 Partners' uses of time by the woman's work status (no. ¼-hr. units/wk.)

	Woman's time allocation			Man's time allocation			Joint time allocation		
	Woman's work status								
	Non-working	Part-time	Full-time	Non-working	Part-time	Full-time	Non-working	Part-time	Full-time
Work	—	75.7	130.0	166.4	161.8	147.8	166.4	237.5	277.8
Travel to work	—	10.7	19.3	21.4	21.4	32.9	21.4	32.1	52.2
Breaks	—	3.0	11.6	10.6	17.1	14.4	10.6	20.1	26.0
All work	—	89.4	160.9	198.4	200.3	195.1	198.4	289.7	356.0
Sleep	240.4	226.2	225.3	221.2	216.2	225.9	461.6	442.6	451.2
Meal preparation	33.9	30.2	20.0	3.4	4.8	8.6	37.3	35.0	28.6
Washing up	13.2	11.0	6.5	2.6	3.8	4.0	15.8	14.8	10.5
Laundry	13.2	13.8	11.5	0.6	0.3	0.5	13.8	14.1	12.0
Tidying	6.6	6.1	3.9	2.8	2.1	1.5	9.4	8.2	5.4
Cleaning	27.9	24.7	8.8	0.1	2.4	0.8	28.0	27.1	9.6
All housework	94.8	85.8	50.7	9.5	13.4	15.4	104.3	99.2	66.1
Shopping	21.2	26.8	19.6	8.4	12.3	16.1	29.6	39.1	35.7
Other household/garden	4.9	9.1	3.3	20.8	13.7	8.4	25.7	22.8	11.7
All household	120.9	121.7	73.6	38.7	39.4	39.9	159.6	161.1	113.5
Eating in home	31.0	25.4	21.6	22.4	24.9	20.5	53.4	50.3	42.1
Personal care	24.6	29.4	29.0	22.8	21.8	20.3	47.4	51.2	49.3

General child care	58.9	19.7	3.8	12.6	4.9	2.3	71.5	24.6	6.1
Playing/teaching	14.9	7.2	1.6	9.1	9.6	1.1	24.0	16.8	2.7
All child care	73.8	26.9	5.4	21.7	14.5	3.4	95.5	41.4	8.8
Watching TV	68.9	57.1	44.9	64.1	70.9	73.5	133.0	128.0	118.4
Reading	9.1	18.4	13.9	10.4	15.1	6.6	19.5	33.5	20.5
Relaxing	27.5	18.6	27.3	21.6	15.4	10.4	49.1	34.0	37.7
All home leisure	105.5	94.1	86.1	96.1	101.4	90.5	201.6	195.5	176.6
Crafts and knitting/sewing	3.1	7.8	6.4	1.9	—	6.6	5.0	7.8	13.0
Seeing family/friends	43.2	32.7	36.0	21.7	24.2	32.0	64.9	56.9	68.0
Sports	5.3	1.9	1.9	9.0	8.3	10.0	14.3	10.2	11.9
Clubs/societies	5.8	1.3	12.9	4.3	3.4	14.3	10.1	4.7	27.2
Pubs	1.0	3.8	0.9	1.6	9.4	3.8	2.6	13.2	4.7
Meals out/cinema	4.5	5.3	2.3	5.3	2.6	2.1	9.8	7.9	4.4
All outside leisure	59.8	45.0	54.0	41.9	47.9	62.2	101.7	92.9	116.2
Away from home	5.0	1.6	—	3.8	1.4	—	8.8	3.0	—
Other	8.0	4.5	10.1	3.0	4.1	7.8	11.0	8.6	17.9
TOTAL	672.1	672.0	672.4	671.9	672.1	672.2	1344.0	1344.1	1344.6

cont. over.

TABLE 6.1 *cont.*

| | Woman's time allocation | | |
| | Woman's work status | | |
	Non-working	Part-time	Full-time
Av. no. meals bought away from home	0.7	1.1	0.4
Time spent in personal care outside home (¼-hr. units/wk.)	0.6	1.4	0.4
Household characteristics			
Disposable income (£s per month)	925.29	1029.86	996.0
Average number of children	1.71	1.43	0.63
% with children	92.9	78.6	21.4
Of those with children % aged:			
0–5	84.6	54.5	—
5–12	7.7	27.3	33.3
12–18	7.7	18.2	66.7
% women aged:			
<30	28.6	28.6	62.5
30–45	57.1	71.4	37.5
46–60	14.3	—	—
Sample size	(14)	(14)	(8)

and 45% of this time saving occurs in the area of meal preparation. As less household time is spent eating in the home and only
slightly more meals are recorded as being purchased away from
home in the diary week in households where the woman works
part-time, the time saving would appear to be primarily attributable to food provided and eaten at work. Thus despite differences in household composition, households where the woman
works part-time make only negligible savings in the area of
housework, but some substitution between partner's time in
housework does appear to occur.

In households where the woman works full-time the woman's
housework time is reduced dramatically. But substitution again
occurs, the male partner puts more time into housework, particularly meal preparation, than his counterparts whose wives spend
less time in paid work. However, the total household time allocated to housework remains substantially below that for the
other types of household. The reduced amount of time spent in
meal preparation and eating in households where the woman
works full-time may again be attributed to more meals being
eaten at work. However, the biggest savings are made in cleaning
and tidying time. This cannot be attributed to the purchase of
cleaning services from outside[9] or cleaning technology, which is
unlikely to vary between households, but may be attributable to
smaller household size, hence, possibly smaller size of house, and
less time spent in the home, all of which would require less cleaning to be done. Alternatively, lower standards may be observed
in households where the woman works full-time.

Substitution out of housework time when women are working
would therefore appear to be limited once different compositional
factors have been taken into account. This is particularly evident
where the woman works part-time. Limited reductions in housework time imply that neither time-saving goods and services nor
domestic labour-saving technology appear to be factors in facilitating the woman's participation in paid work. While some time-
saving in meal preparation, probably due to food being eaten at
work, does occur, previous results of reduced housework time for
working women seem to result, at least in part, from the increased
involvement of her partner, so relieving her of some of these
responsibilities. Even where women work full-time and considerable reallocation of time from housework does seem possible, the

male partner contributes over a third of the difference between her time and her non-working counterpart's time in meal preparation time, and time savings in cleaning may be better explained by compositional factors rather than the time spent in work by the woman.

Other household work activities largely confirm the picture that emerges from housework time. Women working part-time spend more time shopping and doing other household and garden activities than non-working women, resulting in a slightly higher total household work time. Women working full-time again reduce the time spent on these activities, although evidence of shopping being more likely to be jointly undertaken by both partners with greater women's involvement in paid work, results in household shopping time being considerably higher in working-wife households. This illuminates previous results where women's shopping time and behaviour is found to be unaffected by the woman's work status (Strober and Weinberg 1980, Piachaud 1982). Men's involvement in traditional male tasks, such as gardening, car, and household maintenance, is reduced with greater women's involvement in paid employment. This leaves total male household work time unaffected by the woman's work status. Instead substitution takes place within male household work categories; the man spends less time on male tasks and becomes more involved in traditionally female tasks where the woman is employed.[10]

Time spent in child care is the main element in time use that differs with the woman's work status.[11] The greater the woman's time committed to paid work the lower both her and her partner's time allocated to child care. Working women have, on average, fewer and older children in the household which, not surprisingly, appears to facilitate their undertaking paid employment.

Time spent by the woman in leisure activities in the home is reduced the more time she has committed to paid work; men's home leisure does not show any consistent relationship with the woman's work status. Working women also spend less time in outside leisure activities, though their partners spend considerably more time doing these, particularly if the woman works full-time. Taking the two types of leisure together, men's leisure increases from 34 hours 59 minutes through 37 hours 20 minutes to 39 hours 50 minutes per week as the woman's involvement in paid work increases. Thus although husbands of working women spend more time in housework, they are able to divert some of the time saved in child care to leisure, particularly leisure taken outside the home. For women the situation is reversed. Total leisure time is 42 hours 6 minutes for non-working women, 36 hours 48 minutes for women working part-time and 36 hours 33 minutes per week for women working full-time. Working women reallocate some of their leisure time to paid work and have less leisure than their husbands, the converse of the situation where the woman is not working.

The reallocation of time by women and by both partners together to cover the hours committed to paid employment is summarized in Table 6.2. The most important time saving is the lesser time devoted to child care in working-wife households; the time saved accounts for approximately half the time the woman is committed to work. A further quarter and seventh of the time is taken from the leisure of women working part-time and full-time

TABLE 6.2 *Women's and household time allocation changes to accommodate the woman's work*[a]

	Woman's time allocation		Household time allocation[b]	
	Part-time	Full-time	Part-time	Full-time
Hours committed to work above non-working wife household:				
	22hr 21min	40hr 14min	22hr 50min	39hr 24min
% work time accounted for by changes in time allocated to:				
Sleep	−15.9	−9.4	−20.8	−6.6
Housework	−10.1	−27.4	−5.6	−24.2
Other household work	+11.0	−2.0	+7.2	−5.0
Eating in the home	−6.3	−5.8	−3.4	−7.2
Personal care	+5.4	+2.7	+4.2	+1.2
Child care	−52.5	−42.5	−59.3	−55.0
Home leisure	−12.8	−12.1	−6.7	−15.9
Crafts	+5.3	+2.1	+3.1	+5.1
Other leisure	−16.6	−3.6	−9.6	+9.2
Other time uses	−7.7	−1.8	−9.0	−1.2

[a] Difference between working and non-working women/household time allocated to each activity as % of average weekly hours committed to work by the women/household above that of the non-working women/household.

[b] Sum of both partners' time uses.

respectively. However, this reduces to a seventh and a sixtieth for the household because of increased male leisure. Sleep is another area where time is saved, accounting for one-fifth of the time devoted to work in households where the woman works part-time. In households where the woman works full-time nearly three-tenths of her work time is reallocated from housework and other household work, but there is no saving in households where the woman works part-time.

Regressions of time use for working-wife households (see Table 6.3) show a notable lack of response of the woman's time allocation to her own wage.[12] An increase in the man's wage has the usual negative effect on women's paid work and positive effect on household production[13] but no effect on leisure. The main effect on women's time allocation is the number of children. As the number of children increases, time spent in paid work and in leisure activities is reduced and time spent in all household production activities increases. Male time allocation is not significantly determined by any of the explanatory variables.

The price and income determinants of the neoclassical time allocation model therefore appear to have limited predictive power for this sample. Although women's time allocation is quite responsive to partner's wage rates, household composition has stronger explanatory power. Men's time allocation appears to be set around norms rather than being responsive to economic or household composition variables. The lack of response of male time use to the number and ages of children has been found elsewhere (Pedersen 1990). The differential effects of children on male and female time allocation is crucial in understanding the constraints on women's time use.

The information on frequency of participation in activities for the larger sample (see Table 6.4) supports the time-budget findings. Men increase their participation in social activities the more the woman works outside the home. Participation in home activities is also increased for men whose wives work part-time. Thus men enjoy greater participation in all activities when their wives are working, although only participation in home activities is significant once other factors have been controlled. Women working part-time participate less in social activities than their non-working counterparts, whereas full-timers participate more. The reverse relationship is exhibited for participation in home activities and gives a frequency of participation in all activities that decreases as the woman's involvement in paid work increases. However, the differences are not significant and are not as large as might have been expected from the time-budget data.

Men are more likely to do social and all activities with other household members where the woman works, although the differences are not significant. Working women, particularly women working full-time, do significantly more social activities with other household members. However, women working part-time do less home activities with other members of the family resulting in their total activities with other household members being slightly lower than for their non-working counterparts.[14] Full-timers are significantly more likely to do all activities with other household members.

These results tend to suggest that although working women have considerably less time allocated to leisure this has only a limited effect on the degree to which they participate in various activities and, for full-timers, increases the likelihood of these activities being done with other household members. Thus less leisure time does not appear to curtail severely the number of activities and frequency with which working women participate in these activities. Instead a more intensive use of leisure time may be suggested. Men's activity participation generally is not affected significantly although there is a tendency for it to be higher where the woman is working. This, however, does not seem to be a product of the woman's work status *per se* but the ability to reallocate time savings in child care to leisure time.

The overall effect of the time allocation changes is to distribute the total work load more evenly between the two partners. If 'all work' activities are classified as time committed to paid work, all household work, and child care, men do a decreasing amount as the woman's work increases. Total work time is almost equalized between women working full-time and part-time but is considerably lower for non-working women. But, contrary to expectation, men's total hours of work are higher than the woman's when she is working part-time or non-working and only 22 minutes lower than the woman's where she is working full-time.

TABLE 6.3 *Time allocation regressions (working-wife households)*[a]

	Constant	Woman's net wage	Man's net wage	Other unearned income	Number of children	Age of youngest child	Age of woman	R^2
Female partner's time spent in:								
Paid work	222.44	−3.50	−16.64	−0.05	−30.70	5.33	−5.81	0.68
	(6.68)*	(−1.45)	(−2.52)*	(−0.52)	(−2.52)*	(2.53)*	(−0.22)	
Household production:	20.43	2.91	12.35	0.06	48.22	−3.27	−3.01	0.79
	(0.74)	(1.45)	(2.26)*	(0.78)	(4.79)*	(−1.87)	(−0.14)	
housework	44.08	3.18	9.14	0.02	32.13	2.22	−42.29*	0.68
	(1.93)	(1.92)	(2.02)	(0.31)	(3.85)*	(1.53)	(−2.36)*	
housework, gardening, shopping, etc.	24.73	3.17	16.49	0.01	28.47	1.39	−25.45	0.67
	(0.95)	(1.68)	(3.19)*	(0.10)	(2.99)*	(0.84)	(−1.24)	
child care	−4.29	−0.27	−4.13	0.05	19.75	−4.66	22.43	0.89
	(−0.48)	(−0.41)	(−2.31)*	(2.08)	(5.98)*	(−8.14)*	(3.17)*	
Leisure:	377.40	0.92	2.41	−0.01	−36.59	−2.47	51.86	0.46
	(9.49)*	(0.32)	(0.31)	(−0.09)	(−2.52)*	(−0.98)	(1.66)	
sleep	232.21	0.56	−3.39	−0.01	−0.26	−0.65	6.08	0.09
	(13.55)*	(0.45)	(−1.00)	(−0.16)	(−0.04)	(−0.60)	(0.45)	
eating and personal care	37.76	0.08	4.22	0.01	−1.64	0.92	−3.14	0.18
	(2.74)*	(0.08)	(1.55)	(0.14)	(−0.33)	(1.05)	(−0.29)	
leisure activities	107.43	0.28	1.58	−0.01	−34.69	−2.74	48.92	0.43
	(2.64)*	(0.09)	(0.20)	(−0.07)	(−2.34)*	(−1.07)	(1.53)	

Male partner's time spent in:

Paid work	227.83 (6.95)*	0.55 (0.23)	-5.92 (-0.91)	-0.01 (-0.09)	-1.52 (-0.13)	1.65 (0.79)	-6.78 (0.26)	0.14
Household production:	34.46 (1.01)	-0.01 (-0.01)	-2.16 (-0.32)	-0.04 (-0.47)	2.42 (0.19)	-0.19 (-0.09)	16.03 (0.60)	0.07
housework	28.31 (2.37)*	-0.69 (-0.79)	-2.49 (-1.05)	-0.02 (-0.75)	4.91 (1.12)	-0.12 (-0.16)	-3.12 (-0.33)	0.21
housework, gardening, shopping, etc.	32.07 (1.31)	0.31 (0.17)	0.55 (0.11)	-0.06 (-0.84)	-4.46 (-0.50)	-0.65 (-0.42)	6.22 (0.32)	0.08
child care	2.38 (0.12)	-0.32 (-0.23)	-2.71 (-0.71)	0.01 (0.22)	6.88 (0.98)	-0.84 (-0.69)	9.82 (0.65)	0.23
Leisure:	388.44 (10.56)*	-0.08 (-0.03)	7.50 (1.03)	0.06 (0.56)	-4.39 (-0.33)	-1.64 (-0.70)	3.48 (0.12)	0.17
sleep	218.20 (12.01)*	2.04 (1.55)	-1.74 (-0.48)	0.07 (1.52)	3.81 (0.57)	-0.83 (-0.72)	-2.00 (-0.14)	0.34
eating and personal care	22.19 (1.96)	-0.75 (-0.91)	2.99 (1.33)	-0.01 (-0.29)	0.24 (0.06)	0.20 (0.27)	7.26 (0.82)	0.27
leisure activities	148.05 (3.95)*	-1.37 (-0.50)	6.25 (0.84)	-0.01 (-0.10)	-8.44 (-0.62)	-1.00 (-0.42)	-1.78 (-0.06)	0.22

Note: * Significant at 5% level.
t ratio in brackets.
[a] dependent variables are number of ¼-hour units spent in each activity per week.

TABLE 6.4 *Partners' participation in activities by the woman's work status*

	Woman's work status:		
	Non-working	Part-time	Full-time
Index of frequency of participation in activities:			
Social activities (12)	127.5	131.9	134.1
Man			
Woman	138.7	127.5	144.1
Home activities (4)			
Man	140.6	165.7	138.4
Woman	158.4	161.3	140.5
All activities (19)			
Man	279.7	308.2	294.3
Woman	336.0	311.0	305.1
Average number of activities done with household members:			
Social (11)			
Man	4.8	4.9	5.6
Woman	4.7	4.9	5.4
Home (4)			
Man	2.4	2.3	2.0
Woman	2.1	1.8	2.1
All activities (15)			
Man	7.4	7.5	8.1
Woman	7.2	7.0	8.0
Sample	(45)	(30)	(35)

Analysis of variance[a]

	Participation in activities		With family members
	Two-way[b]	Three-way[c]	Two-way[b]
Social activities			
Man			
Woman			W
Home activities			
Man	W	W	
Woman	W AW^2		
All activities			
Man			
Woman			WA

[a] Inclusion of symbol Y (disposable income), W (woman's work status), A (age of youngest child), implies significance of 5% or more. Squared terms indicate interaction effects.

[b] Woman's work status and age of youngest child.

[c] Woman's work status, age of youngest child and disposable income.

SUMMARY AND DISCUSSION

Housework is an area in which time saving possibilities appear to be limited, particularly in households where the woman works part-time. Indeed time savings do not appear to occur primarily through the substitution of market goods and services, with the exception of meals at work; instead a substantial amount of any time saving made in housework by the woman is offset by the increased, if small, involvement of her partner. While men's contribution to housework time remains small this increased involvement supports Dolan and Scannell's (1987) finding and is of primary importance in highlighting the substitution of time between partners, an aspect which is not generally acknowledged in the existing literature. Thus substitution, in conjunction with reduced amounts of child care necessitated from both partners in households where women are working, serves to equalize men's and women's involvement in 'all work' as women's hours spent in the labour market increase. Of interest here is the nature of men's involvement in household work. Husbands of working wives do increase their contribution to primary housework but they also make a similarly increased contribution to shopping. Furthermore these increases are nearly entirely offset by a reduction in the time spent in traditionally male tasks, such as gardening and care maintenance. Thus men are not actually putting more time into their traditional household work when women are working but are getting more involved in the traditionally female tasks. This may be viewed optimistically as a move towards the breaking down of traditional gender segregation within the home, although a more cynical view may suggest that increased male participation in shopping may result from a desire to control expenditures within the household which may be less easily achieved when the woman is working unless the husband oversees or participates in the activity himself.

Working women find approximately half the time they devote to paid employment from reduced child care requirements. This is obviously consistent with female life-cycle patterns of employment and would also support historical findings of reduced fertility and increased female labour supply being inextricably related (Folbre 1982; Sprague 1988).

Leisure and sleep are the other main areas from which women reallocate time towards paid work. However, this has little effect on the number of activities in which they participate and instead may suggest that leisure time is used more intensively.

The standard neoclassical model appears to have limited explanatory power for household time allocation. Time uses are remarkably unresponsive to price and income variables and substitution between partners would not be predicted by models that require specialization to achieve gains from marriage. Housework time is little affected by wage variables or time spent in paid work; instead, cultural and social norms would appear to have more explanatory power. The invariance of housework time would imply only limited substitution between market goods and home-produced commodities and few differences in domestic production technology used in working-wife and non-working-wife households. The neoclassical emphasis on substitution out of household production into labour market work for women appears misplaced. Child care and leisure are the main areas from which time reallocation occurs, although the degree to which this reallocation occurs as a response to price and income variables is unclear. The neoclassical model needs to incorporate factors such as necessary housework time and limited market substitutes if a closer representation of reality is to be achieved. Life-cycle fertility decisions do appear to be relevant to labour market participation decisions and it is in this area, rather than home production, that the New Home Economics has something to offer. Leisure is the other area of interest; home production should be included in standard work/leisure models but only to the extent that it reduces the time available for substitution out of leisure.

There is some support for the more realistic two-person household time-allocation model discussed earlier. Partners do appear to be complements in the production of the child commodity; child-care time increases for both partners as the average household composition tends towards more and younger children. This complementarity is argued to reduce the degree of specialization in other time uses; the time-budget data indicates that both partners are likely to participate in all household production activities. Such a model allows substitution of time of the partners in these activities to be feasible, and the data suggest this is an option which may be used, particularly for meal preparation and washing up. The classification of household production activities is also useful. Housework can reasonably be classified as production which has few market substitutes as the time use in this activity remains fairly constant. However, the substitute commodity needs more careful definition, covering activities such as eating out, gardening, household maintenance, and crafts. In addition, the possibility of a leisure component in these should be allowed. Leisure could also be subdivided to cover leisure inside and outside the home, sleeping, and personal care time, with market goods categorized in a way which is associated with these time uses. The results from such a small sample can only be tentative but the time-substitution effects, in particular, suggest further research in this area could be fruitful and underline Becker's (1965) admonition that both time and money budget data are needed to fully examine household commodity demands and labour supply.

It was argued earlier that time uses can be linked to the structure of demand (Morgensen 1990) and here differences in working-wife and non-working-wife households' time uses are compared with the expenditure effects of women working identified in another study (Horrell 1991).

Using Family Expenditure Survey (FES) data for 1984, having a woman working in the household was found to decrease household expenditures on housing and fuel and increase expenditures on clothing, food purchased away from home (with a consequent decrease in expenditure on food prepared and eaten at home), domestic and personal care services, and alcohol,[15] once other factors were controlled.

Partners in working-wife households spend less time eating in the home; although these households did not report eating out more often in the time-budget week, this would fit with the substitution of expenditure on food eaten in the home by expenditure on food eaten outside the home found from FES data. The increased expenditure on alcohol found for households where the wife works full-time may also be linked to eating out more often. An alternative explanation offered by the time budgets is that the increased amount of leisure spent outside the home by the man may account for this increased expenditure. Additional time spent in personal care in working-wife households is reflected in increased expenditures on personal care services by these types of household. The increased expenditure on clothes may also relate to this time use.

Any reduction in housework time has been argued to be largely a result of smaller household size and possibly smaller size of house. This explanation accords with the finding of lower housing expenditure by working-wife households and also relates to the expenditure on fuel. The differences in housework time do not seem to be explainable by more labour-saving appliances in working-wife households as durables expenditure was unaffected by the woman's work status.

Plausible links between time use and expenditure effects in working-wife households can be established and there would appear to be a strong case for arguing that the time-use consequences of increased numbers of married women participating in the labour market can be followed through to the expenditure effects. The time-use investigation has highlighted the ways in which demand structure may alter. The neoclassical model's emphasis on reallocation of time away from household production when women work has been shown to be misplaced, and the compatible expenditure and time-use effects illustrate how both the allocation of time and money need to be jointly investigated to give rise to reliable predictions.

NOTES

1. For a single-person household the model is $Z = Z(X, L)$ where L is leisure and X goods. Goods can be home produced or purchased in the market, $X = X_M + X_H$ where $X_H = f(H)$, the time spent in home production, and is subject to diminishing marginal productivity. Work at home and work in the market are perfect substitutes as far as the direct utility they generate is concerned and the person is indifferent between consuming home-produced and market goods. Utility is maximized subject to the budget constraint $X_M = wN + \mu$, where μ is unearned income and N hours worked, and the time constraint $L + H + N = T$. Maximization results in the optimizing condition that the marginal rate of substitution for goods and leisure should equal the person's marginal productivity in home production, which in turn equals the wage rate if the person works in the market or the shadow price of time if the person does not work in the market: $U_L/U_X = f' = w$ (or w^*).

2. See Horrell (1991) for a full development of the arguments in this section.

3. With the Becker model a rise in the woman's wage rate with diminishing marginal productivity in home production would imply either that she does less household work or that the man does more; alternatively, both can alter their time allocations in the above directions.

4. Housework time was not clearly defined in this survey. Respondents gave the average time per week spent in this activity and may have included child care.

5. The time-budget part of the Social Change and Economic Life Initiative was instigated and organized by Professor Johnathan Gershuny, now of the University of Essex. I would like to thank him for making the diaries for Northampton households available to me.

6. Options for frequency of doing an activity were; once a week, once a fortnight, once a month, every few months, once or twice a year, or never. Who the activity was normally done with can be broadly classified as alone, with other household members, or with people from outside the household.

7. Social activities include swimming, playing sport, watching live sport, going to the theatre or a concert, to the cinema, to a pub or club, to a religious service, paying a social visit to someone's house, having someone round for a social visit, attending leisure activity groups, evening classes, and meetings of local groups. Home activities cover work in the garden, watching TV, reading a book or magazine, and going for a walk. All activities include going to the library, doing unpaid voluntary work, and doing unpaid help for people outside your household in addition to the above mentioned. The questionnaire did not ask who the unpaid voluntary work, unpaid help, and meetings for local groups or political parties were done with.

8. Time committed to work includes time spent working and taking breaks at the place of work, time spent travelling to work, and time spent doing, for instance, paperwork at home. Break times used for shopping, sports, and other activities are classified under these headings. For an argument in support of taking time committed to work rather than usual weekly hours as the relevant variable in determining other time allocations and the feasibility of women undertaking paid employment see Marsh (1991). Gronau (1977) also uses time committed to work rather than paid hours of work.

9. The household survey asked about outside help for a range of domestic activities, but only two households in the present sample reported help with cleaning, washing up, and laundry. One of these

employed paid help, the other received unpaid help; however, these were both households where the woman worked part-time.

10. This is supported by answers in the household survey asking which partner usually performed various household tasks. Men were more likely usually to do the washing up, cleaning, and cooking for the family when the woman worked full-time. Women working part-time were as likely usually to do these tasks as their non-working counterparts.

11. Child-care activities were included as such if they were direct and main activity child care (for instance, playing with a child, taking a child to school or activities, putting a child to bed, physically feeding the child, and dressing a child). Activities such as meal preparation and laundry which were done for all household members are classified under these headings.

12. This is even true for paid work but may result from consideration of time committed to work rather than hours of paid work. However, other studies using time committed to work have not found the own-wage variable insignificant (Gronau 1977; Pedersen 1990).

13. This appears to increase the woman's time spent in gardening, shopping, and other household production activities and reduce the time spent in child care, but has an insignificant effect on housework.

14. Women working part-time are quite likely to be involved in work that requires unsocial hours (Horrell and Rubery 1991), which may explain this result.

15. Alcohol expenditure was only increased for households where the woman worked full-time.

7

Money in the Household*

CAROLYN VOGLER

Recent changes in labour market conditions have led to specula-
tion about their possible impact on household relations. The
most striking of these changes has been married women's
increased participation in the labour market, combined with high
levels of unemployment (particularly male unemployment).
Between 1971 and 1986 the proportion of women in the
employed labour force rose from 38% to 45%, while unemployment rose from a mere 3.4% in 1972 to 13% in 1985 (and male
unemployment from 4.9% in 1972 to 15.6% in 1985). While the
increase in women's employment has mostly been in part-time
work, women are nevertheless coming to spend an increasing
proportion of their lives in employment and differences in the
total amount of time spent in employment by men and women
are declining (Martin and Roberts 1984). Recent evidence also
points to a polarization between no-earner and dual-earner
households, since male unemployment tends to be associated with
a wife's non-employment, whereas when husbands are in employment wives are also likely to be employed (McKee and Bell
1983). At the level of individual households, evidence thus points
to a great homogeneity of employment statuses between spouses,
as both tend to be either in or out of paid employment.

There are two broad interpretations of these changes for
household relations. Some commentators (Young and Willmott
1973) suggest the family is becoming a more egalitarian unit of
consumption, as power over decision making, access to financial
resources, and the distribution of domestic work are coming to
be shared more equally between spouses. Others (Morris and

* The author would especially like to thank Jan Pahl for invaluable help with
question design, advice in early discussions, and comments on the paper. Thanks
are also due to Muriel Egerton for advice on logistic analysis and to Duncan
Gallie for insightful comments and suggestions.

Ruance 1989) have, however, suggested that changes in labour markets are reinforcing rather than reducing inequalities in access to power and financial resources within the home. From this point of view, part-time work is seen as a way of increasing household income (and meeting employers' needs for labour) without upsetting the traditional division of labour between male breadwinners and female childbearers/secondary earners. Women's increased labour market participation is thought to have modified but failed to overcome inequalities in power, access to financial resources, and the division of labour within the home. The debate has wide ramifications in the social sciences since much economic and sociological analysis rests on the assumption that households operate as collective decision-making units within which partners have equal access to power over decision making, equal access to financial resources, and thus share the same living standard.

The objective of this paper is to assess the plausibility of these arguments with respect to patterns of financial allocation used within households. Using data acquired as part of a comparative study of six urban labour markets in Britain, we begin by classifying the main methods couples use to organize household money, in terms of Pahl's (1983) typology of household allocative systems. We then show how these are related to gender inequalities between spouses in control over financial decision making and in access to money as a resource. Finally, we discuss the main determinants of different allocatory systems and the extent to which they change over time.

The analysis is based on data from 1,211 couples interviewed as part of the Household and Community survey. Interviews were conducted jointly with both partners. In order to reduce the risk of consensus answers, a large proportion of questions were answered by means of self-completion booklets. Each partner was given a self-completion booklet in which they ticked their own answers, without conferring with each other. For a large proportion of questions we thus obtained independent answers from both husbands and wives. Whenever possible, analysis is based on both husbands' and wives' answers.

PATTERNS OF FINANCIAL ALLOCATION WITHIN HOUSEHOLDS

Early post-war studies of working-class families painted a graphic picture of marked inequalities between individuals in the same household. Husbands were often economic masters, enjoying greater power over decision making and higher living standards than wives (Young 1952; Dennis *et al.* 1956; Klein 1965). While two subsequent studies of the family claimed to have shown a long-term trend to greater equality in marriage consequent upon women's increased labour market participation, they failed to collect data either on inequalities in access to money as a resource or on inequalities in financial decision making (Bott, 1957; Young and Willmott 1973). They were thus unable to show how far financial decision making was genuinely becoming more consensual, rather than dominated by one partner, or how far financial resources were genuinely coming to be shared more equally.

Our first aim was to classify the main ways in which couples organized their household money using Pahl's (1989) typology of household financial allocative systems. Pahl identifies five basic systems of money management, four of which can be thought of as involving separate spheres of responsibility for household money—the female whole wage system, the male whole wage system, the housekeeping allowance system, and the independent management system—while the remaining pooling system involves joint or non-segregated spheres of responsibility for household finances.

1. In the *female whole wage system* wives have sole responsibility for managing all household finances. Husbands hand over the whole of their wage packet (minus their personal spending money) to wives, and the husband's responsibility for budgeting or making ends meet, ends with the handing over of the wage. Wives responding to Oakley's (1974) questionnaire resented this, on the grounds that they were the ones who had to worry about paying bills, while husbands could spend without worrying.

2. In the *male whole wage system* husbands have sole responsibility for managing all household finances, which may leave non-employed wives with no personal spending money.

3. The *housekeeping allowance system* involves separate spheres of responsibility for household expenditure. Husbands give their wives a fixed sum of money for housekeeping expenses, while the rest of the money remains in the husband's control and he pays for other items. Husbands have traditionally had the final say over the amount of the housekeeping allowance as well as over the purchase of other items. Wives who do not earn may have no personal spending money separate from the housekeeping money which is allocated for collective expenditure (Mays 1954; Dennis *et al.* 1956; Klein 1965; Zweig 1961). This system has traditionally been associated with higher-paid workers and middle-class couples in which the husband is the only earner (Dennis, Henriques and Slaughter 1956; Zweig 1961; Klein 1965; Oakley 1974; Edgell 1980).

4. In the *pooling system*, financial responsibilities are in principle non-segregated. Both partners are thought to have joint access to all or nearly all household money and both are thought to be responsible for management and expenditure from the common pool. This is thought to be typical of middle-class households where wives are in employment (Hunt 1980; Wilson 1987) although the mechanisms by which it operates on a daily basis are unclear. The ways in which management and control are exercised and the processes of conflict resolution are unspecified.

5. Finally, in the *independent management system*, both partners have independent incomes and neither has access to all the household money.

Respondents were asked to say which type of allocative system came closest to the way in which they currently organized their own household finances. It was clear from the data that the most commonly used system was undoubtedly the pool, chosen by a full half of all our respondents with the remaining half selecting one of the segregated systems. The most frequently used segregated system was the female whole wage system, used by more than half of those using a segregated system (26% of the overall sample). The male whole wage and housekeeping allowance systems were used by 10% and 12% respectively of the overall sample, and the independent management system by only 2%. The latter was too small for independent analysis and has thus been omitted from the subsequent discussion.

A first question to ask about the budgetary categories is how far the most commonly selected option, pooling, simply reflected a generalized ideological commitment to sharing and equality, as opposed to any real practices of joint financial management (Pahl 1989). We were able to explore this further by means of a separate indicator of money management which could be cross-checked against responses to the budgetary categories. The independent measure of money management asked *both* respondents and their partners to say who in their household had ultimate responsibility for organizing household money and paying the bills: the male partner, the female partner, or both equally. Each couple's responses were combined into a single five-point scale showing both partners' perceptions of money management, as well as the extent of agreement or disagreement between them.[1] The independent indicator of financial management clearly validated the segregated systems,[2] but confirmed that the pool was in fact very heterogeneous in terms of management practices. Only 39% of pooling couples both perceived finances as jointly managed, with almost as many disagreeing with each other—16% over whether they were jointly or husband managed and 18% over whether they were jointly or wife managed. A substantial minority of pooling couples also agreed that finances were managed by only one partner, the wife in 14% of pooling households and the husband in the remaining 13% of pooling households. In short, in as many as 61% of pooling households, at least one and often both partners nominated one or the other of them as ultimately responsible for management. These results clearly indicate that the general 'pool' category masks the existence of three analytically different forms of pool—the male pool, female pool, and the jointly managed pool—which need to be analysed separately rather than assumed a priori to be similar or the same as each other. It may be, for example, that in practice husband- and wife-managed pools are rather more similar to the male and female segregated systems than they are to the joint pool. Pooling couples have therefore been subdivided into three categories on the basis of both partners' responses to the management indicator. Those in which one or both partners claimed husbands were responsible for management have been classified as using a *male-managed pool*, and those in which one or both partners claimed wives were responsible for management were said to be using a *female-managed pool*, (there were no occasions where one spouse claimed male management and the other female management). The term *joint pool* was reserved for households in which both partners agreed that both were equally responsible for management. This produced the six-fold classification of allocatory systems shown in Table 7.1. The real or joint pool now accounts for only 20% of the overall sample with the nominal male- and female-managed pools accounting for a further 15% each.[3]

A second point to note about the allocatory systems is that they varied slightly by labour market. If we divide them into those involving female management, those involving male management, and the jointly managed pool, the male managed systems, especially the male whole wage system, were most prevalent in Coventry—traditionally a skilled working-class area with no historical tradition of married women's employment. The joint pool, on the other hand was most prevalent in Kirkcaldy—traditionally a coal-mining area which also provided good opportunities for women's employment, initially in linoleum and tex-

TABLE 7.1 *Household allocative systems showing different forms of pooling*

	%
Female whole wage	27
Female-managed pool	15
Joint pool	20
Male-managed pool	15
Male whole wage	10
Housekeeping allowance	13
TOTAL	100
Number [a] = (1 165)	

Note: These estimates are based on the *full* sample, from which the household survey respondents were drawn as a subsample. As a result of weighting, the total number of respondents in subsequent tables is higher.

[a] Number of respondents.

tiles and later in electrical engineering. Finally, traditionally low-wage Aberdeen was marked by a slightly higher proportion of female managed systems.

How far then were the different allocatory systems associated with differences in living standards between husbands and wives within the same household?

SYSTEMS OF FINANCIAL ALLOCATION AND INEQUALITIES IN THE HOUSEHOLD

Inequalities in Decision Making

Systems of financial allocation provide some indication of the different ways in which money is *managed* within households, but are they linked to inequalities either in financial decision making or in access to money as a resource? One way in which systems of money management may be related to differences in living standards between individuals in the same household is through the way in which they are related to inequalities in power over financial decision making. Inequalities in power over financial decision making may facilitate inequalities in access to money as a resource, which may culminate in differences in living standards between spouses in the same household.

As a point of departure, we distinguish between strategic control over household finances and financial management as an executive function, recognizing that the person exercising strategic control may be different from the person responsible for managing money on a day-to-day basis. Our previous question on ultimate responsibility for organizing household money and paying bills was an indicator of executive management, whereas strategic control can be thought of as referring to control over infrequent but important decisions such as which allocative system should be used, how much should be spent on collective domestic expenditure as opposed to personal spending money, and who has the final say over big financial decisions. Previous studies have shown that while wives are more likely to manage household finances, control is more often a male prerogative, associated with the breadwinning, primary-earner status (Edwards 1981*a*, 1981*b*; Wilson 1987).

Our main indicator of strategic financial control asked respondents to say who in their households had the final say in big
financial decisions, the male partner, the female partner, or both
equally. In the sample as a whole, 70% of respondents indicated
that financial decision making was joint, nearly a quarter (23%)
that the husband had the final say, and 7% that the wife had the
final say. There were no significant differences between male and
female respondents. However, strategic control varied markedly
with the type of allocative system used in the household. The
joint or female-managed systems were much more likely to be
equally controlled than the male-managed systems. Of couples
using the joint pool, 81% claimed to have equal control over
finances, as did 79% of couples using the female pool and 74% of
those using the female whole wage system, compared with only
61% of couples using the male pool, 56% of couples using the
male whole wage system and 50% of couples using the housekeeping allowance system.[4]

A very similar picture emerged from a more general indicator
of control over the most important decisions made in the household. Respondents and partners were both asked who in their
households had the most say over the most important decisions:
the male partner, the female partner, or both equally. When partners disagreed, this usually took the form of one person claiming
that control was joint whereas the other partner saw control as
either male or female dominated: when this kind of disagreement
took place the answer was coded as 'male control' or 'female
control' respectively. Couples using the joint or female-managed
systems were much more likely to have an equal say over the
most important decisions (78% and 70% respectively) than those
using the male whole wage or the housekeeping allowance systems (54% and 46% respectively). The two explicitly male-managed systems—the male whole wage and the housekeeping
allowance systems—were also associated with higher levels of disagreement between partners over who exercised control, than was
the case with households using the more egalitarian joint or
female-managed systems.

In order to construct a rough summary index of power within
the household which took account of both spouses' answers as
well as decision making in both the financial and the general
spheres, respondents' answers to the financial control indicator

making indicator. Households in which husbands exercised control in both spheres were said to be characterized by strong male
power, those in which wives exercised control in both spheres
were said to be characterized by strong female power and those
in which both partners exercised equal control in both spheres
were characterized by strong equality. Households in which husbands (or indeed wives) exercised control in one sphere while
decisions were made jointly in other spheres were said to be characterized by weaker male or female power. Two points emerge
from the data (see Figure 7.1). First, couples using the joint or
female-managed systems were markedly more egalitarian than
those using the male-managed systems, particularly the male
whole wage and the housekeeping allowance systems. Second,
husbands were much more likely to control finances than wives
and husbands were most likely to control finances when they also
managed them. In other words, when husbands managed finances
they were also likely to control them, whereas both wife and

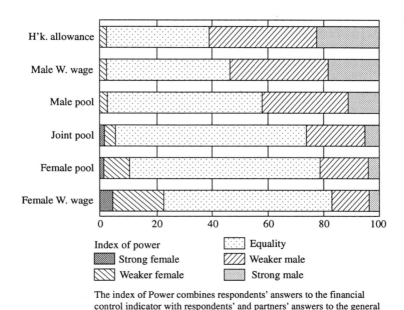

The index of Power combines respondents' answers to the financial
control indicator with respondents' and partners' answers to the general
decision-making indicator.

FIG. 7.1 Household and allocative systems by the index of power

joint management were much more likely to be subject to joint control. The implication is that male control is in fact exercised through male management whereas other forms of management, notably joint or wife management, are almost invariably circumscribed by joint control.

How far then can inequalities in power over financial decision making, in turn, be seen as laying the basis for inequalities in access to money as a resource?

Inequalities in Access to Money as a Resource

Individuals living in the same household may experience two rather different kinds of inequalities in access to money as a resource. Spouses may experience different levels of financial deprivation and also inequalities in access to personal spending money.

In order to provide a general picture of the experience of financial deprivation, respondents and partners were both asked to say which economies, if any, 'you *yourself* have had to do over the last two years to make ends meet when your household was short of money'. The focus of the question was clearly on the individual. The list which was presented to individuals included fourteen different items running from missing a meal or turning down the heat to borrowing money and getting into debt. The commonest things on which people had cut back were social activities, clothing, and holidays. Much rarer were reductions in heating and expenditure on food, together with measures such as getting into debt and borrowing (see Table 7.2).[5]

To provide a rough summary index of the experience of financial deprivation, we gave people a score of one for each action that they had taken to cope with financial difficulty. A measure of the difference in financial deprivation between husbands and wives living in the same household was then obtained by subtracting husbands' financial deprivation scores from those of their own wives. A minus score would indicate that husbands experienced higher levels of financial deprivation than wives, whereas a positive score would indicate that wives experienced higher levels of financial deprivation than husbands. As Table 7.3 shows, all the scores were positive, indicating that wives generally experienced greater financial deprivation than husbands, but the extent to which this was the case varied markedly with the type of allocatory system. The largest differences between spouses emerged among couples using the female pool, the female whole wage, and the housekeeping allowance systems, with index scores of 0.55, 0.52 and 0.44 respectively. Those using the male whole wage scored 0.15 and those using the male pool 0.11. Differences between spouses were smallest among couples using the jointly managed pool (0.07). These differences between spouses persisted within income groups and within classes. In households where inequalities between spouses were greatest—that is, those characterized by the two female-managed or housekeeping allowance systems—inequalities clearly increased as income declined (see Table 7.4). It can be argued, therefore, that wives in medium- and low-income female-managed and allowance households were doubly disadvantaged, since financial constraints emanating from outside the household (presumably from the labour market) were reinforced by clear gender inequalities in access to financial resources within households.

The second way in which allocatory systems may be associated with inequalities between spouses in access to money, is through their relationship with personal spending money (PSM). Access to personal spending money was measured by asking both respondents and partners who in their household had the most personal spending money: the male partner, the female partner, or both equally.[6] In the sample as a whole just over half (58%) of all couples both perceived personal spending money as equally distributed. A further 12% agreed that the husband had the most personal spending money, a tiny 4% agreed that the wife had most personal spending money, while the rest disagreed. Couples who disagreed over whether the wife had more personal spending money or whether they had equal amounts were coded as 'female more PSM', while disagreements over whether the man had more or whether spending money was shared equally were coded as 'male more PSM'. As Table 7.5 shows, inequalities in access to personal spending money varied markedly with the type of allocatory system used in the household. In households using the two female-managed and the housekeeping allowance systems husbands clearly had greater access to personal spending money than wives, even after controlling for social class. Similar results were found by Pahl (1989).

TABLE 7.2 *Household allocative systems and financial deprivation (%)[ab]*

	Female whole wage	Female pool	Joint pool	Male pool	Male whole wage	House keeping allowance	Total	Sig. of allocative system
Missed a meal								
Husband	6	1	4	2	4	5	4	not
Wife	9	7	4	4	3	7	6	not
Reduce meals spending								
Husband	17	15	16	12	12	7	14	5%
Wife	34	28	27	24	26	29	28	not
Turned down heat								
Husband	29	23	25	26	30	27	27	not
Wife	30	27	19	28	28	26	26	not
Cut down on social life								
Husband	51	49	47	46	39	36	46	5%
Wife	54	61	48	45	39	37	49	1%
Given up holiday								
Husband	41	42	37	36	31	25	37	5%
Wife	42	42	41	38	32	31	39	not
Cut back on clothes								
Husband	42	40	38	41	25	24	37	1%
Wife	59	60	46	54	46	52	54	6%
Reduced savings								
Husband	30	32	32	37	31	27	31	not
Wife	39	39	30	34	21	25	33	5%

Got into debt								
Husband	18	20	24	14	8	16	18	5%
Wife	17	18	18	10	7	12	15	5%
Financial help/others								
Husband	18	17	15	14	9	8	15	not
Wife	18	13	15	9	9	10	14	5%
Borrowed Money								
Husband	13	17	15	14	9	12	14	not
Wife	14	13	12	5	3	7	10	1%
Other[c]								
Husband	8	13	8	4	8	13	8	not
Wife	8	10	8	5	6	6	8	not
Number[d]								
Husband	(343)	(205)	(250)	(191)	(118)	(153)	(1 260)	
Wife	(343)	(205)	(250)	(191)	(118)	(153)	(1 260)	

[a] The question wording was as follows: 'Please tick *any* of the following that *you yourself* have had to do *over the last two years* to make ends meet when your household was short of money.'

[b] The percentages given are of those respondents who had done any of the items listed during the last two years when their households were short of money.

[c] For example, hire purchase goods repossessed.

[d] Number of cases on which percentages are based.

TABLE 7.3 *Differences between husbands and wives in financial deprivation (1)*

Allocative systems	Difference between spouses in financial deprivation (mean: 0.33)
Female-managed pool	0.55
Female whole wage	0.52
Housekeeping allowance	0.44
Male whole wage	0.15
Male-managed pool	0.11
Jointly managed pool	0.07
(Significance < 0.01)	

Note: To obtain a measure of the difference in financial deprivation between individual husbands and wives, husbands' financial deprivation scores were subtracted from those of their own wives. A minus score indicated that husbands experienced higher levels of financial deprivation than wives, whereas a positive score indicated that wives experienced higher levels of financial deprivation than husbands. The scale ranged from –7 to +9 with a mean of 0.324 and a standard deviation of 1.9.

TABLE 7.4 *Differences between husbands and wives in financial deprivation (2)[a]*

Standardized household income	Female-managed pool	Female whole wage	Housekeeping allowance
High income	0.4	0.3	–0.02
Medium income	0.7	0.7	0.5
Low income	0.7	0.7	0.7
Number[b]	(205)	(343)	(153)

(Significance of allocative systems <0.01 (no interaction) Significance of whole table <0.007)

[a] By allocative system, and controlling for total standardized household income. Total household income was standardized according to DHSS conventions, by the number of adults and children in the household, and then split into three equal categories: high, medium, and low.

[b] Number of cases on which figures are based.

TABLE 7.5 *Household allocative systems and differences between spouses in personal spending money (PSM)*

	All households						Total
	Female whole wage	Female pool	Joint pool	Male pool	Male whole wage	House keeping allowance	
Male more PSM	34	24	18	20	26	42	27
Agree equal PSM	50	61	67	70	55	47	58
Female more PSM	15	15	15	11	20	13	15
TOTAL	100	100	100	100	100	100	100
Number[a]	(324)	(196)	(232)	(179)	(109)	(138)	(1 178)
(Significance <0.0001)							

[a] Number of cases on which percentages are based.

Inequalities between spouses in financial deprivation and personal spending money thus tended to hang together. The two female-managed and the housekeeping allowance systems were clearly associated with the largest inequalities between husbands and wives, both in financial deprivation and in access to personal spending money. The joint, and to a lesser extent, the male-managed pools, on the other hand, were associated with greater equality both in financial deprivation and in access to personal spending money.

Patterns of Equality and Inequality within Households

How far then were inequalities in strategic financial control in turn associated with inequalities in access to money as a resource? Patterns of financial control and distribution point to the existence of three main types of household: those using the joint pooling system, those using one of the male-managed systems, and those using one of the female-managed systems. First, joint pooling households stood out from others in the extent to which there was equal strategic control over finances and equal access to money as a resource. Equal financial control appeared to reflect and reinforce equality in access to money as a resource. Secondly, in households using the three male-managed systems husbands were much more likely to control finances, and in allowance households male control was associated with marked inequalities in access to financial resources. In allowance households, finances were more likely to be both managed and controlled by husbands who suffered less financial deprivation than wives, and had greater access to personal spending money. Inequalities in strategic control over finances thus appeared to be translated into inequalities in the distribution of financial resources within households. This implies that the allowance system itself has changed little since Michael Young's description in 1952. Far from having slowly evolved into a less inegalitarian system (as some have suggested) the separation of responsibilities for household expenditure continues to privilege husbands at the expense of wives. In male whole wage and male pool households, however, where male control was associated with greater equality in access to money, a wife's access to financial resources may have been rather more conditional on the husband's continued good will, than among joint pooling couples, who were more likely to control their finances jointly. Finally, households using one of the two female-managed systems were characterized by a disjunction between strategic control over finances and access to money. Despite egalitarian or even female strategic control over finances, wives in these households experienced significantly higher levels of financial deprivation than husbands, while husbands had greater access than wives to personal spending money. This raises questions about the real meaning of equal or indeed independent female control in these households, suggesting it may be more nominal than real, heavily circumscribed by the husbands' needs for personal spending money and (as we see later) by labour market constraints. As Wilson (1987) argues, equal control in these households may thus serve an important ideological role in masking the real extent of inequality in access to money as a resource.

In summary, therefore, the data point to marked differences between three main types of household that render problematic singular conceptions of *the* household. The orthodox model of households as egalitarian decision-making units, within which resources are shared equally, applied to only a fifth (20%) of the households in our sample, notably to those using the joint pooling system.[7]

THE MAIN DETERMINANTS OF FINANCIAL ALLOCATORY SYSTEMS

What then were the main determinants of different allocative systems? Financial allocative systems have been seen in the literature as related to a range of highly interrelated labour market and life-cycle variables, as well as to class, education, parental socialization, the domestic division of labour, and normative attitudes to gender roles. Wilson (1987), for example, argues that the level of income is an important determinant of which allocatory system couples use, although other writers (Hunt 1980; Morris 1988) emphasize the importance of the source of income, particularly the extent to which income is derived from state benefits. Heavy dependence on state benefits, particularly with male unemployment, is thought to be associated with the female whole wage system. A third view is that allocative systems are shaped by both

TABLE 7.6 *Household allocative systems by standard-*
ized household income (£s per month)[a]

	Standardized household income
Female whole wage	624
Female-managed pool	658
Jointly managed pool	719
Male-managed pool	728
Male whole wage	755
Housekeeping allowance system	697
(Significance <0.05)	

[a] Total household income was standardized according to DHSS convention, by the number of adults and children in the household.

spouses' employment statuses mediated by class, socialization and normative attitudes to gender roles (Pahl 1984). Underlying this is a notion of the resource theory of power, according to which equal positions in the labour market are thought to be conducive to equality in financial arrangements within households, with unequal labour market positions being conducive to inequalities within households. Pahl (1989), for example, argues that women's power over financial decision making increases when they have an independent income from employment. The direction of causation, however, is unclear since egalitarian attitudes could be conducive both to egalitarian household relations, and to women's

TABLE 7.7 *Household allocative systems by male respondent's low pay (%)*

Male respondents	Female whole wage	Female pool	Joint pool	Male pool	Male whole wage	House-keeping allowance	Total
Low paid	30	24	14	17	17	11	20
Not low paid	70	76	87	83	83	89	80
TOTAL	100	100	100	100	100	100	100
Number[a]	(110)	(80)	(93)	(78)	(48)	(43)	(452)

Note: Low pay is defined on the basis of the Low Pay Unit's 1986 definition (i.e. gross earnings of less than £3.50 per hour).
[a] Number of cases on which percentages are based.

TABLE 7.8 *Household allocative systems by falling into arrears over payment of various bills* (%)

	Female whole wage	Female pool	Joint pool	Male pool	Male whole wage	House-keeping allowance	Total
Rent/mortgage	12	10	7	6	6	11	9
Gas bills	10	4	5	3	4	5	5
Electric bills	7	5	4	3	3	3	5

labour market participation. Most previous studies, however, have been too small scale to distinguish between women's full-time and part-time work to disentangle the direct and indirect effects of the various labour market and other factors. Finally, allocative systems have traditionally been seen in the literature as determined by the broader division of labour within the home.

Allocative Systems and Labour Market Factors

Turning first to labour market factors, allocative systems were found to be clearly related to the level of income, to both spouses' employment statuses, and to class, but not to the proportion of income derived from state benefits.

Table 7.6 shows the mean standardized household income for each allocatory system. The two female-managed systems (the female whole wage and female pool) were associated with the lowest household incomes, while two of the male-managed systems (the male whole wage and the male pool) were associated with the highest household incomes. The association between the two female-managed systems and the lowest household incomes also emerges from a number of other indicators. As Table 7.7 indicates, male respondents using these systems were more likely to be classified as low paid (Low Pay Unit's definition of less than £3.50 per hour (Low Pay Unit 1988)), while couples using these systems were more likely to have fallen into arrears with payments of rent, gas, and electricity (see Table 7.8).

In short the data confirm the finding that women are most likely to manage finances single-handedly in low-income households where financial management is likely to be a burden rather than a source of power, whereas men are more likely to manage

TABLE 7.9 *Household allocative systems by household employment status* (%)

	Both full-time	Both unemployed	Husband unemployed, wife full-time	Wife unemployed, husband full-time	Husband full-time, wife part-time	Husband full-time, wife non-employed	Husband unemployed, wife part-time or non-employed	Both non-employed	All systems
Segregated systems									
Female whole wage	27	16	19	20	30	24	38	28	27
Male whole wage	8	11	0	10	8	13	8	9	9
Housekeeping allowance	4	5	16	11	14	18	10	18	12
Pooling systems									
Equal pools	25	20	6	16	17	19	24	17	20
Male pools	17	19	24	18	14	13	14	12	15
Female pools	20	30	35	25	17	13	5	16	16
All pooling systems									
Sub-total	62	69	65	59	48	45	43	45	51
TOTAL	100	100	100	100	100	100	100	100	100
Number[a]	(340)	(14)	(18)	(61)	(377)	(279)	(77)	(44)	(1 210)

[a] Number of cases on which percentages are based.

money in higher-income households where the task is (presumably) less onerous. One of the main reasons why spouses in male whole wage and male pool households shared expenditure cuts reasonably equally may simply have been that their higher total household income necessitated fewer cuts. Interestingly, the two most polarized systems in terms of the distribution of financial resources within the household—namely, the housekeeping allowance system and the joint pool—were characterized by very similar average levels of total household income. This implies that the higher levels of financial deprivation and reduced access to personal spending money experienced by wives in allowance households were more the result of the rigid demarcation of financial responsibilities than particularly low total household incomes. As Morris (1989) argues, the rigid demarcation of financial responsibility in these households has traditionally served to protect husbands' personal spending money and limit wives' access to husbands' earnings.

Household allocative systems were also found to be clearly related to both spouses' employment statuses (see Table 7.9). Our measure of employment status makes two distinctions. Those currently in employment were classified as being in either part-time or full-time employment, those not currently in employment as either unemployed or non-employed. Part-time work was defined as less than 30 hours a week. Individuals were classified as 'unemployed' if they were *either* registered as unemployed *or* had been without work and looking for work in the previous four weeks.

The most important finding to emerge was that households in which wives were in full-time employment were significantly different, in terms of financial arrangements, from households in which wives were employed part-time or were non-employed. If the six methods of financial allocation are divided into the three pooling systems on the one hand and the three segregated systems on the other hand, women's full-time employment (and indeed women's unemployment) were associated with one of the pooling systems, whereas women's part-time and non-employment were associated with the segregated systems.

Some form of pooling was used in 62% of households where both partners were in full-time employment, 69% of households where both partners were unemployed, 65% of households where husbands were unemployed while wives worked full-time, and

59% of households where wives were unemployed while husbands worked full-time (see Table 7.9). Less than half the households where wives were in part-time employment or non-employed used a pooling system. The joint pool was most commonly used where *both* partners were in full-time employment (25%) and the female pool where one or both partners were unemployed. The latter are probably best conceptualized as relatively low-income households characterized by a relative homogeneity of spouses' commitment to the labour market. The relative homogeneity of labour market participation may be ideologically acknowledged by the term 'pool', while their low income may tend towards the use of the female-managed rather than the jointly managed pool. In households, however, where wives were in part-time employment or non-employed, couples' were less likely to use one of the pooling systems and more likely to opt for one of the segregated systems, although which one depended on the husband's employment status. Where husbands were unemployed (while wives were non-employed or worked part-time) the female whole wage system was most commonly used (38%), whereas where husbands were in full-time employment or non-employed (while wives were non-employed or worked part-time) housekeeping allowances or the male whole wage system were more common. In short, the key factor predicting whether or not couples called their system a pool was not whether wives participated in the labour market or not, but whether they were in *full-time* employment.[8] This supports Morris' (1984) argument that financial equality depends on a wife's full-time employment, since part-time work simply operates to reduce calls on the husband's wage, without increasing wives' influence over finances. These findings point to a modified and indeed stronger version of the resource theory of power, according to which equality in household financial arrangements depends crucially on women's full-time employment, rather than simply on employment *per se*. The length of time wives had been in full-time employment, however, was found to be unrelated to financial allocatory systems, which implies either that allocatory systems may play a role in determining wives' employment patterns or that both are mediated by another variable, such as attitudes.

Finally, household allocative systems were also found to be related to class as measured on the Goldthorpe schema (Goldthorpe 1987). Allocatory systems were more strongly

TABLE 7.10 *Household allocative systems by joint class* (%)

	Both service	Both intermediate	Both working	Husband higher	Wife higher	Total
Segregated systems						
Female whole wage	12	20	37	21	37	27
Male whole wage	11	10	7	12	8	9
Housekeeping allowance	8	20	9	17	7	12
Pooling systems						
Joint pool	27	19	19	20	17	20
Male pool	23	14	13	16	13	15
Female pool	20	17	14	15	18	16
All pooling systems						
Sub-total	70	50	46	51	63	51
TOTAL	100	100	100	100	100	100
Number[a]	(156)	(118)	(318)	(383)	(258)	(1 233)

(Significance <0.00001)

Note: Husbands' and wives' last class was measured on the Goldthorpe seven-class schema. Joint class was constructed by combining husbands' and wives' own current or last class position as measured on the Goldthorpe three-class model.

[a] Number of cases on which percentages are based.

related to husbands' current or last class than to wives' current or last class; they were more related to Erickson's dominance model of household class (Erickson 1984) than to husband's class; and finally they were more related to a model of joint class based on husbands' and wives' own current or last class than they were to Erickson's dominance model. On the basis of the joint class model, the female whole wage system was most commonly used where both partners were working class or where wives were in a higher class than husbands (especially where the wife was in the intermediate class and the husband in the working class, 39% of whom used this system). The explicitly male-managed systems were most commonly used in households where both partners were in the intermediate class or where husbands were in a higher class than wives (particularly where husbands were in the service class and wives were in the working class). All forms of pooling, but especially the joint pool were most commonly used where both partners were in the service class (see Table 7.10).

In summary, then, two points emerge from the data. First, there is support for Morris's stronger version of the resource theory of power. The joint pool was clearly associated with both partners being in similar labour market positions—namely, in full-time employment and in the service class. By contrast the male-managed systems were more characteristic of higher-income, service-, or intermediate-class households with the traditional disparity in spouses' labour market participation: typically, husbands were in full-time employment and wives in part-time or non-employment.

Secondly, the data also confirm the finding that women are most likely to manage money single-handedly where labour market constraints are most severe, namely, low-income, working-class households where husbands are unemployed or in low-paid work. In these circumstances, inequalities deriving from the labour market were reinforced by intrahousehold gender inequalities in terms of standards of living and access to personal spending money, with the brunt of both falling squarely on women.

The Implications of Parental Socialization, Education, and Generation

Allocative systems were found to be strongly related to the systems used by parents when respondents were young, to husbands' educational qualifications, and to respondents' age cohort or generation. Respondents and partners were both (independently) asked to say which allocative system their parents had used when they themselves were in their early teens. Almost all parents had used either the female whole wage system or the housekeeping allowance system (35% and 36% respectively) with only a small proportion using some form of pooling or the male whole wage system (19% and 9% respectively).[9]

Comparing respondents with their parents indicates a large decline in the housekeeping allowance system (36% to 12%), a marginal decline in the female whole wage system (35% to 27%), and a marked increase in some form of pooling (19% to 50%). However, despite these changes there was also considerable intergenerational continuity, especially among couples using allocatory systems that were more widespread in the 1950s and 1960s.

Nearly half of those using the female whole wage and housekeeping allowance systems, for example, had been brought up in households using these systems when they were young (46%) compared with only a quarter (25%) of those using some form of pooling (see Table 7.11). Socialization was weakest in the service class and strongest in the working class where the female whole wage system exercised much greater holding power than in other classes. Service-class couples were more likely than those in other classes to shift to the joint or male pool, regardless of which system their parents had used.[10]

Household allocative systems were also related to husbands' but not wives' educational qualifications. The most highly qualified men (i.e. those with A levels or above) were approximately twice as likely as those with fewer qualifications to use the joint pool: 32% of men with A levels used the joint pool as compared with 15% of men with O levels and 17% of men with no qualifications. Conversely men with no qualifications or only O levels were more than twice as likely as those with A levels to use the female whole wage system (31%, 30%, and 12% respectively). In other words, the most egalitarian form of financial management was most commonly used in households where husbands were highly educated.

Table 7.12 shows the relationship between allocative systems and the respondents' age cohort or generation. Consistent with

TABLE 7.11 *Household allocative systems and parental socialization*

Respondent's system

Parents' allocatory system	Female whole wage	Male whole wage	House-keeping allowances	Pool	Total
Female whole wage	46	38	33	29	35
Male whole wage	10	17	8	8	9
Housekeeping allowance	31	38	46	37	36
Pool	13	8	13	25	19
TOTAL	100	100	100	100	100
Number[a]	(283)	(105)	(125)	(551)	(1 064)
(Significance <0.0001)					

[a] Number of cases on which percentages are based.

the intergenerational shift away from the housekeeping allowance system, those aged over 40 were found to be more likely than those aged under 40 to use one of the explicitly male-managed systems (27% and 16% respectively). Those aged 30 to 39 were more likely than those in other age groups to use the female pool, which is consistent with a drift to greater quality at the ideological level, while those aged 20 to 29 were (interestingly) more likely than those in other age groups to use the female whole wage system. These patterns will be discussed in greater detail in the final section. While these differences could be interpreted either as age or as generational effects, as we show later, the lack of any longitudinal change within individual households strongly supports the generational interpretation.

The Domestic Division of Labour and Attitudes to Gender Roles

Patterns of financial allocation have traditionally been seen in the literature as strongly related to, or indeed part of, a broader

TABLE 7.12 *Household allocative system by respondent's age (%)*

| | Age of respondent | | | | | | |
	20–29	30–39	40–49	50–61	All under 40	All over 40	Total
Segregated systems							
Female whole wage	34	24	26	28	27	2	27
Male whole wage	8	5	15	10	6	13	9
Housekeeping allowance	8	12	14	15	10	14	12
Pooling systems							
Joint pool	20	21	18	20	21	19	20
Male pool	15	17	13	15	17	14	15
Female pool	16	21	14	13	19	13	16
All pooling systems							
Sub-total	51	59	45	48	57	46	51
TOTAL	100	100	100	100	100	100	100
Number[a]	(264)	(410)	(351)	(253)	(674)	(604)	(1 278)
(Significance <0.0002)							

[a] Number of cases on which percentages are based.

overall division of labour within the home. Jointness in financial management is thought to be an aspect of segregation or jointness in the general division of domestic labour (Bott 1957). Recent case study literature, however, suggests that the key factor underlying access to household resources is a self-identity as a breadwinner. This is supported by our own data, showing that allocatory systems were more strongly related to the allocation of breadwinning responsibilities than they were to the domestic division of labour *per se*.

Our measures of the domestic division of labour attempt to take seriously the argument that the crucial factor structuring behaviour and attitudes may not necessarily be who undertakes a specific task at any specific time (which may vary considerably depending on circumstances) but who has ultimate responsibility for ensuring broad areas of household work are undertaken

TABLE 7.13 *Household allocative systems and the domestic division of labour* (%)

	Female whole wage	Female pool	Joint pool	Male pool	Male whole wage	House-keeping allowance	Total
Who has ultimate responsibility for income							
Both agree male	45	44	35	53	65	80	50
Disputed male	21	29	26	26	16	13	23
Both agree equal	27	23	37	19	18	6	24
Disputed or agree female	7	5	2	2	1	1	3
TOTAL	100	100	100	100	100	100	100
Number[a]	(291)	(189)	(225)	(172)	(104)	(138)	(1 119)
(Significance <0.00001, Cramers V. 18)							
Who has ultimate responsibility for housework							
Both agree female	79	74	67	66	78	86	75
Disputed female	13	20	19	24	17	9	17
Agree equal or disputed male	7	5	14	11	6	5	8
TOTAL	100	100	100	100	100	100	100
Number[a]	(330)	(198)	(234)	(184)	(108)	(149)	(1 203)
(Significance <0.00003, Cramers V.12)							

[a] Number of cases on which percentages are based.

adequately, which is likely to be more stable over time. Respondents and partners were both asked whether the husband, wife, or both equally had *ultimate responsibility* for two broad areas of domestic life: ensuring the family had an adequate income and ensuring the housework was done properly. Table 7.13 shows couples' answers. Two points emerge from the data. First, patterns of financial allocation were more strongly related to responsibilities for breadwinning than they were to responsibilities for housework: the vast majority agreed that wives were responsible for housework. The second point is that couples using the joint pool were most likely to agree that responsibilities for breadwinning and housework were shared equally, whereas those using the housekeeping allowance system were most likely to give traditional gendered responses in both areas. This pattern persisted within classes, income groups, and dual/single-earner households, indicating that it was associated with the budgetary categories *per se*, rather than being an artefact of other variables.

The current division of domestic responsibilities (i.e. couples' current behaviour) may not necessarily correspond with their individual attitudes to gender roles, either inside or outside the household. Individuals, for example, may not regard their current domestic division of labour as legitimate and financial allocatory systems may be more related to individuals' normative attitudes than to their current behaviour. In order to test this hypothesis, couples were questioned on their attitudes to gender roles both inside and outside the home.

Normative attitudes to gender roles *within* the home were measured by asking both respondents and partners whether they thought the husband, the wife, or both equally *should* have ultimate responsibility for: ensuring the family had an adequate income and ensuring the housework was done properly.[11] As can be seen in Table 7.14 systems of money management were most strongly related to normative views on who should be responsible for breadwinning and less strongly related to normative views about who should be responsible for housework. Couples using the joint pool were more likely to hold relatively egalitarian attitudes towards breadwinning and housework, than those using other systems, particularly the housekeeping allowance system.

In order to construct a rough summary index of traditionalism in individuals' attitudes to the domestic division of labour, indi-

TABLE 7.14 *Couples' normative attitudes to gender roles: perceptions of who should be responsible for income and housework* (%)

	Female whole wage	Female pool	Joint pool	Male pool	Male whole wage	House-keeping allowance	Total
Income							
Agreed male	43	39	30	40	50	62	42
Disputed male	27	30	30	31	32	31	30
Agree equal	22	29	40	27	18	6	25
Female agree/							
disagree	8	2	—	2	—	1	3
TOTAL	100	100	100	100	100	100	100
Number[a]	(314)	(197)	(229)	(179)	(109)	(144)	(1 172)
(Significance <0.00001, Cramers V. 16)							
Housework							
Male agree/							
disagree	2	—	2	3	3	—	2
Agree equal	11	16	27	23	10	7	16
Disputed female	29	24	28	26	31	26	27
Agree female	57	60	43	47	56	66	54
Total							
disagreement	2	1	1	1	1	1	1
TOTAL	100	100	100	100	100	100	100
Number[a]	(332)	(202)	(234)	(187)	(111)	(150)	(1 216)
(Significance <0.00003, Cramers V.16)							

[a] Number of cases on which percentages are based.

viduals were given a score of one for each traditional response to the normative questions on who should be responsible for bread-winning and housework.[12] Individuals' scores were then summed, producing a scale ranging from 0 to 2, with low scores indicating non-traditional attitudes and high scores indicating traditional attitudes. As can be seen in Table 7.15, after controlling for household class, individuals using the joint pool were least traditional in their views about how domestic responsibilities should be allocated, while those using the housekeeping allowance system were most traditional in their attitudes.

Normative attitudes to gender roles *outside* the home were measured by a series of Likert scales relating to inequalities in

TABLE 7.15 *Allocative systems by traditional attitudes to the domestic division of labour*[a]

	Female whole wage	Female pool	Equal pool	Male pool	Male whole wage	House-keeping allowance
Male respondents						
All	1.4	1.3	0.9	1.1	1.3	1.6
Service class	1.4	1.0	0.8	0.9	1.3	1.6
Intermediate class	1.2	1.6	1.0	1.4	1.4	1.6
Working class	1.4	1.5	1.1	1.3	1.3	1.6

(Significance of class <0.009; Significance of allocation system <0.001; Significance of whole table <0.001)

	Female whole wage	Female pool	Equal pool	Male pool	Male whole wage	House-keeping allowance
Female respondents						
All	1.3	1.1	1.0	1.3	1.3	1.6
Service class	0.9	0.9	0.8	1.0	1.4	1.6
Intermediate class	1.2	0.9	0.9	1.0	1.2	1.6
Working class	1.5	1.4	1.1	1.7	1.4	1.5

(Significance of class <0.001; Significance of allocation system <0.002; Significance of whole table <0.001)

Note: The higher the score the more traditional the views on who *should* be responsible for the housework and ensuring the family has an adequate income.

[a] Controlling for household class.

men's and women's labour market participation. Individuals were asked to say how far they agreed or disagreed with the following three statements:

1. 'Men are more suitable than women for positions of responsibility at work.'
2. 'I'm not against women working but men should still be the main breadwinner in the family.'
3. 'In times of high unemployment married women should stay at home.'

Individuals' responses to each of the three items were aggregated into an index of *sexist attitudes*, with high scores denoting sexist attitudes, and low scores, less sexist attitudes.[13] Men's sexist attitudes were found to be clearly related to the allocatory system

TABLE 7.16 *Allocative systems by husband's sexist attitudes to women's labour-market participation*[a]

	Female whole wage	Female pool	Equal pool	Male pool	Male whole wage	House-keeping allowance
Male respondents						
All	8.3	7.7	6.7	7.4	8.9	9.2
Service class	7.9	7.2	6.1	7.1	8.5	8.1
Intermediate class	7.3	7.9	6.6	8.2	8.5	9.9
Working class	9.1	8.0	8.0	7.6	10.1	10.1

(Significance of class <0.001; Significance of allocation system <0.001; Significance of whole table <0.001)

Note: The higher the score the more sexist the views on women's labour market participation.

[a] Controlling for household class, which was constructed by combining each partner's Goldthorpe class according to Erickson's dominance model.

used in the household, whereas women's were not. As can be seen in Table 7.16, men using the joint pool were least sexist in their attitudes to women's labour market participation, while those using the housekeeping allowance and male whole wage systems were most sexist in their attitudes.[14]

The Relative Importance of Determinants of Allocative Systems

Up to this point we have considered variables singly or in groups. In order to assess the relative importance of labour market-factors, socialization, education, generation, and attitudes, we carried out a series of logistic regressions on the two allocative systems which seemed to be at opposite extremes in terms of many of the variables examined: those were the joint pool and the housekeeping allowance system. As can be seen in Table 7.17 the four strongest influences on the joint pool were both spouses' socialization, the husband's educational qualifications, the husband's attitudes to the domestic division of labour, and the wife's employment status. Husbands brought up in pooling households when they were young and husbands with A levels, were nearly twice as likely to use the joint pool as husbands

TABLE 7.17 *Logistic regressions on the joint pool and housekeeping allowance systems*

Variables	Estimate	Standard error	Odds ratio	Chi-sq	df	p*
Joint pool						
Husband's parents used pool	0.6138	0.2094	1.8	16.4	1	<0.001
Wife's parents used pool	0.4450	0.2095	1.6	6.2	1	<0.025
Both in full-time employment	0.1684	0.1855	1.2	5.7	1	<0.025
Male has A levels	0.5973	0.2041	1.8	10.3	1	<0.005
Husband has traditional attitudes	−0.4306	0.09911	0.3	16.9	1	<0.001
Kirkcaldy	0.5189	0.1959	1.7	6.7	1	<0.025
Constant	−3.7	0.5191	0.02			
Number^a = (1 063) pseudo G^2 = 0.06						
Housekeeping allowance						
Both over 40 years old	0.6743	0.1952	2.0	11.5	1	<0.001
Both in intermediate class	1.033	0.2502	2.8	14.2	1	<0.001
Husband in service class	0.8918	0.2556	2.4	9.4	1	<0.005
Husband full-time, wife non-employed	0.7164	0.2435	2.1	10.4	1	<0.005
Husband full-time, wife part-time employed	0.4160	0.2276	1.5	5.9	1	<0.025
Husband's parents used Allowance	0.4637	0.1970	1.6	5.3	1	<0.025
Male has A levels	−0.5511	0.3226	0.6	4.9	1	<0.05
Husband has sexist attitudes	0.09875	0.04382	3.6	7.3	1	<0.01
Husband has traditional attitudes	0.3804	0.1408	3.1	7.8	1	<0.01
Constant	−4.319	0.4478	0.01			
Number^a = (1 079) pseudo G^2 = 0.09						

^{a} Number of cases on which the statistics are based.

not brought up in pooling households and husbands without A levels. Conversely husbands with traditional attitudes to the domestic division of labour were 70% less likely to use the joint pool than those with traditional attitudes.[15] Wives brought up in pooling households when they were young were 1.6 times more likely to use the joint pool than those not brought up in such households and wives currently in full-time employment were slightly more likely to use the joint pool than wives in other employment statuses. The husband's socialization and education thus appear to have a stronger impact on the use of the joint pool than either the wife's socialization or the wife's current employment status. Finally, we have one area effect. Couples living in Kirkcaldy were more likely than those in other areas to use the joint pool, after controlling for other factors.[16]

The four strongest influences on the housekeeping allowance system, however, were husbands' attitudes to women's labour market participation, husbands' attitudes to the domestic division of labour, spouses' joint class position and the husband's class position. Husbands with sexist attitudes to women's labour market participation[17] and traditional attitudes to the domestic division of labour were over three times more likely to use the housekeeping allowance system than husbands with less traditional attitudes. Intermediate-class couples (as measured on the joint-class model) were 2.8 times more likely to use the allowance system than couples in other classes and service-class husbands were 2.4 times more likely to use allowances than husbands in other classes. Use of the allowance system, however, was also related to both spouses' age cohort, wives' employment status, husbands' socialization, and husbands' education. Couples over 40 years old were twice as likely to use the allowance system as those under 40 years old. Non-employed wives and wives in part-time employment were (respectively) 2.1 and 1.5 times more likely to use allowances than wives in other employment statuses. Husbands brought up in families using the allowance system when they were young were 1.6 times more likely to use this system themselves, while husbands with A levels were 40% less likely to use allowances than those without A levels.

In short, then, after controlling for other factors, allocatory systems were found to be more strongly related to the husband's characteristics, particularly his attitudes, education, socialization, and social class, than they were to the wife's characteristics, notably her employment status. Wives' normative attitudes were found to be insignificant.

How, then, were the various labour market and attitudinal factors actually related to the system of financial allocation used

TABLE 7.18 *Logistic regressions on the joint pool and housekeeping allowance systems—including the male breadwinner variable*

Variables	Estimate	Standard error	Odds ratio	Chi-sq	df	p*
Joint pool						
Husband's parents used pool	0.6230	0.2107	1.9	16.4	1	<0.001
Wife's parents used pool	0.4242	0.2108	1.5	6.2	1	<0.025
Both in full-time employment	0.015	0.1953	1.02	5.7	1	<0.025
Male has A levels	0.6428	0.2059	1.9	10.3	1	<0.005
Husband has traditional attitudes	−0.3418	0.1060	0.4	16.9	1	<0.001
Kirkcaldy	0.5074	0.1968	1.7	6.7	1	<0.01
Agree male is breadwinner	−0.4568	0.1914	0.6	5.7	1	<0.025
Constant	−3.011	0.5915	0.05			
Number[a] = (1 063) pseudo G^2 = 0.07						
Housekeeping allowance						
Both over 40 years old	0.7830	0.1995	2.2	11.6	1	<0.001
Both in intermediate class	1.090	0.2564	3.0	14.2	1	<0.001
Husband in service class	0.7914	0.2590	2.2	9.4	1	<0.01
Husband full-time, wife non-employed	0.2786	0.2564	1.3	10.4	1	<0.01
Husband full-time, wife part-time employed	0.2121	0.2353	1.2	6.0	1	<0.01
Husband's parents used Allowance	0.4514	0.2005	1.6	5.3	1	<0.02
Male has A levels	−0.5603	0.3238	0.6	4.9	1	<0.05
Husband has sexist attitudes	0.09344	0.0445	3.4	7.3	1	<0.01
Husband has traditional attitudes	0.09615	0.1489	1.3	7.8	1	<0.01
Agree male is breadwinner	1.288	0.2459	3.6	25.5	1	<0.001
Constant	−4.523	0.4595	0.01			
Number[a] = (1 079) pseudo G^2 = 0.13						

[a] Number of cases on which the statistics are based.

within the household? We showed earlier that budgetary arrangements were strongly related to whether husbands occupied the status of primary breadwinner in the family (see Table 7.13). When a dummy variable indicating whether both partners agreed that husbands were ultimately responsible for breadwinning was entered into the equations (as in Table 7.18) the husband's status as breadwinner was found to have a clear impact on the association between budgetary arrangements and both labour market factors and husbands' normative attitudes.[18] In allowance households, the addition of the male breadwinner variable reduced the coefficients for wives' non-employment and part-time employment from 0.7 and 0.4 to 0.3 and 0.2 respectively and for husbands' attitudes to the domestic division of labour from 0.38 to 0.1. In joint-pooling households, the addition of the male breadwinner variable reduced the coefficient for wives' full-time employment to insignificance (i.e. from 0.17 to 0.02) and that for husbands' attitudes to the domestic division of labour from 0.4 to 0.3. At the same time, however, the male breadwinner variable increased the pseudo G^2 for each equation, thus indicating that it was adding something over and above employment status and attitudes *per se*. It was clearly the most important variable predicting the housekeeping allowance system and the third most important variable (after husbands' socialization and education) predicting the joint pool. When husbands occupied the status of primary breadwinner, couples were three and a half times *more* likely to use the housekeeping allowance system and 40% *less* likely to use the joint pool, even after controlling for the wife's employment status and the husband's attitudes.

That breadwinning is so clearly related to employment status and attitudes and also plays such a key role in explaining allocatory systems, even after controlling for employment status and attitudes, implies that it also plays an important role in mediating the latter. This is in fact supported by a number of qualitative studies. Hunt (1980), Brannen and Moss (1987), and Mansfield and Collard (1988), for example, show how the gendering of breadwinning occurs very early on in marriage, as a prefiguration of future expectations of parenthood roles.

In the early days of marriage, often when both partners are in full-time employment, couples come to adopt a gendered notion of a primary breadwinner, which then plays a fundamental role in structuring both partners' future behaviour both in the labour market and in the home. Men's jobs come to be regarded as more fundamental in providing for basic family expenditure than women's jobs, which are regarded as temporary and potentially disposable. This is partly because of men's greater earning power in the longer if not the shorter term and partly because of men's disinclination to stay home to look after children should it become necessary for one partner to do so. Men themselves thus come to be afforded the status and prestige of being primary breadwinners, while women on the other hand are expected to assume primary responsibility for the care of pre-school children, together with most of the domestic work. While this may not necessarily be regarded as legitimate, especially by wives, it tends to be regarded as inevitable and thus plays a key role in structuring social relations within the household. This is thought to be one of the main reasons why increases in women's labour market participation have so far failed to challenge fundamentally the traditional division of labour within the home.

In summary, then, the data point to the importance of the gendering of the breadwinner role, both in determining which allocatory system couples use and in mediating the relation between allocatory systems and other variables.

TOWARDS EQUALITY? CHANGES IN ALLOCATORY SYSTEMS OVER TIME

How far, then, has women's increasing participation in the labour market been associated, as the literature has suggested, with a shift to greater equality in household financial arrangements over time?

The data make it possible to examine changes in household financial arrangements in three different ways: first, intergenerationally (comparing couples with their parents); second, on a cohort basis (comparing age groups with each other); and third, longitudinally, focusing on changes within individual households as spouses move between different employment statuses. If the thesis of a progressive shift to greater equality in household financial arrangements were correct we would expect to find significant shifts from the relatively inegalitarian female whole wage, male whole wage and housekeeping allowance systems, to the relatively egalitarian joint pool, on all three measures.

As we have seen, comparing couples with their parents indicated a large decline in the housekeeping allowance system (36% to 12%), a marginal decline in the female whole wage system (35% to 27%), and a large increase in some form of pooling (19% to 50%). Only 20% of respondents, however, used the egalitarian joint pool. If we assume that parents as well as respondents could be divided into the three roughly equal pooling categories (i.e. the male, female, and joint pools), we estimate a moderate 14% increase in the use of the joint pool, together with moderate increases in the ideologically equal but practically inegalitarian male and female pools (14% and 11% respectively). The decline of the housekeeping allowance system would not appear, then, to have been associated with any significant intergenerational shift to greater equality in household financial arrangements. The most pronounced change has in fact been to one of the female managed systems.[19]

The thesis that intergenerational shifts have not been associated with any very marked increase in greater equality in household financial arrangements is also supported by the cohort analysis shown earlier in Table 7.12. While those under 40 years old were less likely to use the housekeeping allowance system than those of 40 years or over, they were no more likely than the latter to use the egalitarian joint pool. As we showed earlier those aged 30–39 were more likely than those in any other age group to use the female pool, which is consistent with increased commitment to sharing and equally at least at the ideological level. Those aged 20–29, however, were more likely than those in other age groups to use the female whole wage system.[20] In the youngest age group, therefore, we may be witnessing the resurgence of a very traditional method of financial allocation associated with marked inequalities between spouses in access to money as a resource.

Finally, we also examined the extent to which budgetary arrangements changed longitudinally within individual households as spouses moved between different employment statuses. Respondents were asked what their last change in employment status had been (becoming unemployed, becoming non-employed, starting work, changing to full-time, or changing to part-time work), and whether they had changed the way they organized their household finances since their last change in employment status. Only 2.1% of the total sample (10% of those with a relevant labour market change) had changed their system of financial allocation since their last change in employment status.[21]

Among women, changes to part-time work were never associated with changes in allocatory systems, although stopping work was associated with a shift from pooling to the housekeeping allowance system. Conversely starting work or changing to a full-time job were associated with shifts from the housekeeping allowance system to the joint and male pools and from the female whole wage system to the joint and female pools. There was no evidence that male unemployment was associated with any shift to the female whole wage system.[22] This implies that the greater prevalence of the female whole wage system among those in the youngest age group is best interpreted as a generational change, related to general increase in job insecurity and financial constraint experienced by those in the lowest social class (who are most vulnerable to unemployment) when they first set up home together, rather than to any specific experience of unemployment.

CONCLUSION

These results do not support the theory that changes in labour market participation are leading to greater equality in household financial arrangements in any deterministic way.

While the inegalitarian housekeeping allowance system is now used much less than in the past, its decline has been associated with a moderate generational increase in the joint pooling system together with somewhat larger increases in the female whole wage system and the female-managed pool. These two female-managed systems have been shown to be associated with marked inequalities between men and women in access to personal spending money and even larger inequalities in financial deprivation than the housekeeping allowance system.

The data are therefore consistent with the thesis of a growing polarization between the two female-managed systems on the one hand, within which women clearly bear the brunt of both an inadequate total household income and an unequal distribution of income within the home, and the joint pool, on the other hand, within which financial resources are much more equally shared. It seems likely that significant shifts to greater equality in household financial arrangements will depend not just on women's greater participation in the labour market as full-time workers but also on effective challenges to the husband's traditional status as the main breadwinner in the family.

NOTES

1. Since almost all disagreement between partners took the form of one partner claiming management was joint while the other claimed it was undertaken by only *one* partner (rather than one partner claiming it was done by one spouse while the other partner claimed it was done by the other spouse) the five-point scale was as follows:

   (a) agree female;
   (b) disagree female or equal;
   (c) agree equal;
   (d) disagree male or equal;
   (e) agree male.

   In the sample as a whole 70% of couples gave exactly the same answer.

2. Of couples using the female whole wage system, 71% agreed that wives were ultimately responsible for organizing money; 77% of couples using the male whole wage system agreed that husbands were ultimately responsible for organizing money; and 49% of couples using the housekeeping allowance system agreed husbands were responsible for organizing money, with a further 25% of those using this system disagreeing over whether responsibility lay with the husband or whether it was joint.

3. While there were no *statistically significant* differences between male and female respondents, male respondents were initially more likely than female respondents to classify their system as a joint pool (55% and 50% respectively), whereas female respondents were somewhat more likely than male respondents to claim that they used the female whole wage system (29% and 24% respectively). In reality, however, the excess of male over female respondents selecting the pool all turned out to be using the male-managed pool, which implies that male respondents were slightly more likely than female respondents to mask their own management of finances under the label of 'pooling'.

4. An interesting difference emerged between male and female respondents using the female whole wage system. Male respondents were twice as likely as female respondents to see wives as exercising independent financial control whereas female respondents were more likely to see financial control as joint or as exercised by husbands. Wives using the female whole wage system thus felt they had less independent control over finances than husbands perceived them as having. This raises a question mark over the extent to which wives using this system really controlled as opposed to simply managed finances, and tends to support findings in the literature emphasizing the constraints on women using this system (Wilson 1987; Pahl 1987).

5. At the aggregate level wives were much more likely than husbands to have experienced cuts in meals expenditure (28% and 14% respectively) and clothing (54% and 37% respectively). The former is likely to reflect both gendered responsibilities for expenditure on food and wives' tendency to protect husbands from the effects of reductions. Charles and Kerr (1987), for example, found that when husbands were in employment, wives deliberately tried to shield them from the effects of reductions in food spending by cutting back on the quality of food for themselves and children so as to ensure that husbands received a disproportionate share of what was available. In short, the husbands in our sample may have been genuinely less aware than wives of reductions in food expenditure and also less subject to the effects of cutbacks.

6. Given the strong normative emphasis on the importance of sharing and equality in marriage, people may have been reluctant to admit to having different amounts of personal spending money, which means we may be underestimating possible inequalities in this respect.

7. It might be objected, of course that the small 2% of households using the independent management system may, in fact, have been the most egalitarian households in our sample, and that omitting them from the analysis led us to underestimate the real extent of equality within households. This is not supported by the data. Somewhat surprisingly perhaps, finances in independent management households were more likely to be controlled by husbands, who also had more access than wives to personal spending money. Only 25% of independent management households were characterized by strong equality in financial and other decision making, and only 30% by equal access to personal spending money. Fully 70% were characterized by strong or weak male power and 45% by greater male access to personal spending money. Independent man-

agement households were very similar to those using the housekeeping allowance system, and in the previous typology, would have been classified in the 'male controlled' category.

8. A wife's employment status was also found to mediate the impact of male unemployment on household finances. When wives were in full-time employment, male unemployment was most likely to be associated with the female pool whereas when wives were in part-time employment or non-employed, couples were more likely to use the female whole wage system.

9. There were no differences between male and female respondents in the systems used by their parents.

10. Amongst intermediate-class respondents the housekeeping allowance system exercised stronger holding power than in other classes, with 21% of those whose parents or parents-in-law had used this system, continuing to use it themselves.

11. At the aggregate level there were no *statistically significant* differences between husbands and wives although husbands were slightly more likely than wives to give traditional answers on breadwinning and housework. The data show relatively weak correlations between individual husbands' and wives' answers (0.3 for breadwinning and 0.3 for housework) and higher levels of disagreement than in the previous behavioural table.

12. Factor analysis of individual's attitudes to housework and breadwinning indicated that they were related to one underlying factor explaining 75% of the overall variance.

13. Factor analysis of the three items revealed that they were highly intercorrelated with each other, with one underlying factor explaining 38% of the overall variance.

14. These differences are consistent with the previous findings on husband's education. Education was found to be strongly related to husband's sexist attitudes, those with no qualifications being significantly more sexist in their attitudes to women's labour market participation than those with A levels or above.

15. All odds ratios relating to husbands' traditional attitudes should be interpreted as referring to the effect of a change over the whole scale, which ranged from 0 to 2. The 70% change in likelihoods was calculated by subtracting the estimate of 0.3 from 1 and multiplying by 100. All negative likelihoods have been calculated in the same way.

16. An interaction was found between living in Kirkcaldy and both spouses being in full-time employment. Couples living in Kirkcaldy who were not both in full-time employment were more likely than their counterparts in other localities to use the joint pool. When the

equation was rerun excluding Kirkcaldy respondents, the effect of parental socialization was reduced while the effect of both partners being in full-time employment was increased. This implies that the Kirkcaldy effect is really the effect of the previous generation's work patterns. Parents in Kirkcaldy were significantly more likely than those in other areas to use the joint pool. This is consistent with the historical tradition of married women's employment in the area—initially in linoleum and textiles and later in electrical engineering. A similar effect did not emerge in Rochdale, which also had a strong historical tradition of married women's employment in textiles. The situation in Kirkcaldy may be partially the result of the conjunction between industrial capitalism (coal-mining and linoleum) and unitarian ideas which were particularly prevalent in Scotland.

17. All odds ratios relating to the husbands' sexist attitudes to women's labour market participation should be interpreted as referring to the effect of a change over the whole scale which ranged from 3 to 15.

18. Amongst couples using the joint pool, an interaction was found between whether husbands were responsible for breadwinning and husband's attitudes to the domestic division of labour. Examination of the tables, however, showed this was simply a correction effect due to the very strong positive association between the two variables.

19. Of those brought up in allowance households when they were young, 42% changed to one of the two female-managed systems, 26% to one of the male-managed systems and only 17% to the egalitarian joint pool.

20. These changes could be interpreted either as age or as generational effects, although the lack of longitudinal change within individual households strongly supports the generational interpretation.

21. There were no significant differences between those who changed their employment status and those who did not, in the methods of financial allocation used at the time of the survey. Male and female respondents were equally likely to have changed their budgetary arrangements: 13% of men and 10% of women with relevant changes in labour market activity had changed their financial system. In practice, of course, two-thirds of changes occurred with changes in women's labour market activity, simply because women changed their labour market activity more often than men.

22. Couples rarely changed their financial arrangements when husbands became unemployed and the few who did were in fact more likely to change from either the female or male whole wage to the *male* pool than from pooling to the female whole wage system.

METHODOLOGICAL APPENDIX

The Social Change and Economic Life Initiative

DUNCAN GALLIE

1. INTRODUCTION

The Social Change and Economic Life Initiative (SCELI) focused on six local labour markets—Aberdeen, Coventry, Kirkcaldy, Northampton, Rochdale, and Swindon. These were selected to provide contrasting patterns of recent and past economic change. In particular, three of the localities—Coventry, Kirkcaldy, and Rochdale—had relatively high levels of unemployment in the early and mid-1980s, while the other three had experienced relatively low levels of unemployment.

In each locality, four surveys were carried out designed to provide a high level of comparability between localities: the Work Attitudes/Histories Survey, the Household and Community Survey, the Baseline Employers Survey, and the 30 Establishment Survey. The interview schedules for these surveys were constructed collectively by representatives of the different teams involved in the research programme. In addition a range of studies was carried out that were specific to particular localities. These were concerned to explore in greater depth a number of themes covered in the comparative surveys.

A distinctive feature of the research programme was that it was designed to provide for the possibility of linkage between the different surveys. The pivotal survey (and the first to be conducted) was the Work Attitudes/Histories Survey. This provided the sampling frame for the Household and Community Survey and for the Employers Baseline Survey. The Baseline Survey in turn provided the listings from which organizations were selected for the 30 Establishment Survey.

The field-work for the Work Attitudes/Histories Survey and for the Household and Community Survey was carried out by Public Attitudes Surveys Research Ltd. The Baseline Employers Survey was a telephone survey conducted by Survey and Fieldwork International (SFI). The interviews for the 30 Establishment Survey were carried out by members of the research teams.

2. THE WORK ATTITUDES/HISTORIES SURVEY

This survey was concerned primarily with people's past work careers, their current experience of employment or unemployment, attitudes to trade unionism, work motivation, broader socio-political values, and the financial position of the household.

Two pilot studies were carried out in the preparation of the Work Attitudes/Histories Survey, testing questionnaire items, the placing of the work history schedule, interview length, and the contact procedure. The main field-work was conducted between June and November 1986. The objective was to secure an achieved sample of 1,000 in each of the six localities. As can be seen in Table A.1, the target was marginally exceeded, providing an overall sample of 6,111.

The sampling areas were defined in terms of the Department of Employment's 1984 Travel to Work areas (TTWA), with the exception of Aberdeen. In Aberdeen, where the TTWA was particularly extensive and included some very sparsely populated areas, the Daily Urban System area was used to provide greater comparability with the other locations.

A random sample was drawn of the non-institutionalized population aged 20–60. The electoral register was used to provide the initial selection of addresses, with probabilities proportional to the number of registered electors at each address. A half open-interval technique was also employed, leading to the identification of a small number of non-registered addresses in each locality. Doorstep enumeration of 20- to 60-year-olds was undertaken at each address followed by a random selection using the Kish procedure of one 20- to 60-year-old at each eligible address.

To provide sufficient numbers for analysis, it was stipulated that there should be a minimum of 150 unemployed respondents in each locality. A booster sample of the unemployed was drawn in the localities where this figure was not achieved through the initial sample. The booster sample was based on a separate random sample of addresses, with a higher sampling fraction in the wards with the highest levels of unemployment. As with the main sample, addresses were selected from the electoral register. But, for the selection of individuals, only the unemployed were eligible for inclusion. This booster sample was implemented in five of the six localities, producing a total of 214 respondents. Response rates for the combined main and booster sample were approximately 75 per cent in each of the localities, ranging from 73 per cent in Northampton to 79 per cent in Kirkcaldy (see Table A.1).

Where appropriate, weights have been used to take account of the booster sample, using the estimates of the proportion of unemployed

TABLE A.1. *The Work Attitudes/Histories Survey 1986: achieved sample*

	Aberdeen	Coventry	Kirkcaldy	Northampton	Rochdale	Swindon	TOTAL
Eligible addresses	1,345	1,312	1,279	1,400	1,350	1,321	8,007
Achieved sample							
Main sample	997	990	1,011	957	987	955	5,897
Booster sample	48	23	—	65	18	60	214
Total interviewed	1,045	1,013	1,011	1,022	1,005	1,015	6,111
Response rate (%)	78	77	79	73	74	77	76

available from the initial sample. There are also weights to provide a Kish adjustment for household size and to correct for an over-representation of women in the achieved sample (3,415 women compared with 2,696 men). The sex weight assumes equal numbers of men and women in the relevant population, as is shown to be almost exactly the case by examination of census data.

The interview consisted of two major sections. The first was a life and work history schedule in which information was collected about various aspects of the individuals' labour market, family, and residential history over the entire period since they had first left full-time education. Information about family and residential history was collected on a year grid basis. Information about labour market history—including spells of unemployment and economic inactivity—was collected on a sequential start-to-finish date-of-event basis. In the case of 'employment events' further information was collected about *inter alia* the nature of the job, the employer, hours of work, number of employees, gender segregation, and trade union membership. The second part of the interview schedule was a conventional attitudinal schedule, with a core of common questions combined with separate subschedules designed specifically for employees, for the self-employed, and for the unemployed and economically inactive.

While the greater part of the questions in the schedules provides direct comparability between localities, some scope was given for teams to introduce questions that would be asked only in their own locality (or in a subset of localities). This usually involved teams introducing a broader range of questions for investigating one or more of the themes covered in the common questions.

3. THE HOUSEHOLD AND COMMUNITY SURVEY

In 1987 a follow-up survey was carried out involving approximately one-third of the respondents to the 1986 Work Attitudes/Histories Survey. This focused primarily on household strategies, the domestic division of labour, leisure activities, sociability, the use of welfare provision, and attitudes to the welfare state. The survey was conducted in each of the localities, with the field-work lasting between March and July. The survey produced an achieved sample of 1,816 respondents, of whom 1,218 were living in partnerships and 588 were living on their own. Where applicable a range of questions was asked of partners as well as of the original respondents.

The sampling lists for the survey were generated from computer listings of respondents to the Work Attitudes/Histories Survey who had agreed to being reinterviewed. To ensure that a sufficiently large number of the unemployed respondents from the Work Attitudes/Histories Survey were reinterviewed, it was decided to specify that, in each locality, approximately 75 of the households in the follow-up survey would be from households where the respondent was unemployed at the time of the Work Attitudes/Histories Survey. For sampling, the lists were stratified into four groups, separating the unemployed from others and people who were single from those with partners. The sampling interval was the same for those of different partnership status, but different sampling intervals were used for the unemployed and for others to obtain the target numbers of people who had been unemployed at the time of the first survey.

In the event, 87 per cent of respondents (ranging from 84.8 per cent in Coventry to 89.7 per cent in Aberdeen) had indicated that they were willing to co-operate in a further phase of the research. Since the sampling areas were once more defined in terms of local labour markets, there was a further attrition of the original eligible sample due to people leaving the area (between 7 per cent and 9 per cent, depending on the locality). Response rates (for those that had agreed to be reinterviewed and were still in the area) were 75 per cent or better in each locality, ranging from 75 per cent in Rochdale and Northampton to 77 per cent in Kirkcaldy. The structure of the achieved sample is given in Table A.2. It should be noted that the table describes respondents with respect to their characteristics at the time of the Work Attitudes/Histories Survey, 1986, since this was the relevant factor for the sampling strategy. The economic and partnership status of a number of respondents had changed by the time of the second interview. For instance, while 1,223 of these respondents were classified as having had partners in 1986, the number with partners at the time of interview in 1987 was 1,218.

The questionnaire for this survey consisted of three sections: an interview schedule including questions of both respondents and partners, a respondent's self-completion, and a partner's self-completion. There was a shorter separate schedule for single people. The questionnaires included an update of the life and work histories of the original respondent and a full work history was collected for partners interviewed. The self-completion for respondents and partners was used at different points in the interview to collect independent responses from partners where it was thought that issues might be sensitive or that there was a danger of contamination of responses. The respondents and their partners filled in the relevant sections of the self-completion in the presence of the interviewer, but without reference to each other. The great majority of questions were common to all localities, but, again, a limited number of locality specific questions were allowed.

The *Time Budget Survey*. The data available through the Household and Community Survey interview was extended through a linked time budget survey. This project was directed by Jonathan Gershuny of the University of Oxford. The final five minutes of the Household and Community Survey were devoted to introducing the time budget diaries to the individual or couple present. The diaries were designed to cover a full week starting from the day following the household interview. They required natural-language descriptions of the diarist's sequences of activities to be kept on a fifteen-minute grid, for the whole week, together with any secondary (i.e. simultaneous) activities and a record of geographical location and whether or not others were present during the activities carried out. Interviewers left behind addressed, reply-paid envelopes for return of the diaries at the end of the diary week.

Forty-four per cent of those eligible (802 of the original 1,816 respondents and 533 of their 1,218 partners) completed usable diaries for the whole week. This low rate of response, though not unexpected from a postal survey, raises the issue of the extent of non-response biases. In anticipation of this problem, a number of questionnaire items were included in the original Household and Community Survey interviews which were intended to 'shadow' or parallel evidence from the diaries (i.e. questions about the frequency of participation in leisure activities and about the distribution of responsibilities for domestic work). An analysis of the two sources of data showed that the distribution of frequencies of the questionnaire responses of those who failed to complete diaries was very similar to the distribution of questionnaire responses for those who did keep diaries. From this we may infer an absence of bias at least with respect to estimates of these leisure and unpaid work activities (for a fuller account, see Gershuny 1990).

4. THE EMPLOYER SURVEYS

The implementation of the Baseline Employers Survey, which was a telephone survey, was the responsibility of Michael White of the Policy Studies Institute. The schedule was drawn up in collaboration with a working party of representatives from the different teams involved in the SCELI programme.

The survey involved a sample of establishments. The major part of the sample was drawn from information provided from the Work Attitudes/Histories Survey about people's employers. Each of the 1,000 individuals interviewed in each locality was asked, if currently employed, to provide the name and address of the employer and the address of the place of work. The sample was confined to establishments located within the travel-to-work areas that formed the basis of the research programme. Approximately 12 per cent of establishments initially listed

TABLE A.2. *The Household and Community Survey 1987: achieved sample by characteristics at time of Work Attitudes/Histories Survey*

	Aberdeen	Coventry	Kirkcaldy	Northampton	Rochdale	Swindon	TOTAL
Total issued	390	400	399	404	402	394	2,389
Achieved sample							
Employed/non-active with partner in 1986	153	162	167	163	155	175	975
Employed/non-active, single in 1986	68	54	62	60	68	48	360
Unemployed with partner in 1986	42	42	40	40	45	39	248
Unemployed, single in 1986	41	44	40	38	32	38	233
Total interviewed	304	302	309	301	300	300	1,816
Response rate (%)	78	76	77	75	75	76	76

could not be included in the sample because of insufficient information or closures. The sample covers all types of employer and both the public and the private sectors.

This method of generating a sample differs from a straight random sample drawn from a frame of all establishments. The latter would have resulted in a very large number of small establishments being included, while there was considerable theoretical interest in medium-sized and large establishments as key actors in the local labour market. The method used in SCELI weights the probability of an establishment's being included by its size: the greater the number of employees at an establishment, the greater its chance of having one or more of its employees included in the sample of individuals (and hence itself being selected).

The above method is closely related to sampling with probability proportional to size (p.p.s.); however, there are generally too few medium-sized and large establishments to generate a true p.p.s. sample. To increase the numbers of these medium-sized and large establishments, an additional sample of private sector employers with fifty or more employees was drawn from market research agency lists, supplemented by information from the research teams. The booster consisted of all identifiable establishments in this size range not accounted for by the basic sampling method. The sampling method, then, was designed to be as comprehensive as possible for medium-sized and larger employers. In practice, 70 per cent to 85 per cent of the sample by different localities were provided through the listings from the Work Attitudes/Histories data, while only 15 per cent to 30 per cent were from the booster sample. The structure of the achieved sample is presented in Table A.3. The sample so generated under-represents smaller, and over-represents larger, establishments, but provides adequate numbers in all size groups. It is also approximately representative of employment in each area, but it is possible to use weighting to achieve an even more precise representation of local employment. This was carried out using tables of employment by size group of establishment within industry group within each local labour market, from the 1984 Census of Employment (by courtesy of the Statistics Division, Department of Employment).

There were five stages of piloting over the summer of 1986, particularly concerned to develop the most effective contact procedure. The main field-work period was from October 1986 to February 1987. The overall response rate was 71 per cent, ranging from 64 per cent in Rochdale to 78 per cent in Aberdeen and Swindon.

The interview schedules focused particularly upon occupational structure, the distribution of jobs by gender, the introduction of new technologies, the use of workers with non-standard employment contracts, relations with trade unions, and product market position. Different

TABLE A.3. *The Baseline Employer Survey*

	Aberdeen	Coventry	Kirkcaldy	Northampton	Rochdale	Swindon	TOTAL
Sample from survey	345	280	229	287	233	273	1,647
Booster sample	52	54	32	51	55	39	283
Out of area	1	30	16	27	11	4	89
Eligible	396	304	245	311	277	308	1,841
Interviews	308	203	174	209	177	240	1,311
Response rate (%)	77.7	66.7	71.0	67.2	63.9	77.9	71.2

questionnaires were used for large and small organizations, with fewer questions being asked of small organizations. There were also minor variations in the schedules for public and private organizations, and for different industries. The four industry subschedules were: (1) manufacturing, wholesale, haulage, extractive, agriculture; (2) retail/hotel, catering/personal, and other consumer services; (3) banks, financial and business services, and (4) construction. These were designed to provide functionally equivalent questions with respect to product market position for different types of organization.

In each locality, there were follow-up interviews in at least thirty establishments—the 30 Establishment Survey—designed in particular to explore the motivation behind particular types of employer policy. While steps were taken to ensure that cases were included across a range of different industries, the composition of the follow-up sample was not a random one, but reflected team research interests. In contrast to the other surveys, the data from this survey should not be assumed to be generalizable to the localities.

5. THE RELATED STUDIES

Finally, most teams also undertook at least one smaller-scale further enquiry in their localities, each being designed exclusively by the team itself and funded separately from the three main surveys. These Related Studies sometimes built upon previous fieldwork a team had undertaken in its locality, and upon the resulting network of research contacts. Adopting for the most part documentary, case-study, or open-ended interviewing techniques of enquiry, the Related Studies dealt with special issues ranging from local socio-economic history to present-day industrial relations trends.

In one sense, then, the Related Studies can be thought of as free-standing research projects. At the same time, however, in interpreting the findings from a related study, a team could take advantage of the extensive contextual data provided by the main surveys. What is more, thanks to their use of methodologies permitting enquiry in depth and over time, the Related Studies could throw more light on many of the quantitative (and at times somewhat summary) findings of the main surveys. Several Related Studies were of particular value in validating and extending core-survey findings.

BIBLIOGRAPHY

ACAS (1988), *Labour Flexibility in Britain: The 1987 ACAS Survey*, occasional paper no. 41 (London: Advisory, Conciliation and Arbitration Service).

Anderson, Michael (1980), *Approaches to the History of the Western Family, 1500–1914* (London: Macmillan).

Andrews, F., Morgan, J., Sonquist, J., and Klein, L. (1973), *Multiple Classification Analysis*, 2nd edn. (Ann Arbor, Mich.: University of Michigan Press).

Askham, Janet (1975), *Fertility and Deprivation: A Study of Differential Fertility amongst Working-Class Families in Aberdeen* (Cambridge: Cambridge University Press).

Barro, Robert (1984), *Macroeconomics* (New York: John Wiley).

Baruch, G. K., and Barnett, R. (1983), 'Correlates of Fathers' Participation in Family Work: A Technical Report', working paper no. 106 (Wellesley, Mass.: The Wellesley College Centre for Research on Women).

Becker, G. S. (1965), 'A Theory of the Allocation of Time', *Economic Journal*, 80: 493–517.

—— (1974), 'A Theory of Marriage: Part I', *Journal of Political Economy*, 81: 813–46.

—— (1981), *A Treatise on the Family* (Cambridge, Mass.: Harvard University Press).

Blackburn, Robert M., and Mann, Michael (1979), *The Working-Class and the Labour Market* (London: Macmillan).

Bott, E. (1957), *Family and Social Network* (London: Tavistock).

Bourdieu, Pierre (1976), 'Marriage Strategies as Strategies of Social Reproduction', in Robert Forster and Orest Ranum (eds.), *Family and Society: Selections from Annales* (Baltimore: Johns Hopkins University Press).

Brannen, J., and Moss, P. (1987), 'Dual Earner Households: Women's Financial Contributions After the Birth of the First Child', in J. Brannen and G. Wilson (eds.), *Give and Take in Families* (London: Allen & Unwin).

Brown, C., and Preece, A. (1987), 'Housework', in *The New Palgrave* (Macmillan: London), 678–80.

CBI (1989), *Hours of Work in British Business*: *A CBI Survey* (London: Confederation of British Industry).

Chadeau, A., and Roy, C. (1981), 'Relating Households' Final Consumption to Household Activities: Substitutability or Complementarity between Market and Non-Market Production', *Review of Income and Wealth*, December, 387–407.

Charles, N., and Kerr, M. (1987), 'Just the Way It Is: Gender and Age Differences in Family Food Consumption', in J. Brannen and G. Wilson (eds.), *Give and Take in Families* (London: Allen & Unwin).

Clark, Kim B., and Summers, Lawrence H. (1982), 'Labour Force Participation: Timing and Persistence', *Review of Economic Studies*, 49: 825–44.

Crowe, Graham (1989), 'The Use of the Concept of "Strategy" in Recent Sociological Literature', *Sociology*, 23(1), 1–24.

Dennis, H., Henriques, L., and Slaughter, C. (1956), *Coal is Our Life* (London: Eyre & Spottiswoode).

Dex, Shirley (1988), *Women's Attitude to Work* (London: Macmillan).

—— and Shaw, Lois B. (1988), 'Women's Working Lives: A Comparison of Women in the United States and Great Britain', in Audrey Hunt (ed.), *Women and Paid Work*: *Issues of Equality* (London: Macmillan), 173–95.

Dolan, E. M., and Scannell, E. (1987), 'Husbands' and Wives' Household Work: Moving towards Egalitarianism?', *Journal of Consumer Studies and Home Economics*, 11: 387–99.

Duesenberry, James (1960), 'Comment on an Economic Analysis of Fertility', in *Demographic and Economic Changes in Developing Countries* (Princeton, NJ: Universities National Bureau Committee for Economic Research).

Edgell, S. (1980), *Middle Class Couples* (London: George Allen & Unwin).

Edwards, M. (1981*a*), *Financial Arrangements Within Families* (Canberra: National Women's Advisory Council).

—— (1981*b*), 'Financial Arrangements Within Families', *Social Security Journal*, December, 1–16.

Edwards, Rosalind, and Ribbens, Jane (1991), 'Meanderings Around Strategy: A Research Note on Strategic Discourse in the Lives of Women', *Sociology*, 25(3), 477–89.

Erickson, R. (1984), 'Social Class of Men, Women and Families', *Sociology*, 18(4), 500–14.

Fallon, P., and Verry, D. (1988), *The Economics of Labour Markets* (Cambridge: Cambridge University Press).

Folbre, N. (1982), 'Exploitation Comes Home: A Critique of the Marxian Theory of Family Labour', *Cambridge Journal of Economics*, 6: 317–29.

Gershuny, J. (1983), *Social Innovation and the Division of Labour* (Oxford: Oxford University Press).

—— (1990), 'International Comparisons of Time Budgets: Methods and Opportunities', in R. von Schweitzer, M. Ehling, and D. Schaeffer (eds.), *Zeitbudgeterhebungen* (Stuttgart: Metzler-Poeschl/Wiesbaden: Statistisches Bundesamt (German Federal Statistical Office)).

—— and Robinson, J. (1988), 'Historical Changes in the Household Division of Labour', *Demography*, 25(4), 537–52.

Goldthorpe, J. (1987), *Social Mobility and Class Structure in Modern Britain* (Oxford: Clarendon Press).

Granovetter, Mark (1985), 'Economic Action and Social Structure: The Problem of Embeddedness', *American Journal of Sociology*, 91(3), 481–510.

Greenhalgh, Christine A., and Stewart, Mark B. (1985), 'The Occupational Status and Mobility of British Men and Women', *Oxford Economic Papers*, 37: 40–71.

Gronau, R. (1973), 'The Intrafamily Allocation of Time: The Value of the Housewife's Time', *American Economic Review*, 63(4), 634–51.

—— (1974), 'The Effect of Children on the Housewife's Value of Time', in T. W. Schultz (ed.), *Economics of the Family* (Chicago: University of Chicago Press), 457–88.

—— (1977), 'Leisure, Home Production and Work—The Theory of the Allocation of Time Revisited', *Journal of Political Economy*, 85, 1099–123.

—— (1980), 'Home Production: A Forgotten Industry', *Review of Economics and Statistics*, 62, 408–14.

Gronmo, S., and Lingsom, S. (1986), 'Increasing Equality in Household Work: Patterns of Time Use in Norway', *European Sociological Review*, 2(3), 176–89.

Hakim, C. (1987), 'Trends in the Flexible Workforce', *Employment Gazette*, November, 549–60.

Hawrylyshyn, O. (1977), 'Towards a Definition of Non-Market Activities', *Review of Income and Wealth*, 23(1), 78–96.

Hochschild, A. (1990), *The Second Shift* (London: Piatkus).

Horrell, S. (1991), 'Working-Wife Households: Inside and Outside the Home', unpublished Ph.D. thesis, Cambridge University.

—— and Rubery, J. (1991), *Employers' Working Time Policies and Women's Employment* (London: HMSO).

Hunt, P. (1978), 'Cash Transactions and Household Tasks', *Sociological Review*, 26(3), 555–71.

—— (1980), *Gender and Class Consciousness* (London: Macmillan).

Klein, J. (1965), *Samples from English Cultures*, 1 (London: Routledge & Kegan Paul).

Knights, David, and Morgan, Glenn (1990), 'The Concept of Strategy in Sociology: A Note of Dissent', *Sociology*, 24(3), 475–83.

Komendi, E. (1990), 'Time Use Trends in Denmark', in G. V. Mortensen (ed.), *Time and Consumption* (Copenhagen: Danmarks Statistik), 51–74.

Levine, David (1977), *Family Formation in an Age of Nascent Capitalism* (New York: Academic Press).

Low Pay Unit (1988), *The Poor Decade: Wage Inequalities in the 1980s* (London: Low Pay Unit).

Lucas, Robert E. jun., and Rapping, Leonard A. (1969), 'Real Wages, Employment, and Inflation', *Journal of Political Economy*, 77, 721–54.

McKee, L., and Bell, C. (1983), 'Marital and Family Relations in Times of Male Unemployment', in B. Roberts, R. Finnegan, and D. Gallie (eds.), *New Approaches to Economic Life* (Manchester: Manchester University Press).

Main, Brian G. M., and Elias, Peter (1987), 'Women Returning to Paid Employment', *International Review of Applied Economics*, 1(1), 86–108.

Mansfield, P., and Collard, J. (1988), *The Beginning of the Rest of Your Life? A Portrait of Newly-Wed Marriage* (Basingstoke: Macmillan).

Marsh, C. (1991), *Hours of Work of Men and Women in Britain* (London: HMSO).

Martin, J., and Roberts, C. (1984), *Women and Employment: A Lifetime Perspective* (London: HMSO).

Mays, J. B. (1954), *Growing Up in the City* (Liverpool: Liverpool University Press).

Meissner, M., Humphries, E. W., Meis, S. M., and Scheu, W. J. (1975), 'No Exit for Wives: Sexual Division of Labour and the Cumulation of Household Demands', *Canadian Review of Sociology and Anthropology*, 12(4), 424–39; reprinted in R. Pahl (1990) (ed.), *On Work* (Oxford: Blackwell).

Mincer, J. (1962), 'Labor Force Participation of Married Women: A Study of Labour Supply', in *Aspects of Economics*, a report of the National Bureau of Economic Research (Princeton, NJ: Princeton University Press).

Modigliani, Franco, and Brumberg, R. E. (1954), 'Utility Analysis and the Consumption Function', in K. K. Kurihara (ed.), *Post-Keynesian Economics* (New Brunswick, NJ: Rutgers University Press).

Morgan, David H. J. (1989), 'Strategies and Sociologists: A Comment on Crowe', *Sociology* 23(1), 25–9.

Morgensen, G. V. (1990), *Time and Consumption* (Copenhagen: Danmarks Statistik).

Morris, L. (1984), 'Redundancy and Patterns of Household Finance', *Sociological Review*, 32: 492–523.

—— (1987), 'Constraints on Gender: The Family Wage, Social Security and the Labour Market: Reflections on Research in Hartlepool', *Work Employment and Society*, 1(1), March.

—— (1988), 'Employment, the Household and Social Networks', in D. Gallie (ed.), *Employment in Britain* (Oxford: Blackwell).

—— and Ruance, S. (1989), *Household Finance, Management and the Labour Market* (Aldershot: Gower).

Niemi, I., and Paakkonen, H. (1990), *Time Use Changes in Finland in the 1980s* (Helsinki: Central Statistical Office of Finland), 174.

Oakley, A. (1974), *The Sociology of Housework* (London: Martin Robertson).

Oppenheimer, Valerie Kincade (1981), 'The Changing Nature of Life-Cycle Squeezes: Implications for the Socioeconomic Position of the Elderly', in Robert W. Fogel *et al.* (eds.), *Aging: Stability and Change in the Family* (New York: Academic Press).

Pahl, J. (1983), 'The Allocation of Money and the Structuring of Inequality within Marriage', *Sociological Review*, 31(2), May, 237–62.

—— (1984), 'The Allocation of Money within the Household', in M. Freeman (ed.), *The State, the Law and the Family* (London: Tavistock).

—— (1987), 'Earning, Sharing, Spending: Married Couples and their Money', in G. Parker and R. Walker (eds.), *Money Matters* (London: Sage).

—— (1989), *Money and Marriage* (London: Macmillan).

Pahl, Ray E. (1984), *Divisions of Labour* (Oxford: Blackwell).

—— and Pahl, Jan (1971), *Managers and their Wives* (London: Allen Lane).

Pedersen, L. (1990), 'Determinants of Time Use Patterns for Men and Women in the Work Force', in G. V. Morgensen (ed.), *Time and Consumption* (Copenhagen: Danmarks Statistik), 95–122.

Piachaud, D. (1982), 'Patterns of Income and Expenditure within Families', *Journal of Social Policy*, 11(4), 469–82.

Robinson, J. (1976), *How Americans Use Time: A Social-Psychological Analysis of Everyday Behaviour* (New York: Praeger).

Rubery, J. (1989), 'Labour Market Flexibility in Britain', in F. Green (ed.), *The Restructuring of the UK Economy* (Brighton: Harvester Press).

Runciman, W. G. (1972), *Relative Deprivation and Social Justice* (Harmondsworth: Penguin).

Saunders, P. (1990), *A Nation of Home Owners* (London: Unwin Hyman).

Shaw, Martin (1990), 'Strategy and Social Process: Military Context and Sociological Analysis', *Sociology*, 24(3), 465–73.

Sprague, A. (1988), 'Post-War Fertility and Female Labour Force Participation Rates', *Economic Journal*, September, 682–700.

Straw, P., and Kendrick, S. (1988), 'The Subtlety of Strategies: towards an Understanding of the Meaning of Family Life Stories', *Life Stories/Recits de Vie*, 4: 36–48.

Strober, M. H., and Weinberg, C. B. (1980), 'Strategies Used by Working and Non-Working Wives to Reduce Time Pressures', *Journal of Consumer Research*, 7: 337–48.

Tilly, Louise A. (1979), 'Individual Lives and Family Strategies in the French Proletariat', *Journal of Family History*, 137–52.

Tunstall, J. (1962), *The Fisherman* (London: MacGibbon & Kee).

Vanek, J. (1974), 'Time Spent in Housework', *Scientific American*, 231, November, 116–20.

Vickery, C. (1979), 'Women's Economic Contribution to the Family', in R. E. Smith (ed.), *The Subtle Revolution: Women at Work* (Washington, DC: The Urban Institute), 159–200.

Walker, K. E., and Woods, M. E. (1976), *Time Use: A Measure of Household Production of Family Goods and Services* (Washington, DC: American Home Economics Association).

Wallman, Sandra (1984), *Eight East London Households* (London: Tavistock).

—— (1986), 'The Boundaries of Household', in Anthony P. Cohen (ed.), *Symbolising Boundaries* (Manchester: Manchester University Press).

Wilson, G. (1987), *Money in the Family* (Aldershot: Avebury).

Wrong, Denis (1961), 'The Oversocialised Conception of Man in Modern Sociology', *American Sociological Review*, 26(2), 183–93.

Young, M. (1952), 'Distribution of Income within the Family', *British Journal of Sociology*, 3, 305–21.

—— and Willmott, P. (1973), *The Symmetrical Family: A Study of Work and Leisure in the London Region* (London: Routledge & Kegan Paul).

Zweig, F. (1961), *The Worker in an Affluent Society* (London: Heinemann).

INDEX